MW00459772

PRAI

"Peter Conti has created a gripping tale of larceny like no other. *Gringo* is an enthralling look inside the drug trade and life on the run against all odds. You can literally smell the inherent sense of fear and danger jumping off the pages. A must read."

—Dante Ross, Grammy-winning producer

"When it's done well, story-telling is an art that can shift our perspective allow us to walk through another man's reality. In this case we experience the highs and lows of a cunning marijuana trafficker and international fugitive. As a story *Gringo* has it all. The fascinating life of Dan 'Tito' Davis is masterfully detailed by Peter Conti in a book that you will not be able to put down."

—Slaine, *La Coka Nostra* and *The Town*

"Sharp and insightful, Conti takes us inside the ultimate fugitive story. You know characters like these exist in the world, but rarely do you get to travel the globe with them."

—Rob Weiss, *Entourage* and *Ballers*

PRAISE FOR *WHATEVER HAPPENED TO MARTIN BARNETT?*

"It's so refreshing to finally read an author who can really write about the streets the right way. Peter Conti makes me feel, taste, and smell everything. It's real. I love real. I always believed in him, which is why I produced three of his plays."

—Joe Pesci, Oscar-winning actor

"I trusted Peter Conti to write the movie about my life. *Whatever Happened to Martin Barnett?* is a major reason why. And you should read this book and you should go see our movie."

—Vinny Paz, five-time world champ

"I read Peter Conti's book in one night. I couldn't put it down. It really captured the underbelly of L.A."

—Johnny Depp, *Donnie Brasco* and *Blow*

GRINGO

GRINGO

My Life on the Edge
As an International Fugitive

DAN "TITO" DAVIS
WITH PETER CONTI

Full Court Press
Englewood Cliffs, New Jersey

First Edition

Copyright © 2016 by Gringo Holdings, LLC

All rights reserved. No part of this book may be reproduced or transmitted in any form or by any means electronic or mechanical, including by photocopying, by recording, or by any information storage and retrieval system, without the express permission of the author, except where permitted by law.

Published in the United States of America
by Full Court Press, 601 Palisade Avenue,
Englewood Cliffs, NJ 07632
fullcourtpressnj.com

ISBN 978-1-938812-84-2
Library of Congress Catalog No. 2016957674

This is a true story. Some of the names of people and places in it have been changed for reasons of privacy.

For more documents and photos pertaining to the book, go to Gringothebook.com.

Book design by Barry Sheinkopf for Bookshapers (bookshapers.com)

Cover design by Deborah Acheson

Author photo by Sasha Burger

To My Mother, Marcelleen Davis
And My Sponsor, Marlyn Erickson
You were always there.

"To live outside the law, you must be honest."
—*Bob Dylan*

Author's Note

I imagine that, when most folks my age tell their friends they are going on a cross-country road trip, they hear things like "You should look up my old college roommate" or "My brother moved to Wisconsin." Not me. My pal Bobby the Chef said, "You gotta go see my friend Eddie, who's doing twenty at Yazoo City . He's looking for a writer." My buddy Vito tried to get me to go see his "guy," who is doing life in Marion—he, too, needed a writer. My friend Mike said I had to stop to see Tito, who was finishing up doing a dime in Wyoming. Tito had written a manuscript Mike said was "a brilliant mess."

My girlfriend and I left New York City en route to Los Angeles on September 1, 2015. Seven days later, we arrived in Gillette, Wyoming, and made our way to the Back to the Rack clothing store. It was closed that day. We sat in the empty parking lot. After a few minutes, Tito emerged through the back door. I had been expecting a Latin American but, instead, we met a white guy from South Dakota whose real name is Dan Davis. He looked like he was in his forties, but I knew from Mike he was in his sixties. He led us to his office in the back of the used-clothing store, where two monitors transmitted news from Mexico and Venezuela.

Tito was on work-release and would finish up a ten-year federal prison sentence two weeks from the day we met him. He said his first order of business, once he was released, was to climb Devil's Tower, the 5,112-foot butte that was featured in *Close Encounters of the Third Kind*. He had never climbed, he told us, but he had been training at a gym during his lunch breaks. It was no surprise to me when, eleven days later, I received a photo in my email of Tito standing triumphantly atop the Tower.

I ASKED HIM TO TELL ME HIS STORY. Tito burst into a fifteen-minute explosion detailing a bus trip in Guatemala during which a baby pig disguised as an infant had pissed on him. For the next two hours he regaled us with stories of life on the run—of living with a drug cartel in Medellín, of being interrogated by the Cuban police, and of being tutored by a hit woman. At the end of our meeting, he handed me a floppy disc (remember those?) that contained his seven-hundred-page-plus manuscript, which he had written on a twenty-five-year-old word processor in prison. He said he needed a real writer to make it work.

A few days later, in Los Angeles, I figured out how to print out the manuscript from the floppy disc, and I began reading it. It was the most fascinating and frustrating piece of writing I had ever encountered. I kept going back over pages because I kept getting lost—I felt the way I had when I attempted to read *Ulysses* in grad school. Characters came out of nowhere and left without any rationalization. There were long, detailed accounts of what Tito ate for breakfast and then a mere sentence about his marriage ceremony in Bali. He would spend page after page writing about a stripper in Cartagena and virtually nothing about his wife. The oddest part was that Tito himself received the least amount of attention. All of a sudden he appears in Mexico, on the run from the feds. We never learn who he is or where he came from. It is almost as if he were a ghost.

I didn't know what to make of it, but I knew there were parts that were riveting. I also believed every word, which was stunning, considering how truly incredible his stories were. I was also confident from our short meeting in Wyoming that Tito was a gifted storyteller—he just had trouble putting it on the page. I also knew I had to rewrite the thing with him. I learned he was in contact with other writers, but I did not sit idly by. I submitted some writing samples, including my script on boxer Vinny Paz and a book—started but not completed—on Tommy DeVito of the Four Seasons, to show I had written nonfiction. I also gave him a copy of my novel *Whatever Happened to Martin Barnett?*, which was based partially on the basketball player Marvin Barnes. Finally, I rewrote the first five pages of Tito's manuscript. A few days later I got a call from Mike saying that he was vouching for me, that Tito was going to offer me the job, and that I had better stay focused and do the right thing. I asked if I should add the threat to our contract.

Sure enough, a week later, Tito gave me the honor of working with him. I flew to Wyoming, where I met his mom and brother. I sat down with Tito, in the shadow of Devil's Tower, where I asked him 288 questions I had about the manuscript. It turned out Tito had an almost photographic memory and was able to provide me with concise details.

I spent a couple of months trying to piece his story together. I talked to Tito several times each day, and I even got him to start texting. But something was missing. I had perused his seven hundred pages many times, and I was in constant contact with the subject; I had a good understanding of Tito, but I realized I had no idea who Dan Davis was. In December, I flew to Key West to stay with him and dig a little deeper. He was living in a luxurious three-bedroom condo that overlooked the water. It belonged to his friend Marlyn Erickson, who was sponsoring him. Every day, Tito received calls from all over the world from people who were checking up on him. Obviously, he had been doing something right all those years.

Slowly but surely I began filling in Tito's missing background. I learned that, while in high school, he'd worked as a jockey and had won over a hundred races. At the University of Nevada–Las Vegas, he'd gotten into the ephedrine business simultaneously with Lilly Pharmaceuticals and the Banditos Motorcycle Club, and by the time he was twenty-four he was earning two hundred thousand dollars a week, which equates to a million a week today. I pressed him to go into greater detail about what it'd been like to never know who was going to turn you in. (The manuscript's narrative voice was much too stoic—I surmised it must have been hell for him during much of his time on the run, and I was right.) Tito also told me that, with the exception of trafficking cocaine, which he had done for a very short time, he'd never felt like he was breaking the law. He also admitted to things he wasn't very proud of—like disappearing on his wife without ever letting her know why. Upon leaving Key West, I was confident I had the details I needed to do his story justice.

I went back to Los Angeles and wrote it. I sent Tito a few chapters at a time. He revised them painstakingly, often finding the most minute of errors. (It turned out he had taught English in prison.) Even if he did not immediately agree when I cut out entire chapters of his work, most of the time he thought it over and saw my point.

I have been very fortunate in having encountered a wide range of individuals who have led exceptional and fascinating lives. I have worked with and/or written about mob bosses, rock stars, boxing champions, Hollywood big shots, Ivy League intellectuals, and Oscar-winning actors. I can honestly say that no one has lived a more fascinating life than Dan "Tito" Davis.

I WOULD LIKE TO THANK the following: My family—especially my mother, who has always supported me, and my brother Bert, who has been my unwavering inspiration. My girlfriend, Cat Lee, who took the road trip, and who silenced my doubts with love and affection. My "sister" JoAnne Colonna, and James Acheson, who built me a clean, well-lighted place in which to live and work in Los Angeles, and their children, Jimmy, Alessandro, and Luca, who have respected my privacy and helped keep me young. Michael Garganese, who has been a loyal friend, and who introduced me to Tito and secured the deal via a veiled threat. Vinny Paz, whose life story was my blueprint. My professors, who taught me to write and think, especially Jascha Kessler, Stephen Dickey, L. Lee Knefelkamp, James Albright, and Ira Shor, and my students, who have kept me on my toes. Finally, my editors, Bob McCormick and Barry Sheinkopf, whose suggestions were concise, detailed, and humbling.

Most of all, I would like to thank Tito, for trusting me with the story of his life. He's a man of his word, the highest compliment I can pay someone.

—Peter Conti
June 14, 2016
Los Angeles, California

TABLE OF CONTENTS

PROLOGUE

I STOOD ON THE PLATFORM of the Chihuahua Train Station, only a few miles from the Texas border, waiting for the Tequila Express. It was already fifty-five minutes late. The sun was burning a hole in my baseball cap, and my T-shirt was soaked with sweat even though it was only 7:15 a.m. and still spring, technically. At five foot ten, I towered over most of the others, but no one seemed to give a damn that I was there. I avoided eye contact, which wasn't difficult, since most of my traveling companions seemed to be sleeping standing up.

Finally the Tequila Express rolled in, and its rusty doors creaked open. The Orient Express it was not. I entered the second-class compartment and took a dusty seat next to an elderly woman who looked me up and down and didn't seem too impressed with what she saw. I wasn't complaining. For the first time in my life, I wasn't trying to impress anyone. I just wanted to blend in. I was just another disillusioned white guy who was turning forty with the realization that life was passing me by; I wanted to get out of the day-to-day grind of nine-to-five corporate America and travel to exotic places, starting with Mexico. My wife had left me, and she'd gotten the house. I needed a change.

I wasn't going to go to Club Med or Cancun or any other place where my friends traveled to blow off steam. When I say I needed change, I meant real, profound change. I was finally going to learn Spanish and start living a life away from the desk I had been sitting at for the past fourteen years. I was trading in my briefcase for a backpack, my Brooks Brothers suit and tie for surf shorts and a tank top. I was on a quest to live life to the fullest and start by finding some excitement in my ho-hum existence.

This, of course, was bullshit. I had never sat at a desk for fourteen minutes, nor had I worked in corporate America. I wasn't bored or disillusioned. I had been living a life that most guys wouldn't have even dared dream. I didn't yearn to learn a language or immerse myself in some bullshit cultural experience. I was a fugitive from the United States justice system who was facing life in prison.

And this was going to be my cover. Backpacking through Mexico and beyond, shoulder to shoulder with travelers and natives, in the hope that it might just be possible to stay off the grid long enough to figure out what I was going to do. Doesn't sound like much of a plan at all, right? Well, where would you go if the FBI, Interpol, and a bevy of other law enforcement agencies were after you? This was the best that I had come up with. True, I didn't give a damn about multiculturalism or traveling in third-world countries or slumming like a trust-fund kid. I enjoyed Five-Star hotels, swanky clubs, and sitting in first class—or better yet, flying my own plane anywhere the hell I wanted to go.

As the train lumbered along the battered tracks and into the highlands of Mexico, I would love to report that it was a tropical paradise with which I instantly fell in love. It wasn't. In fact, it was not even as stimulating as my home state of South Dakota. But I couldn't think about home—not of my mother, working in the shadow of the Devil's Tower, who would be worried sick about me; or my wife, whom I, in fact, had left; or my stepdaughter, whom I would not get to see grow up; or my houses, my planes, or my cars. Every one of my possessions was in my backpack. (Except for some money, twenty-eight thousand dollars of which was hidden in cash in a money belt strapped between my legs like a chastity device.)

Money was not going to be a problem—at least for a while.

I sat back and watched the crummy landscape pass me by at an alarmingly slow rate. It would take twenty-two hours to get to Mexico City, which I calculated was about an average of seventeen miles per hour. I tried to remain calm as the vendors—skinny, dirty kids who smiled broadly, apparently not ashamed of their rotting or missing teeth—sold tacos, two for an American dollar. I tried to remain calm as *federales*[1] strolled down the aisle, muttering away in Spanish. I tried to remain calm when a couple from Indiana boarded the train, sat across from me, and made small talk. But most of all I tried to remain calm about Marvin Schumacher.

Not that I knew where he was. That was not for lack of trying. But even with all of my connections back in the States and all the money that I had been able to throw around back then, it is next to impossible to find someone who is in the Witness Protection Program. And I would have given almost anything then to spend a few quality minutes with Marvin Schumacher.

I'm not about to claim that I have been a Boy Scout. I did a five-year bid[2] back in the 1980s, and I did so without ever claiming that I had been set up. But the truth is, this time, I had been. Marvin was a friend I had known since grade school. He was a wanna-be drug dealer who always bragged that he would never rat on his friends if he got caught—that he could "do a dime standing on his head." Believe me, I have come to know that it is always those guys, the ones who swore they would never talk, who are the first to flip. Legend has it that the feds had to slap Marvin to get him to stop talking.

But that isn't what had me so riled up about Marvin Schumacher. Anyone who actually believes there is honor among thieves (or drug dealers) has been watching too many movies. The reason I was so enraged (besides the fact that I really didn't have anything to do with the two pounds of meth in question) is that I had saved the bastard's life a few years back.

Out of pity, I had brought him along on a hunting trip even though he wasn't much of a hunter, and that in itself should have been a red flag, since every Midwestern kid back then grew up hunting. One thing led to another, and the stupid bastard got shot, at close range, with a twelve-gauge shotgun. He instantly went into shock and would have bled out in fifteen minutes had I not tied him off with my own damn shirt and rushed him fifty miles to the nearest hospital, where they were not only able to save his life, but salvage his leg, too. And for this, he had told the police that his two pounds of meth was mine, and that they should put me in prison until I was a senior citizen or dead.

But I knew that, if I was going to survive, I would have to get Marvin Schumacher out of my mind.

I may have had some serious grip back in the States but now I was entering a country where I had absolutely none. Sure, I knew some people who knew some people, but I was in no position to reach out to any of them. It would be awfully tempting to mention where I was staying in lieu of, say, sixty months[3] in prison, or for a few pesos. I had enough cash to keep me afloat in that shithole country for quite a while. My real worry was my lack of documentation. I had a fake California driver's license, but I was pretty sure that I could be required to provide a passport at any bureaucrat's whim. As I said, I had plenty of money, but I was not going to get too confident because money without the right connections, when you're dealing with counterfeiters and black marketeers, could prove disastrous.

I tried to remain positive. I wouldn't have my home, but neither would I have my ridiculous mortgage. I wouldn't have to worry about the police impounding my cars. I wouldn't feel my stomach tighten every time I checked my bank accounts, for fear the government had frozen my assets again. As much as I would miss my wife, I wouldn't miss the stress I was causing her. Of course, I would miss my stepdaughter, but I had to convince myself that she would be better off without me. (That was the most difficult.)

Still, I couldn't get over how far I had fallen, especially when I thought about how far I had come to get there.

1

A MIDWESTERN BOYHOOD

I WAS BORN ON JULY 10, 1953, in Pierre, the capital of South Dakota, which is not much of a capital. There were only about 5,200 of us when I came into the world. My mom had grown up during the Depression, and much of her childhood was spent in a sod house[4] on a farm. At night, the farm animals were ushered into the house to sleep with her and her family. Often, she walked to school barefoot—for as long as she was able to attend school. But my grandparents persevered. They saved their hard-earned money selling milk from their lone cow, and eventually they bought another cow. Then another. They stocked away every penny and were ultimately able to move into a wooden house.

My father, the youngest of thirteen, was raised by his older siblings because his mom had died the year he was born and his father had bolted soon after. Dad became a mechanic at twelve and stayed in that business his entire life. My parents had five kids; I was the oldest. We didn't grow up in abject poverty as our parents had, but there wasn't much money to spare, not that I had reason to complain.

Growing up in South Dakota before the Internet and social media was a kid's dream. There were no gangs or drugs. We fished, hunted, and hiked, and we played sports. We weren't aware of the material advantages we lacked. There was only one channel on the black-and-white TV, and we spent most of our time outside, in Nature. It was the perfect place and perfect time to grow up. Boys aspired to be Daniel Boone, not Kanye West, and girls didn't have Kim Kardashian as their role model.

Our world was small. I had no idea that people came in colors other than white until one day when my mother brought my sisters and me school shopping at Crazy Days, a makeshift outdoor mall. I must have been about eight when I heard a commotion break out in front of the JC Penney store. I dragged my mom by the hand to see what was going on. When I got there, I saw a guy of about eighteen who seemed to be made out of chocolate.

Some of the kids went up and began to touch him. I heard an adult say, "Oh, my God, look at that. A real live nigger."

My mother didn't say anything but hurried us off to another store. When I asked her about him, she told me to mind my own p's and q's.

I didn't actually meet a black person or a Latino until college, and even at UNLV I only remember meeting a few—mostly athletes. It's ironic, considering that I've spent most of my adult life with hardly any whites.

I enjoyed school and took it seriously. I was taught that it was a privilege, given that my parents hadn't been able to stay in school when they were kids. The best part about it was that it taught me there was life outside my little world.

One day my fifth-grade teacher, Mrs. Eliason, hosted a Career Day that featured her son Tom, who was a horse-racing trainer. He mesmerized us with tales of traveling and racing. I peppered him with questions, so much so that after the Q & A, Tom told his mom that she should bring me over to the ranch someday. A few weeks later she drove me the thirty-six miles, and I got to hang out in the stalls with Tom and make friends with the horses. I asked if I could be a jockey; he said not until I was sixteen. I asked him what I should do until then. He said, "I'll tell you what you shouldn't—gain weight."

About then I got my first real job, as a flag boy for the crop dusters—spray planes, they call them. A bunch of us kids marked the routes for them. It wasn't your typical job for a ten-year-old, but they liked to use us because we were agile and we could sit by the feet of the pilots who flew from one field to another. There were no seat belts. Hell, there weren't even any masks. I made $1.20 an hour (about $7.50 today). I worked weekends and every day after school for the two months that it lasted.

In high school, I wanted to play sports, but at ninety-two pounds I didn't have many options. I ended up wrestling all four years, and while I wasn't great, I certainly won many more matches than I lost. My biggest challenge was my weight. My sophomore year I had a growth spurt of six inches. I stood five-feet-five but was wrestling in the ninety-eight-pound weight class.

During that season, Tom Eliason showed up at one of my tournaments. Horse trainers recruited at the wrestling tournaments, because where else were they going to find graceful athletes under a hundred pounds? They also recruited us because we knew all the tricks to lose weight quickly. He remembered me and asked if I wanted to start working at his stable and begin training to be a jockey.

I started at Eliason Farms the summer before high school, grooming the horses, cleaning the stables, and learning how to ride. I was paid a hundred and twenty bucks a month—a big cut from the money I'd made as a flag boy, but I didn't mind because they said that I had natural talent and a shot at being a pro.

They were right. The following spring I began my career on the "leaky roof" circuit, where I entered eight to ten races a day. I was paid a minimum of five dollars-a-race and, depending on the race, could earn up to two hundred for a first-place finish. And I won plenty of races—over a hundred in my short career. In fact, I earned about ten thousand that summer, well more than my father made in a year.

But making weight was killing me. I never enjoyed a meal, because if I did indulge in one, I knew what I'd be having for dessert—either a couple dozen chocolate Ex-Lax, or a finger down the throat. It wasn't as if I was going out on dinner dates anyway.

I had no idea what I wanted to do with my life. I had plenty of money saved—almost eleven thousand dollars, along with a new car and more experiences than most people had in their entire lives. The Vietnam War was raging, and though my draft number in the lottery was 333, very low, I still thought it might be better to go to college. I had always been a good student in high school. I'd made the honor roll most semesters. I was not tempted by pot or any other illegal drugs because, believe it or not, there were none. I rarely finished a beer, because I always had to be in tiptop shape for horse racing half the year and wrestling the other half. I was looking forward to moving into the dorms, but I knew I didn't want to do the whole starving-student thing. I had been making a decent living since I was ten, and I had grown accustomed to buying what I wanted when I wanted it.

IN THE FALL OF 1972, I drove my brand-new powder blue Chevy SS 454, considered the baddest muscle car in the Midwest at the time, onto the campus of Black Hills State College in Spearfish, South Dakota. My father had nicknamed that car the Blue Coffin, because he thought for sure I was going to end up dead in it. I didn't die, but not for lack of trying—I drove like a maniac, and the campus police grew alert each time I started my car.

For the first semester, I shared a room in Thomas Hall with a square kid from the other end of South Dakota. There were plenty of attractive coeds strutting around campus, but I lacked confidence to approach them. I guess it was because, too focused on sports, I hadn't dated in high school. In college I didn't have that excuse.

I couldn't figure out what to major in, but since I had always been interested in health and fitness, I took science courses—biology, chemistry, calculus, and physics. I think I also gravitated toward those classes because my adviser said that taking hard courses early in my academic career would afford me more options down the line, which made sense to me.

But I got a little lazy. I wasn't working out, instead eating everything I could in the cafeteria. It was the first time since I started wrestling at twelve that I could eat sweets, and I made the most of it.

I don't know if it was because of all the carbs but I also started getting lethargic. I slept later and even missed a few classes. While other kids were pounding beers from kegs in their rooms, I was posted up by the soda fountain drinking Coke. The only exercise I remember getting was during an intramural wrestling tournament, which I won pretty easily. The diligent adolescent, courtesy of the Midwestern work ethic that my parents had forcefully instilled in me for the first eighteen years of my life, was suddenly replaced by a kid who listened to The Doors until the wee hours of the morning and slept until afternoon. As a result, I got behind in my studies.

One night I was cramming for a biology test and desperate because I only had about eight hours before my 8 a.m. class. My buddy Ted Jenkins wandered into the library. I guess I complained I was getting drowsy, because he handed me a white pill with a cross on it.

I had never done a drug in my life, never even smoked pot, but it seemed as though all the serious students who studied in the library late at night were taking White Crosses. The weak students who were carrying C averages were usually stoned on pot in their dorm rooms.

I held it in my hand.

"Stop being so lame," said Ted. "I take them every day, and I'm passing all my classes." This in itself was astounding, since Ted Jenkins was no genius. He'd grown up on the wrong side of the tracks in the ironically named Winner, South Dakota, and was best known for winning the South Dakota Gold Gloves several times and a number of AAU boxing tournaments. The fact that these pills helped him pass his college classes made me want to give them a try.

I walked over to the men's room and put the pill in my mouth. I just stood there. Frozen. I just could not get myself to swallow the damn pill. In fact, I spit it into the sink. Luckily, it got stuck right before the drain.

It's odd: I'd had the balls to work with the crop dusters at ten and raced horses at sixteen, but I was deathly afraid of a drug that almost all of the smart kids were taking to study. I picked it out of the sink, put it back in my mouth, cupped some water into my hands and swallowed it. I looked into the mirror, waiting to see a change. Of course, nothing happened.

I returned to my study table and opened my biology book, trying to memorize the material. I could feel myself getting even more tired. I thought for sure that Ted was pulling a prank on me.

But after about twenty minutes—*bang!*—it hit me. The hair on my body felt like it was standing on edge and my balls began to tighten. Beads of sweat slid down my forehead and fell onto my textbook. My mouth hadn't been that dry since my days working with the crop dusters. I began to read the dense material, and I immediately became immersed in it, as if it was the greatest writing in the history of Western language. I rolled into class the next morning on no sleep and aced my bio exam.

White Crosses were the drug of choice in colleges (or should I say college libraries) in the early 1970s. It was our Adderall, our Ritalin, our Red Bull. They were cheap. Ted bought bags of 100 pills for twenty bucks and sold them for a quarter each. He said that he wasn't getting rich but he was able to take as many as he wanted for free.

I finished the semester strong, passing all my difficult classes; however, I was no closer to deciding what I wanted to major in. The one thing I knew for certain was that I didn't want to be broke. That summer, no matter how much I exercised and starved myself, I could not make weight to be a jockey. I had grown to five-feet-ten, and I was walking around at 175 pounds. There was no way I was going to lose more than fifty pounds no matter how much Ex-Lax I ate.

When I came back to school the next semester, I was worried about my finances. I had gone through most of my savings. I got a job washing dishes at a local diner. It was a pretty easy job, but I wanted more. I had never minded working hard but I felt bad making less money as a college sophomore than I had as a fourth-grader.

I was also *dying* of boredom. Snow covered the campus for much of the school year, and there was nothing to do except study and party. And when I say party, I mean drink cheap beer and smoke bad weed. I especially hated pot, because it made me feel lethargic and gave me the munchies. There was one drug, however, that interested me—White Crosses.

I did some research at our local library during Christmas break. White Crosses were methamphetamine pills. Crystal Meth, as it is more commonly called today, is methamphetamine in powder form. White Crosses, the mainstay of college students and truck drivers, was more for work. Crystal Meth was more of a recreational drug, which was sometimes smoked or even shot up.

I realize that it is easy to pass judgment today about the dangers of Crystal Meth—I know many people have become experts from watching *Breaking Bad*. But, then, Crystal Meth didn't carry the stigma that it does now, any more than OxyContin did ten years ago. Yet, if you have been paying attention, many parts of the country are now in the grips of a major Oxy epidemic.

I went to the library and did some more research, this time on methamphetamine. A powerful amphetamine, it had first been made in

1887 in Germany; methamphetamine, which was more potent and easier to make than anything before it, was developed in Japan in 1919. Meth went into wide use during World War II, when both sides employed it to keep troops awake. In the 1950s, methamphetamine was prescribed in the United States as a diet aid and a treatment for depression. Easily available, it was used as a non-medical stimulant by college students, truck drivers, and athletes. Eventually the popularity of the drug spread. By the mid-1960s, the increased availability of injectable methamphetamine led to a much darker and dangerous habit.

I was definitely afraid of it, but I was confident there was serious money in White Crosses, much more than what Ted was making.

Still, I didn't want to go to jail. Richard Nixon had created the Drug Enforcement Administration (DEA) two years earlier, and drug cases were beginning to make the news. But this was just the beginning of America's war against drugs. Vigilant parents were the DEA when I was growing up.

I'd have given up on my dream of selling White Crosses had it not been for the brilliance of my sophomore year roommate. Ed Buanno looked like most nineteen-year-old college students: awkward, sleep-deprived, a bit out of shape, and he put little effort into his wardrobe or overall appearance. But he was a genius. Not only was he running a 4.0 GPA as a chemistry major, he simultaneously attended chiropractor school.

One day, I asked him about White Crosses. He'd seen them around campus, but he hadn't tried one. (Ed was a Sanka junkie.) He suggested that we test the pills. He told me to get him about a dozen, because it wasn't going to be easy to break them down. Three days later I got a call from him on the pay phone in the hall of the frat house where I was living. He told me to come to the chemistry lab right away.

When I got there, he was bouncing around. "Dan, you're never going to *believe* this," he said.

"You finally got laid."

"Your White Crosses aren't methamphetamine," he said, ignoring the wisecrack.

"What are they, then?"

"Ephedrine."

". . .What's that?"

He explained that ephedrine was derived from the herb ephedra, a staple of traditional Chinese medicine. While it had a very similar molecular structure to methamphetamine and worked in a similar way, it had several differences that I really didn't fully comprehend. But there was something that Ed mentioned that *did* pique my curiosity—it was *legal*.

That was all that I needed to hear.

I got my pal Ted to let me tag along with him when he went down to B & B and Back Porch, where he introduced me to Fonzie, the doorman, and, more importantly, his White Cross connection. Named after the hero of the hit sitcom *Happy Days*, Fonzie rode a motorcycle and wore a leather jacket. His arms were covered with tattoos long before tattoos became cool. It was rumored that he was a prospect[5] for the Bandidos.

In 1966, Don Chambers founded the Bandidos Motorcycle Club, also known as Bandido Nation, in San Leon, Texas. Chambers, a Vietnam vet, had modeled the club's colors, red and gold, after those of the U.S. Marine Corps. They took pride in being known as One Percenters—unlike ninety-nine percent of bikers, they were not law-abiding citizens. Their motto was, "We are the people that our parents warned us about."

About six months before my introduction to Fonzie, Don Chambers had been given a life sentence for his part in the double murder of two drug dealers in El Paso, Texas. The dealers had sold baking soda to the Bandidos, claiming it was meth. Chambers and two other Bandidos had driven the two dealers into the desert north of El Paso and forced them to dig their own graves, after which the bikers shot them and set their bodies on fire.

"This is my friend Dan," Ted said, "who I knew from high school. He wants to get some White Crosses."

"Twenty bucks for a hundred," Fonzie said, barely looking in my direction.

"Actually," I said, "I want a jar."[6] This got his attention.

Soon I was selling White Crosses to the entire school and to many of the townies.[7] But there was a problem. Fonzie, being a prospect, only had limited amount of grip, and he couldn't lay his hands on nearly enough to supply my clients. Not only that, the Bandidos had been having internal problems since the departure of Don Chambers, so Fonzie said that it was difficult for him to get what I needed. As a result, I started making enemies on campus. Students would get angry if I couldn't come up with the pills, especially when they had a paper was due or an exam was coming up.

I had made a couple thousand dollars, but I realized that, if I was going to make any real money, I had to get out of Black Hills. I knew that I had to stay in college if I was going to build my business, since that is where my potential customers were.

One night I was sitting in the library, looking out of the window, watching the snow pile up around me. I was trying to write a paper on Heisenberg's Uncertainty Principle, but my fellow nerds kept interrupting me for White Crosses. I had completely run out, which probably explained why I had read the first paragraph of the article five times. The truth was, I was sick of being a big fish in a little pond. I decided that night that that would be my last semester at Black Hills.

I walked over to the Reference Room and started perusing a book that described all the colleges in the United States. It took me all night, but by the end I decided there was only one place where I needed to be.

2

RUNNING REBEL

I ENTERED THE UNIVERSITY OF NEVADA AT LAS VEGAS (UNLV) in the fall of 1974, about the same time as Jerry Tarkanian.[8] My new college could not have been more different than my old one. Temperatures reached triple digits most of my first week of classes. The students were certainly more hip at UNLV, and the girls dressed much sexier. At Black Hills State College, we'd had a few bars and restaurants to party at. At UNLV we had the Las Vegas Strip.

It took me a few months to link up with the main dealer on campus, a Mexican American kid named Billy Valdez, who also worked as a waiter at the Sombrero Room in Binion's Horseshoe in downtown Las Vegas. I couldn't figure out why he was keeping his waiter job. He not only supplied most of the campus but also sold to the truck stops. I told Billy that I was looking for some serious weight. Of course he didn't believe me until I paid him fifteen hundred bucks up front for ten jars—ten thousand pills.

Three days later, I bought ten more. The next week I bought another ten. I was shipping as much as I could to Ted Jenkins and his buddy Fonzie. By then Fonzie had become a full-fledged member of the Bandidos, and they were moving the White Crosses through South Dakota to the truck stops in Iowa and then eventually to the oil fields in Wyoming. But my supply still wasn't meeting their demand. They were threatening to take their business somewhere else.

Then I got hit with more bad news: Billy Valdez was moving back to Arizona.

I surprised him at work. I sat down at a two-top table in the Sombrero Room at Binion's.

He came to my table. "What are you *doing* here?" he asked.

"I heard you're moving back to Arizona," I said.

"Me and my brother bought a house. My girl is pregnant."

"Congratulations," I said. "But what about our business?"

He shrugged and went to another table to take an order. When he came back, I hit him with an offer. I had saved up almost ten grand. I wanted to buy a hundred thousand pills.

"You *loco*, Dan," he said, laughing.

"I'm serious."

". . .I'm moving back on Saturday. I'll talk to my uncle. If he wants to do the deal, you'll have to bring the cash to Arizona and take the pills yourself," he said.

"Sure thing," I said, even though I had no idea how I was going to move all that merchandise from Arizona to South Dakota.

For the next two weeks I couldn't focus on school. Fonzie and Ted were still threatening to link up with another supplier. I was pretty sure that they hadn't made a connection, but it would only be a matter of time.

Then one night, after attending my first Running Rebels basketball game, I got a call on the hall phone from Billy's brother Angel, whom I had met a few times on campus when he came to visit him. He said that their uncle usually didn't do business with gringos, but that, since Billy was vouching for me, the man would make an exception. But there was a catch. The lowest amount he would sell me would be two hundred thousand hits, for twenty grand.

"But I only need a hundred thousand," I said. "Down the line, I'm sure—"

"There's no down the line, *guero*.[9] Either it's two hundred or it's *nada*."

"Let's do it," I said.

I tried to get Fonzie to loan me the extra ten thousand. But since he was already pissed off that I wasn't meeting his orders, and he hung up in my ear.

The next day I borrowed the money from my folks—they took out a second mortgage on their home. I had made up a big lie about staking Ted Jenkins in a pro boxing career. I knew this would get over on my dad—he was a big boxing fan, and Ted was a local legend.

When I picked up the money that my folks had wired me the next morning, I justified my behavior—I would pay them back with interest. And if my business took off as I anticipated, I would pay off their original mortgage. I would also buy my mom a mink coat and my dad a Cadillac.

But the truth is they wouldn't have known what to do with those things. My folks were extremely conservative and frowned upon any excess. If my plan worked, I would do better to buy them a cow or something. Looking back at it, I'm not proud of my behavior, but I wasn't the first, nor will I be the last, twenty-year-old who got some help from his parents to start a business.

I waited another four days for Billy or his brother to call. It seemed like the twenty grand was burning a hole in the center of my mattress. I finally got the call, from Angel, and I couldn't contain my excitement. I boarded a quick flight on a Yellow Banana[10] to Phoenix, money in hand, and took a taxi to Billy and Angel's. Angel greeted me at the door and led me into their modest house.

"Where's Billy?" I asked.

"He's working, but he should be here any minute. He said to make yourself at home. Crash here tonight if you want."

"Sounds good. You got the pills?"

"Yeah. You got the 20 Gs?"

"Of course."

"Well, let's get this done," he said. "My uncle is right across the street."

"Cool," I said, getting up. "Let's go."

"Nah, man, you can't go over there."

"Why not?"

"Let's just say you're the wrong shade."

We laughed. "He's right across the street?" I asked.

"Yeah, man. I'll be back in fifteen minutes."

I pulled out two stacks of hundred-dollar bills from my gym bag. "You want to count it?" I asked.

"My brother says you're a good guy. I trust you," he said, snatching the money and sticking it in the pockets of his windbreaker. "I'll be right back. *Mi casa, su casa*." Then he left.

I didn't start to worry until about an hour later. I walked outside to see if there was any police activity. Nothing. I went back inside and paced around the living room. About two hours after Angel left, the door opened. It was Billy, wearing yet another waiter's uniform.

"Danny? What the hell you doing here?" he asked, shocked to see me.

"Funny," I said. "I'm waiting for your brother."

After a few minutes of "Who's On First?" we came to the realization that Billy's brother had robbed me.

"Half this money is my parents'," I said. "They're going to lose their house. We have to talk to your uncle."

It took me about an hour and a half bottle of tequila to convince

Billy to take me over to his uncle's house.

Babe was in his mid-forties, which looked like ninety when I was twenty-one. He was a short, well-built guy who seemed to be smiling the entire time I was in his company, even when he was screaming bloody murder. He greeted us from the second-floor balcony of his two-story mansion—the most palatial residence that I had ever seen.

"You lost your *mind*, Billy?" he barked. "Why you bringing a gringo to my house?"

"Uncle Babe, this is Danny, the guy I was telling you about from UNLV."

"I don't know what you're talking about," Babe said. "Get him gone. *Pronto*!"

Babe walked back inside. Billy pleaded with his uncle to let us in. After a couple of neighbors screamed for Billy to shut up, Babe let us into his garage. I explained what his other nephew had done and the predicament that it'd put me in, how my family was going to lose their house.

"That sucks, Gringo," Babe said. "But what does it have to do with me?"

"I know it doesn't," I said. "But I have no one else."

There was a long silence. Babe left the garage, and we followed him into his back yard to a built-in swimming pool that was shaped like Mexico with the colors of the Mexican flag, green, white, and red, painted on the bottom, and Our Lady of Guadalupe painted on the diving board. He pulled off his shirt and pants. The only thing he kept on was his tighty-whities. He climbed into the pool.

"If you want to talk business, get in the pool," Babe said.

I looked at Billy, who nodded.

I slowly pulled off my polo shirt and began to unbutton my cargo shorts.

"Gringo, if I wanted to fuck you, I would have brought you upstairs," Babe said.

"Uncle Babe wants to make sure you're not wired," Billy said.

"But I don't have any underwear on," I said, loud enough for Babe to hear.

"You gringos are nasty," he said, laughing. "I guess we can't talk, then. Billy, show your friend out."

I pulled down my pants and climbed into the pool.

"It's no big thing, *esse*." He laughed again.

I explained that I had a huge market, but that Angel's theft of my money left me tapped out, and that, if we couldn't come up with a solution, I'd lose all of my customers.

"You said that you came here with twenty grand and you were supposed to get two hundred thousand pills," he said.

I nodded.

". . .Here's what we're gonna do," he finally said after staring into my eyes for a while and sucking on the inside of his cheek. "I'll front you all the pills. And then you bring me back twenty-one grand within two weeks, or it's a thousand a week vig.[11] And if I don't get my money, your parents are gonna have a lot more to worry about than losing their house."

I nodded.

"You sure you can handle this much weight?" he asked.

Two days later I brought him back the twenty-one thousand dollars. Once he saw that I was real, we set up a credit line, and within a month he was fronting me a million White Crosses, and I was selling them just as fast.

After I paid back my parents and bought them a cow, one of the first things that I did was start taking flying lessons, at an accelerated pace. I very quickly I earned my pilot's license.

I didn't stop there. I went on to get a commercial pilot's license, and I bought a small fleet of planes and opened a flying school. I didn't much care about the school, but I figured that the planes might come in handy.

Within six months from the time I met Babe, I was making forty thousand bucks[12] a week, twice what my father made in a year.

But I knew I could make much more.

I had discovered two main flaws in our partnership, neither of which was going to be an easy fix. First, Babe wasn't able to supply me with enough product. A million pills a week was simply not enough. Second, the quality was lousy. I lost about ten percent of each batch because the pills were chipped or ground to powder. From what I heard, Babe transported them in tires from Mexico to Arizona.

I went to work with my roommate Ed, whom I had convinced to transfer to UNLV. After a few bad batches, he figured out how to make an almost perfect White Cross. The trouble was duplicating it in volume. We bought a press, but we couldn't figure it out. Every time we tried, the pills would either come out the wrong size or the cross would be incomplete. Though the contents of the pill were exactly the same, in the drug business, as in most businesses, marketing matters.

I was investing all the money that I was earning, and we were about to go tits up, when Ed suggested that we partner up with a drug company.

That was a stroke of genius.

We formed our own company, Pucci Pet Products. Our first and only product was Super Dog multi vitamins. Then we found our partner.

Colonel Eli Lilly, a pharmaceutical chemist and Union Army veteran of the American Civil War, had founded Eli Lilly and Company and served as its president until his death in 1898. To this day, a stylized version of his signature appears in the company's red logo. Just before and after World War I, the Lilly company experienced rapid change, and by World War II they had partnered with the American Red Cross and had facilities in thirty-seven countries. By 1975, they were one of the biggest drug manufacturers in the world.

We made a deal with them to produce our "dog vitamins," and although they were traded on the New York Stock Exchange, they asked very few questions. They ran a small batch at their Los Angeles plant and mailed it to us in Las Vegas. I had to admit they did look like the ones we got from Babe. Still, we weren't expecting much; the previous two had been busts.

Ed and I stood in front of a movie theater on Fremont Street and each took two hits from the new batch. We walked into the theater to see *Jaws*. We stopped and got candy and popcorn and made our way to our seats. By the time that shark came barreling out of the water at that fishing boat, my balls were tightening up. Soon, I was totally engrossed in the film. When the lights went up, I noticed that Ed and I had not touched our popcorn and candy.

As we strolled outside into the cool Las Vegas night, I turned to him and said, "We're gonna be millionaires."

I wasn't wrong.

Babe was apprehensive at first. "You out of your fucking mind, Gringo? You want me to cut ties with my peoples in Mexico so I can do business with a college boy?" But eventually he came around, and soon I was supplying, through him, most of the White Crosses being sold in Arizona, California, and Nevada.

And I wasn't done. I hadn't told him that I was manufacturing them; instead I'd said I had a strong connect in California. He didn't have the remotest idea that my supplier, at the time I started writing this book, was valued at about eighty-seven billion dollars. (An interesting side note: In 2009, Lilly pleaded guilty to illegally marketing the drug Zyprexa for off-label uses not approved by the U.S. Food and Drug Administration, particularly in the treatment of dementia in the elderly. The company paid a $515 million criminal fine, at the time the largest in history.)

I also convinced Fonzie to introduce me to Dusty La Sarge, who was the sergeant-at-arms of the Bandidos' national chapter. He arranged a meeting with Ronny Hodge, another ex-Marine, who had taken over as president when Chambers went to prison.

Dusty and I went down to the Bandidos' headquarters in Austin, Texas, to meet him. Ronny was pretty easy to do business with. In fact, we did the deal at a strip club. He reminded us that the founder of the club was away in prison for murdering a drug dealer who had sold them phony meth. I failed to mention that our White crosses were not technically meth, but I assured him that they were top-quality, much better than the shit he had been getting.

Soon they were moving a few million pills a week. Then I got a call from the Bandidos—their one plane had crashed in Idaho. This proved to be a boon for me, since I had three planes at my disposal and my commercial pilot license. I would fly my 320 Twin Cessna, which at the time was considered a poor man's Lear Jet, around the country, dropping off millions of White Crosses. I met Bandidos at various airports, and more often than not they would drive right up onto the tarmac, where we would load the pills from the plane into their trucks. The smaller orders, say a hundred thousand pills, were even easier. We would buy a ticket from Las Vegas to, say, Boston. We would check our bags, which were loaded with White Crosses, but not make our flights. Our buyers would pick up the bags at Logan. The airlines were actually delivering the product for us for free. That's how wide-open the 1970s were.

Before long the feds grew curious about where these perfect pills were being manufactured. It was obvious that they were coming out of professional presses in the United States. They began using ballistics tests, which they are performed on the pills, but we were able to stay one step ahead of them. We switched the dyes in the presses every ten million pills, which fooled them into believing the pills were being manufactured by several presses at different locations. At my peak, I was selling about ten million White Crosses a week, and it was relatively easy. There weren't many DEA agents in Middle America. Hell, I doubt that they knew what they were looking for anyway. Don't forget, our pills were ephedrine, which was perfectly legal back then.

This was a curse and a blessing. Whenever one of the Bandidos did get arrested, which wasn't often, they would ultimately walk once the Feds tested the pills in their laboratories. While the Bandidos may have been relived to be free from jail, they weren't thrilled that our product was not meth. Not that anyone could tell, except for the tiny minority of users who shot it—they apparently failed to get the same rush as they did with meth. They also didn't die as often, but that didn't seem to matter, because we started to get complaints.

By 1978, I was clearing two hundred thousand bucks a week, which equates to about a million a week today. I was twenty-four years old.

In retrospect, I should have set up distribution centers all around the country and taken out ads in magazines. White Crosses could have been Red Bull. But I *was* only twenty-four, and I couldn't see the big picture. Instead of working with what I had, I gave up on White Crosses. *Gringo stupido.*

I sold some weed, and the truth is that I could have made a good living from it. But I was so spoiled by the money that I had made with White Crosses that the money that I was earning from pot felt slight, and I let my greed take me into a business that I should have stayed away from.

Why was I obsessed with making money? I guess in part because my parents came from such abject poverty, and even though my siblings and I grew up middle-class, we were constantly reminded of what life was like during the Depression. It scared me.

Another reason was that I had fallen in love, and that scared me, too. Lisa Lien, the young woman that I fell for, happened to come from one of the wealthiest and most prominent families in South Dakota, but I would never have guessed it when I met her.

I stopped at a French restaurant—high-class, with white tablecloths, one of the nicest dining spots in the state—before flying my plane back to Las Vegas. My waitress was adorable, a student at the University of

South Dakota. She was absolutely stunning in the soft light of the restaurant. She had a flowing mane of blond hair that was almost white and fell halfway down her back, and she wore little makeup, which made her freckles visible. She was wearing a crisp French waitress uniform, complete with a short white apron, and I thought she was the most beautiful woman that I had ever met.

There was, however, something peculiar about her. First of all, she wasn't impressed when I left her a hundred bucks for a coffee and a piece of pie. Nor was she impressed that I lived in Las Vegas, or that I flew my own plane. What was the deal? I wondered.

I tried to hang out with her after work, but she wasn't having it. She gave me her number, though, and I called her two days later.

"Hey, Lisa," I said. "It's Dan."

"Hi," she said. "I was expecting your call."

"Oh, really," I said, a bit surprised at her confidence. "Are you working tomorrow night?"

"No."

"Okay, give me your address, and I'll pick you up for dinner. We'll eat at my favorite Italian restaurant."

"Sounds good," she said, not even bothering to get further details.

The next night I drove to her dorm. When I pulled up she was sitting on the steps, smiling widely.

"Jump in," I said.

She got in the car and kissed me on the cheek. She was wearing bell bottom jeans and a light blue cashmere sweater that was much more flattering than the uniform.

We made small talk for the next few minutes, until we returned to the airport.

"I thought we were having dinner," she said.

"We are," I said. "We're going to Piero's."

"Piero's?" she asked. "Where's that?"

"Convention Center Drive, Las Vegas."

"We're going to *Las Vegas?*"

"We can't get good Italian food in South Dakota."

Before she could answer, I grabbed her hand and led her onto my plane.

That night we ate *osso buco* and drank Italian wine. Lisa told me that she was twenty-one (she was really eighteen), and that her last name was Lien. I almost fell off my chair. This girl was a *Lien?* They were a prominent Republican family that had pull all the way to the White House. I asked her why she was working as a waitress. She explained that her father and uncle had started out doing back-breaking work in the quarries long before they started their company, and that her father felt the kids should all work.

She stayed with me a few days in Las Vegas but insisted that she couldn't miss any more classes. The rest of that semester, I'd pick her up on her free days and fly to different cities—New Orleans, San Francisco, and so forth—often just for the night. When spring break came, we boarded the Concord and headed to Paris to shop.

That summer, I met her family, and believe it or not, they really took to me. The fact that I was six years older than Lisa didn't seem to matter. I tried my best to convince them to let her transfer to UNLV, but they weren't having it. They did ultimately concede to allow her to attend of Arizona State, where her brother was a senior. I immediately bought the best house I could find in Tempe, which was featured in the back of the *Arizona Yellow Pages*; the owner was the president of Pepsi.

We were married on my twenty-ninth birthday. Lisa was twenty-three. When I came home one day, she almost tackled me. She was giddy with excitement. She was pregnant. I couldn't have been happier. I held my wife tight, and I promised her that I would do everything in my power to be the best husband and father on the planet Earth.

The truth, though, is that things weren't going that well for me. I had extricated myself completely from the White Crosses trade, and I was looking for a new venture.

About that time I met a couple of old bikers who were manufacturing meth in their trailer and offered me two pounds. Meth, they told me, was "the drug of the future." They were way ahead of their time, because it took another twenty-five years for it to make its way from the fringes of the desert into the gay dance scene and finally the mainstream. But I declined their offer. Meth scared me. Besides, there was another drug that had grabbed America by the nose.

Cocaine was the drug of choice for rich, cool folks. For a hundred dollars a gram, you could fantasize that you were partying with Andy Warhol and Bianca Jagger at Studio 54, having a shootout with Sonny and Crocket on the mean streets of Miami, or breaking off a bit from one of Tony Montana's bricks. Coke did not carry the negative connotations that crack did when it came along a few years later. I suspect that's because of the racial dynamics—cocaine was considered a white person's drug whereas crack, which didn't come along until I was out of the game, got labeled a ghetto drug that blacks smoked.

One night at a club, I was introduced to a sharply dressed nineteen-year-old named Chris Robinson, who was throwing around Benjamins like they were Washingtons . He looked like a preppy you'd expect to break out a lacrosse stick way before a coke spoon. But there he was, snorting it with a gold spoon and tipping the bouncers so no one would bother him. He was from a wealthy Bel-Air family and had attended Dartmouth for a year but dropped out because he yearned to "get his education on the streets."

Chris may have been a rich kid, but he sure had balls. When he visited Colombia with his family, he asked the concierge at the Bogota Hilton, in entitled American rich-kid form, if he knew anyone who could get him cocaine. The concierge's contact actually had people in Miami and was willing to put Chris in the distribution chain. For the previous six months, Chris had been buying coke in Miami and transporting it to Las Vegas.

Someone tipped him off about what I had been doing with White

Crosses, and that I was a good pilot. He propositioned me, claiming that we could get a kilo of coke in Miami for forty thousand dollars and sell it in California for sixty. Do the math—one flight from Miami to California with fifty kilos would yield a million bucks in profit.

As good as the money was, however, I didn't trust Chris—he was a loose cannon. I could tell that the Colombians thought he was disrespectful. They came to meetings wearing suits while he showed up in surfer shorts and a tank top. He wound up ripping them off. Soon, they came looking for him. After I convinced them that I didn't know where he'd gone, they offered to work with me directly.

I set up my old buddy Ted in business, too. I handled Vegas, mostly from my house in Tempe, and he worked out of Denver. After a few months, we were rolling, but unlike the White Cross business, I hated cocaine. There was just too much money at stake. Where sixty thousand dollars got you a million White Crosses, it didn't even get you two kilos of cocaine.

My foray into the cocaine trade came, anyhow, to a quick end. I got a troubling call from Ted in Denver. "I think I'm under surveillance," he said. "They're rummaging through our trash outside the townhouse."

That was before cell phone technology, of course, so I always used pay phones to call Ted and my other associates. While I was in the cocaine business, I never called Ted from my house—except once. One night I needed to reach him. I kept calling from different pay phones, but I couldn't. Lisa was pissed off that I kept going out, because it was pouring like hell that night, which in itself was very odd in Tempe. And to tell the truth, I got a little lazy. About 9:30, I gave in and called from my house. There was no answer; by then, the DEA had found ten kilos in a storage bin they'd tracked him to. Ten kilos was, at that time, a huge bust in a non-border state.

They rounded up Ted and some other guys, and a few months later I got a call that they were going to indict me. My lawyer advised me to fly to Denver and turn myself in. I got in touch with my father-in-law Chuck Lien and asked him very politely to help me out. They were going to hold a Forfeiture Hearing on me to try to figure out where the money was coming from, and I needed him to put up my bond of a hundred and fifty thousand dollars, which he paid with a cashier's check.[13]

I was charged with a slew of crimes. The feds acted like I was Tony Montana when in fact I was moving very little weight, especially compared to what I had done with White Crosses.

They even tried their best to hit me with a RICO.[14] At that time the government mostly used it against the Italian-American Mafia,[15] but they seemed pretty excited to try it out on me. They indicted me on a slew of charges but they never did get to indict me with a RICO; I learned very quickly how the Republican Party worked. The Attorney General of the United States had to sign off on the indictment. At the time, Allan K. Simpson was the Senate Minority Whip. More importantly, Senator Simpson had been a college roommate of Bruce Lien, Chuck's brother. When my case came to trial I had letters from three U.S. senators and one governor—eighty-four in all. The judge said that he had never seen anything like it.

I finally pled out to tax evasion and illegal use of a telephone. I was sentenced to 102 months. The feds were crying that I'd used my political influence to get "only" 102 months. They tried to ship me to a prison on the East Coast, where I had no contacts. I told my attorney, Joe Saint Veltri, a lifelong Democrat, that I wanted to stay on the West Coast. He said I was really pushing my luck. When I told him that I was going to reach out to my father-in-law, Chuck Lien, he said, "If they could pull this off, I'll join the Republican Party." I assume Joe voted for Bush in '88, because I was switched to the Boron Federal Prison Camp in sunny California.

I had been the biggest supplier of White Crosses in the world by the time I was twenty-four. I had burned through millions of dollars.

It's not worth going into, but suffice it to say that I wasn't as prudent with my money as my parents were. I spoiled my wife with shopping sprees in New York. I bought huge houses, wore flashy clothes, rocked a thick gold rope chain. I even wore a diamond pinkie ring. Who did I think I was, Joe Pesci?

Now the only thing that was on my mind was that I had a child to support. My son was born on October 10, 1985. We named him Hunter. I may have been biased, but I honestly had never seen a handsomer baby in my entire life.

I got to enjoy my son for all of six days before I was shipped off.

3

BACK TO SCHOOL

AS WE RODE THROUGH the Mojave Desert, there was not a single blade of grass in sight. And it was hot. To put it in perspective, the hottest temperature ever recorded on Earth was not in Africa or the Middle East but in nearby Death Valley (137 degrees). When I got out of the van, the heat took my breath away.

Remember when I was bragging about how I'd used my political clout to get transferred to a West Coast prison—a *camp*, no less? It may have been the worst thing that could have happened to me.

The Boron Air Force Station was part of the second segment of the Air Defense Command radar network, which began during the Korean War. The 750th Aircraft Control and Warning Squadron was assigned to the newly built radar command center in 1952, with the duty of guiding interceptor aircraft toward unidentified intruders picked up on the unit's radar scopes. In the 1960s, the Federal Aviation Administration (FAA) joined with the Air Force in operating the radar facility.

In 1978, the federal government found a new use for this site: they opened the Boron Federal Prison Camp. At the time, this was one of forty-seven federal prison camps in the country and housed about 540 male inmates. There was no wall around the prison, not even a fence. It sounds pretty good, but I would have much rather been in Attica than stuck in that shithole.

Though it was no longer a base, they still had air-raid testing with the new B1 and Stealth bomber. My job for my first six months there was raking rocks. We slept in the original barracks, which had been built in the 1940s. I have heard people refer to Boron as Club Fed. They must be out of their minds.

Luckily they had a weight pile, and it was there I made some pretty cool friends, including mobster Joey Cusumano, marijuana legend Warren "Blackie" Anderson, and my soon-to-be best friend, Paul Holt.

I did my best to stay busy and stay out of trouble.

When Hunter was about a month old, Lisa started bringing him on visits. You can't believe how fast your son grows when you only get to see him every two weeks. I enjoyed every second of our two-hour visits, even on those occasions when he slept through them. He was an easy child who seldom cried. One of my favorite things was when he held onto my pinky finger with his tiny hand.

About four months into my sentence I was out raking rocks when one of the COs[16] came up to me and said that I had to go to the warden's office. Why the hell for? I wondered. When I arrived, I was greeted by my counselor, who said they'd gotten a call from my wife. She had found Hunter in his crib with his eyes rolled back in his head. They had rushed him to the emergency room and done everything they could, but he had died in Lisa's arms of sudden infant death syndrome as soon as they took him off life support. The poor kid. My poor wife.

I would have given anything to be there to comfort her. My lawyers, along with her family, convinced a judge to give me a furlough to go to the funeral. The problem was that they were going to require me to be handcuffed and accompanied by two marshals. I was catching a lot of ink up there, and the local media would have had a field day. Not only had they painted me as a kingpin (which I wasn't); they'd never failed to mention that I was part of the Lien family. We decided that it would be better for everyone if I stayed put. It destroyed me not to be able to bury my son, but I couldn't be selfish—I had to think about my wife.

Understandably, Lisa went into a period of mourning. The day after the funeral, she flew to California to visit me. I heard that she was in such a frenzied state when she arrived that they'd let her cut the long line of visitors. In fact, the warden let us use his office for that first visit.

After the initial shock began to wear off, I tried to stay busy, and I began taking college courses. Within a couple of years I earned my B.S. in Business, which I never had finished at UNLV. I even taught English to some of my fellow inmates.

I was such a model prisoner that, after about thirty-six months, I was able to transfer to Geiger Federal Prison in Spokane, Washington. Prison is never easy, but we used to joke that people would pay to do time in Geiger. In the eighteen months that I served there, I ate pretty well, weight-trained regularly, and had decent phone and visiting privileges. The best part of Geiger was that I was able to see and socialize with beautiful women every day.

Yes, you're reading right. Geiger was a co-ed prison. Many of the women were *traffacantes*'[17] girlfriends or drug mules. They were some of the hottest women in the world, and for the most part they ran the prison. That was because they had the COs wrapped around their little fingers. For instance, if one of these hotties had a boyfriend who pissed them off, she would tell the CO that she was banging, and the chump would give the boyfriend thirty days in the hole.[18] The women had the keys to all the closets, and they brought their boyfriends in for quickies.

The hottest of the hot was Maria Rosa, a dark-haired Mexican beauty in her late twenties. She was the longtime girlfriend of Gacha,[19] who, along with Pablo Escobar and the Ochoa brothers, ran the Medellín cartel. In 1988, while Maria Rosa was in prison, *Forbes* listed Gacha on its annual list of the world's billionaires.

Weight training has been a staple of prison life for decades, but given that the men wanted to impress the women, at Geiger it meant even more. I partnered up with a Colombian named Manny, who was the head of a powerful family in Medellín. Manny had immigrated to America in the 1960s and somehow obtained citizenship. He worked in New York as a taxi driver, made some connections, and was one of the first *traffacantes* to bring cocaine into New York. I think he had a thing for Maria Rosa, but he didn't make a move on her because of her boyfriend back in Colombia.

Gacha and the other *trafficantes* didn't stop the women from dressing to the nines. One of the most amazing things about the prison was that we were able to wear our street clothes. I say it's amazing because some of the female inmates had wardrobes worth tens of thousands of dollars. On Movie Night, it was common for them to come correct in Gucci and Versace.

Though life wasn't bad at Geiger, it was still a prison, and I fell to my knees and thanked God when I was granted my first furlough in the fall of 1988. It was for twelve hours, and I wasn't allowed to travel more than twenty miles from the prison. That was fine with me. There was a motel only a few minutes away. Lisa flew in and greeted me at the door in a black negligee. I probably spent eleven and a half of my first twelve hours on the outside inside my beautiful wife.

We couldn't have been more in love. She told me that her family still wanted us together, and that once I was released we would start making another baby. I remember going back to Geiger the next morning floating on air. I had two more years to serve, but it was going to be all right. My honey was going to wait for me.

On Valentine's Day, 1990, about two months before I was scheduled for release, I was taking a nap in my cell when I was called to the warden's office. A constable was standing there waiting for me. He handed me a manila envelope and wished me a good day. As the CO walked me out of the office, the warden said, "It happens to all of us, Davis."

In my cell I opened it up to find my divorce papers. How could this possibly be? I asked myself. A few months earlier, I had been granted a seventy-two-hour furlough and I been able to spend Christmas with my in-laws. After dinner on Christmas day, Lisa's father and uncle had met me in Chuck's study, where they promised me that, once I got out of prison, I would go to work for them in the family business. Unlike Lisa's dad, who had nine children, her uncle Bruce, who had none, said that I was going to be his protégé. Bruce had wrapped his arm around me and said, "You kids got through the hard part. It's going to be smooth sailing from here."

He couldn't have been more wrong. Lisa not only divorced me, she made my life miserable. In April, I was released from Geiger—well, almost released. I was walking towards the van that was supposed to bring me to my halfway house in Rapid City when one of the COs called out, "Davis, get back here!" Seriously?

He took me to Solitary and told me that I wasn't going anywhere. The next day my lawyer paid me a visit. Lisa had reached out to the halfway house, claiming that she was afraid that I would cause her or her new boyfriend harm if I were allowed to reside in town. Bullshit: She knew damn well that I had never committed a violent crime, let alone a domestic.

I was mandated to spend another sixty days in Geiger, mostly in solitary, because they had given away my cell and the prison was packed. I reached out to Lisa's brother Pete, who was as shocked as I was. He said he would try to get to the bottom of it. When I spoke to him a couple of days later, he told me Lisa had fallen for a guy from her softball team. Pete ended up sponsoring me; his wife Nancy even picked me up at the airport and drove me to the halfway house. To this day, I have nothing but love for Lisa's family.

Almost all of my property and cars were in her name, and she wasted little time taking everything that the government had left behind.

When I entered prison I owned homes, planes, apartment buildings, and oil wells. When I was released, I had nothing. But I had made a promise to myself when I entered prison, and I repeated the promise to my parole board: Once I got released, I would never deal in cocaine again. I guess prison really did rehabilitate me, because I have kept my promise to this day.

4

THERE'S MONEY IN MARIJUANA?

I WAS BROKE. The government had put tax liens on practically everything I owned. The feds had taken all the money that I had earned, legitimately or not. My wife had grabbed everything else. Who do you think ended up coming to my rescue? One of the guys that I had helped make rich selling White Crosses? No. How about one of the women I'd sponsored? Hell, no.

My mother was the one person who came to the rescue. I did my probation in Rapid City, South Dakota, not far from where I grew up. She linked me up with a developer named Billy Durst. Within days of our first meeting, he set us up with a small ice cream parlor at the base of Mount Rushmore. Soon Mom and I expanded and started selling pizzas. We worked our tails off—7 a.m. to midnight, seven days a week. And we started to make money. The problem was that it was a seasonal business, and the winter starts pretty early in South Dakota.

When the snow arrived, I was lucky enough to get transferred back to Las Vegas,[20] where I met the love of my life, Julie. My cousin Jim introduced me to her; she was looking for someone to go to the gym with, and I, fresh from prison, was in top shape. I wasn't expecting much effort because I had been told that she was a rich girl—her family owned the largest meat company in Nevada. But she was a hard worker, and we very quickly transformed her body to be as stunning as her face.

Like my first wife, Julie came from a wealthy family. She was raised with the Las Vegas elite and eventually sent her daughter to the renowned Meadows School to carry on the family tradition. It was a trip when I picked her up at school and saw a line of limousines fetching her classmates. We would have the kids over on weekends, and no matter who they were or from what enormous wealth, they just wanted to be kids and we would have races in the back yard and eat hot dogs off the grill.

Unlike my first wife, Julie never had to work. Her father bought her a large house and gave her, and the entire family, brand-new BMWs every year. Julie's daughter, Amber, was her father's particular favorite because she shared the same birthday as the old man. I'm sure some folks think that, when a guy hooks up a wealthy woman, he is all set. That was not my case. In fact, it made me feel less than a man, and being around tremendous wealth made me more motivated to earn money. I had refused to take handouts from Lisa's family, and I certainly was not about to start with Julie. But I quickly learned that life as a felon wasn't going to be easy.

Many people fail to realize, when they consider recidivism rates in American prisons, just how difficult it is to survive legitimately. For instance, when I was released, I not only had to face the stigma of being a felon, I found it nearly impossible to get a job. I wanted to fly commercially, but the government forbade it. I thought about selling real estate, but Nevada state law wouldn't allow ex-felons to be licensed. I *could* probably have gotten hired at McDonald's, but I chose to go another route.

There was a dead spot in the early 1990s, before the cartels took over Mexico, when small-time growers could deliver quality marijuana with limited risk. I snuck down to Nogales, Mexico, on the border of Nogales, Arizona, where I linked up with my old pal Pepe. I had known him before I went to prison, and I remembered that he had an impeccable reputation in my circles. He must have felt the same about me, because he immediately set me up with a credit line, one even larger than I had hoped for.

Pepe was a short, skinny Mexican at whom you wouldn't look twice, who drove a red pickup truck and had a humble and nonchalant demeanor. You'd have thought he mowed lawns for a living when, in fact, he was moving tons of marijuana. Not just any marijuana—high-grade *sinsimella*,[21] which was the bud of choice for serious pot heads across the country. The demand for it was extremely high, but it was difficult to get given the challenges of transporting it from Mexico.

We struck a deal and we began transporting the product via a tunnel from Nogales, Mexico, to Nogales, Arizona. Once we got it into Arizona, I used an old trick I had heard about from my days as a horse racer. Horse trailers are usually two- or four-horse. We had a custom-designed trailer that looked like a four-horse but held only three horses; the fourth space was a stash compartment. You would be shocked how much weed that fourth stall could hold if you stacked it correctly. Once I got rolling, I figured that I would earn a thousand bucks a pound, less the hundred a pound I paid my driver. Do the math.

Just as had once been true with White Crosses, the Mexicans could not supply enough to me. Often we could only get half the amount we asked for, which was troubling, especially when you consider that the risk was the same whether it was a hundred pounds, or a thousand, or ten thousand . I racked my brain trying to figure out how I could cut out my Mexican connects and, as I'd done with the White Crosses, work the entire business from within the United States. I was not able to figure it out, but eventually someone did—the United States government.

Besides the problem of Pepe not being able to meet our demands, the operation ran pretty smoothly—until it didn't, when I lost Pepe, who was the best partner that I ever had. One day when I went down to Mexico, he pretended not to know me. His guys started telling me to get lost. It turned out that the *federales* had hung poor Pepe over the side of a bridge and forced him to give up tons of marijuana and some cash. That was his last day in business.

Luckily, I found a new contact in Tijuana, Bruce, who could supply us. He was able to get the pot transported to Los Angeles. In prison, I had made friends with one of the high-ranking members of the Crips. Bruce's crew would shove a big load of weed in the trunk of a rental car and leave it for them in a predetermined spot at about 9 a.m. His crew would pick up the car, drop off the weed somewhere, and return the car to us by 5 p.m., cash in hand.

I wasn't making the kind of money I made with the White Crosses, but within eighteen months I was clearing about fifty thousand a week. The difference was that, this time, I was smart enough to save my money and live below, not beyond, my means. I was also much smarter about where I put my money. The first time I made serious money, I'd put my profits in U.S. banks and invested it in American companies, which made the government's job pretty easy when they hit me with tax liens, froze and then emptied my accounts, and seized my properties. This time I sent my money south of the border into bank accounts in Mexico City. One of my connects had introduced me to a banker named Carlos, who was more than happy to take my U.S. dollars and store them safely for me. This may have been the wisest move that I ever made.

I eventually married Julie and helped raise her daughter, whom I grew to love like my own. I purchased modest homes in Las Vegas and in Arizona. I had nothing to prove—I didn't need the gold chains, the fancy cars, the mansions, and certainly not the damn diamond pinkie ring. I was more than content being a responsible husband and a devoted father. This was the happiest time of my life—until my grade-school chum Marvin Schumacher paid me a visit.

5

WITH FRIENDS LIKE THESE, WHO NEEDS FRIENDS?

MARV WANTED TO GET INTO the weed business. I invited him to stay a few days with me, during which time I took a hard look at him. On paper, he seemed like the perfect candidate. He had been a tough kid—probably the toughest—in my high school. To be more precise, he'd been pretty good with his hands but more of a bully than a tough guy. He wasn't married. He had no kids. He had no record (I don't think he had even been arrested), so if he did get caught he would probably get a suspended sentence or, at worst, a 365.[22]

I agreed to front him twenty-five pounds of pot. He did pretty well with it, and the next time I saw him I fronted him fifty.

I didn't know that Marv had partnered up with a meth cook in Wyoming who had a prior meth manufacturing conviction. Had I possessed that tidbit of information, I would have sent him packing. One thing led to another, and the feds put him on surveillance and caught him with twenty-eight thousand cash and two ounces of meth.

The feds pressed Marv. Though getting caught dealing meth was a much more serious offense than getting caught dealing weed, as a first-time offender, there was no way he could have gotten sentenced to more than a year in jail. In fact, he'd probably have gotten a suspended sentence. But instead of keeping his mouth shut and calling a lawyer, he led them to a car in Wyoming where he had stashed another two pounds of meth. Yes, you are reading this right. The feds had known *nothing* about the car. But for some reason that I still cannot fathom, Marv felt compelled to tell them about it.

Then it was on. They probably left him alone in a hot office. He was thirsty as hell. A cop would come in and give him a big cold can of Pepsi. Then he would have to use the rest room, but it would be broken, and they would make him wait, almost pissing his pants. Six hours later, the cop would tell him that he'd done some checking, that Marv was a good guy but that, even if it was his first offense, the D.A. was coming down hard on first timers and was going to make an example out of Marv. He'd probably get thirty years and have to serve twenty-five. Poor Marv would not get out until he was he was almost seventy. A pity. They told him tall tales about the racial strife in prison and how the brothers fucked white guys, especially white guys from the sticks. It would only be a matter of time before he had to marry one of them. And after a few minutes of this nonsense, Marv, like most bullies, folded like a Texas Hold 'Em player with an off-suit deuce-seven.

When the feds heard *my* name, they must have felt they'd hit the lottery. They knew that I had beaten the system selling the White Crosses made of ephedrine, and they had been itching to get me ever since. Marv explained to the DEA that we went way back, that we'd been friends in grade school, even Sunday school. I assume that he missed the part about Thou Shalt Not Lie Or Frame Thy Fucking Friend. When the DEA added this information to Marv's false sworn testimony that his two pounds of meth was actually mine, and that I was a meth distributor, they tagged him incredibly as "credible" and nailed my coffin shut, since I was the perfect fall guy. The police never even checked the bags of meth or the car for my fingerprints, interviewed the neighbors to find out whether I had ever been in the vicinity, or polygraphed Marv.

It made no difference that he had made innumerable phone calls from his home telephone, not to me, but to chemical companies and pharmacies, clearly to acquire the ingredients needed to manufacture his own meth. Additionally, his partner had a prior meth conviction. None of that mattered.

The feds also ignored the very strong possibility that Marv was lying about the meth being mine. They had no incriminating tapes or photos of Marv and me hanging out together or transacting business payments or deliveries. All they had was a drug dealer's word. And a little thing like the truth was not going to stop them from building a case against someone like me—a case that would help the careers of everyone involved.

At the time, Marv was in debt to me for the weed that I had fronted to him. He was always crying poverty and putting me off, which, in retrospect, was strange considering that he could have paid me back any time because he was running a crystal meth cooking and sales operation of his own.

But I was unaware of any of this. One day I called Marv to ask him when he could come up to see me. He said that he would call me right back, but he didn't call. I was getting pissed off—I'd fronted him the weed, and I wanted my money. I called him the next day, and somebody else, whom I did not recognize, answered the phone. I assumed that it was one of his friends, but it was a cop. Now they had my location, but I made it even easier for them. When Marv called me back later, I told him I was flying into South Dakota the next day, and that we could meet up then.

It was a cold day in Deadwood. When I finally got the chance to listen to the tape that Marv made for the DEA, I could hear the snow crunching beneath our feet as we walked to Kevin Costner's casino to sit and drink a cup of coffee.

Marv sat down and handed me ten grand wrapped in a McDonald's burger bag; without the least suspicion that I was on tape, I began to quiz him. "Is this all you have for me? You've got to start picking things up and bring in more of your accounts receivable, buddy."

People have gone to the electric chair on less evidence than I had just given Marv and his recording crew. It was a perfect tape for their purposes and, from my perspective, a noose. I asked him if he'd like to spend the night at my mom's, but he said he had to get back home to feed his dogs and put more pellets in his wood stove before his pipes started to freeze. Let me translate: "The feds want me back at my place so they can transcribe the tape I just made and get it to a magistrate in the morning."

We walked out of the casino onto Main Street and were heading toward the Franklin Hotel when I noticed a couple of uniformed municipal police officers across the street. I thought nothing of it, since the street was lined with casinos and other businesses that required heightened security.

We crossed the street. Before we could enter the hotel, those uniformed cops, and plain-clothed DEA personnel, tackled us and pointed guns at our heads. The cops cuffed me and took me away in a patrol car. I presumed that they had done the same to my old friend Marv. I still had no clue he was working for them. In hindsight, I imagine that he simply got in his pickup truck and drove back to the house where he kept his Vaseline.

Once they had me in the patrol car, the cops asked if I had large amounts of cash and, before I could answer, reached into my ski jacket and pulled out their burger bag. They took me to the local jail, where they began ordering me to give up my connections. I kept silent. When they put me in the holding cell, I ate the paper that contained the UPS and FedEx tracking numbers for our weed shipments. I thought I was going to choke to death because all that I had to wash it down with was my spit. But it was worth it, for, had they been able to track those shipments, my partners and I would have been in for even more pain.

I called my attorney friend Dan Kelley. He said he'd be up to see me that night, but he was forced to wait until the next day to visit me. As I lay in my bunk in that shithole of a jail in Deadwood, my mind was racing, running dozens of questions, scenarios, and possibilities through my knowledge and experience, trying to get the tumblers to line up so I might unlock some answers.

The next day Kelley met me in a phone booth-sized room to consult long enough to tell me that I needed somebody with a hell of a lot more experience in criminal cases than he. The room was unbearably hot, which, as I pointed out earlier, was a calculated part of their routine. As the heat and claustrophobia set in, you start thinking about getting out, almost panicking, desperate for normal temperatures. I tried to remain calm.

Then my memory lit on Carol, a woman with whom I'd been a friend in college. She'd gone on to marry a former South Dakota Attorney General named Roger Tellinghuisen, who was now a criminal defense attorney with his own practice.

I knew it was just a matter of time before the feds stepped in and started dribbling the ball against me. I needed help, so I called Roger. He was extremely cordial and familiar with state criminal defense, but he lacked federal experience. He recommended Bob Van Norman of Rapid City, South Dakota. It turned out to be the best damned advice I may ever have received.

The next day, Bob told me, as he removed his tie and sports coat, that the feds were certainly going to step in, and that there'd be only one chance to get me bailed out of jail, which I should pay via cashier's check, so the origin of the money could be confirmed. He said he was going to try his best to avoid a Forfeiture Hearing concerning the source of my funds.

Just then I recalled that I had some pot, lots of it, in the pipeline. UPS had sent the merchandise back to the company I had used to ship it because the intended recipients weren't home to sign for it, and I hadn't been able to call them and get things straight at the destinations. Somehow I was able to convey this in code to Paul Holt, my old prison buddy, when we spoke on the phone; he had the wherewithal to send somebody to reclaim the shipments so the stuff was safe.

My wife, Julie, and my brother, came to see me. She was waiting for the school year to end before she and our daughter moved up to Wyoming. It was a sad scene with Julie, looking into each other's eyes through the Plexiglas. My cell smelled like a toilet with bad breath, which made the guards smell a lot better whenever they escorted me anywhere. My food came to me through a slot in the door, and my sanity came in the form of a reprieve on the part of the loony in the next cell, who occasionally stopped screaming at the top of his lungs. Unlike me, that nut belonged in the maximum security section of the jail.

On my second night there, the jail filled up quickly. There was a brawl that apparently involved several members of the Black Hills State University football team. The jail became so overcrowded that the guards were forced to put some of the more boisterous offenders in Maximum with the nut and me. I really liked the kids, and they must have thought I was Al Capone because they treated me with respect. By the end of the night, the football players and I were working out together, having contests in pushups, burpies, and so forth. In the morning they all promised me that they would stay out of jail.

A couple of days later, my attorney paid me another visit to tell me that, if the feds put a detainer on me, there would be no bail reduction hearing where he could argue for my release. He said we needed the hearing as soon as possible—that this would be a one-shot deal, and that we had to make it count.

He was able to get a bail hearing scheduled in state court and, luckily, a blizzard hit the area, paralyzing much of the travel and commuting in and around town. Fortunately, he had a 4x4-wheel drive—they weren't as ubiquitous in 1994 as they are now—so he made it to the hearing, but the prosecutor did not. It was left to a third-string assistant prosecutor to mount the oral arguments at my bail hearing.

My entire family was at the hearing, including my wife, stepdaughter, mother and father, my brother Tim, and other friends. Since they all were staying at my brother's place a few blocks away, they were able to walk to the courthouse.

My bail was set at a hundred and fifty thousand, but the state agreed to take only ten percent as a security, leaving me to pay just fifteen thousand dollars by certified check Tim drew from a local bank. I was promptly released on bail and ordered to check in by phone with the sheriff every day.

I immediately went to the federal building in Rapid City to tell my parole officer in person what had happened. Although luck was with me, I knew that the feds could arrest me whenever they wanted to, and that I'd be in prison for many, many years.

My wife and stepdaughter stayed the next night but we both agreed that it would be better if they went back to Las Vegas. I tried to get a pass to go there, but they laughed in my face. Since I had lost twenty pounds in jail, my first order of business was to eat a pile of pizza. After stuffing myself, I went to my brother's house to see my family. They saw my release on bail as a good thing, but they were somber nonetheless, fully cognizant of the fact that this was the calm before the storm of legal problems that would surely follow. As much as I tried to keep a cool front, I knew inside that being innocent of the crimes that I was charged with wasn't going to matter. There were some powerful people who had been waiting for the opportunity to put me away since the 1970s, and they were not going to let a little thing like the truth stand in their way.

Loose ends were few. My main concern was my wife and stepdaughter. I knew that I would lose Julie, and I thought losing her as a "free" man was better than getting her letter while in prison telling me she'd moving on. I had only recently wed Julie, but I understood that I had to abandon her and Amber.

The DEA had of course offered me a deal, but there was no way I could live with myself if I gave up the people who had taken care of me in the past—I would be no better than Marvin.

So I made the decision to run. Run far away.

I had a few dollars put away from some investments, and I figured that I could live decently in Latin America even if I didn't work. But, at forty, I also knew that wasn't likely. I was my parents' son, and the truth is that I had always enjoyed a hard day's work. I had no idea what I would do, but I would worry about that later. I had to get a new identity first, and build a life. Not too many people get an opportunity to start over. This was mine.

Every time I crunched the numbers on my options, flight from justice came up as the solution. I remember meeting with my lawyer the day before I left, hoping that he would tell me something, anything, that would convince me to stay and fight for my freedom.

Instead, he looked me in the eyes for a few seconds and said, "I can't believe you're still here."

The next day I vanished into Mexico and beyond, not breathing a word to my family or friends.

6

GO SOUTH, YOUNG MAN

MY GUIDEBOOK PROMISED THAT San Miguel de Allende would be both "quaint and cosmopolitan." They weren't lying. European and American writers and artists mixed with Mexican retirees amid well-preserved colonial and Spanish architecture. The coolest thing I saw was a mammoth statue of General Ignacio Allende, a prominent figure in Mexico's War of Independence. But I had not come there to play tourist. I had two objectives: (a) get identification, and (b) learn Spanish.

The only ID I possessed was an old fake California driver's license with the name Judson Allen. And that was going to be *no bueno* in Mexico. Even legitimate local licenses are pretty much useless when dealing with Latin American authorities. If you get pulled over, check into a hotel, rent a car, board a plane, they will most likely ask you for your papers, which means your passport. And a passport, legitimate or otherwise, was much more difficult to obtain than a driver's license.

I walked over to *Academia Hispano Americano*, a top-notch Spanish language school that catered to Americans and Europeans who wanted a fast and intense immersion in the language. I signed up for the next semester, which was to begin in two weeks, and I was directed to the student center. From a board, I jotted down some student housing options. I also took down the name of a few tutors - I wanted to begin my studies immediately.

Later that day, I rented a room in a large colonial mansion that housed seven other students. My rent included three meals a day. My first night there, I ate a plate of *nopal*[23] and drank a few glasses of sangria.

I stumbled into my room. Despite the maid's instructions, the taps for the shower—marked C for *caliente* (hot) and F for *frio* (cold)—defeated me. I ended up burning myself. *Gringo stupido*. I slept well—too well, in fact. I woke up at 10:30 a.m., a bit hung over.

I had missed breakfast, so I wandered outside, bought four tacos from a street vendor, and wolfed them down. An hour later, I felt as if I was in labor, and for the next day I lay rolled up on the bathroom floor, climbing on the toilet every hour or so to pray to the porcelain god, all the while experiencing excruciating diarrhea.

This went on for two days. Since I never planned to go back to the United States, it was fortunate that I had the experience, because I was told that my body needed to become immune to the foreign bacteria. The upshot was that I only got sick a couple more times in Mexico.

The following day, sitting on the corner of my bed, I made a decision that turned out to be one of the best ones that I made while I was on the run: I was going to stay completely clean and sober for the rest of my life. My thinking was this - I had to be of clear mind every second, and even then the odds were stacked against me. If I added alcohol or weed to the program, I knew that I would not last. I am proud to say that I have kept my promise, and that, though I have made mistakes, I've never made them because I was drunk or high or hung over.

I also made a "do not" list that I promised I would try to adhere to:

1. *Do not break any U.S. laws.*
2. *Do not break any local laws.*
3. *Do not drink alcohol.*
4. *Do not do drugs.*
5. *Do not socialize with anyone from my first life.*
6. *Do not enter the United States.*
7. *Do not make emotional decisions.*

Later that day I met a tutor with whom I would work until the semester commenced.

Maria was a dark-haired and dark-skinned graduate student who majored in English. She was serious about studies, and she worked diligently with me every moment we were together. She was polite, but it was obvious that something was weighing on her, as I found out soon enough. She tutored to help support her father, who was battling cancer; a few months earlier, the doctors had given him three months to live. Maria, on the advice of an American student, had taken all of her savings and bought a big shipment of Herbalife supplements. The student had advised her that, taken in large doses, Herbalife was known to cure cancer.

She had been elated when the shipment arrived at the post office. I even accompanied her on a two-hour bus ride to her father's *pueblo,*[24] where I wasn't about to bust her bubble. She instructed me to try out the few expressions I had learned on our fellow passengers. I struggled mightily, but after a week of lessons Maria said that I was the most focused student that she had ever met. She couldn't quite understand why I was driven to learn Spanish—had she only known why!

Of course the supplements could not cure cancer. In fact, Herbalife would gain notoriety years later by being accused of running an elaborate Ponzi scheme that employed thousands of employees in almost a hundred countries.

Maria's father passed away the day before classes began.

THE STORY LINE THAT I DEVELOPED in those two weeks of private lessons was the basis for who I was to become during my stay in Mexico. I was Judson Allen, a thirty-four-year-old amateur surfer, an only child who had just divorced his wife of six years. Originally from Long Beach, I owned a small travel agency in nearby Hermosa Beach that catered to my surfing buddies. My goal was to expand my business, now that I had realized I was never going to be a champion surfer. I wanted to learn Spanish and travel off the beaten paths of Latin America to find surfing destinations that none of the other travel agencies could offer.

In retrospect, it was a pretty solid business plan.

Within a few months I had set up a voice mail with a Los Angeles phone number and made business cards and stationery. (This was before the rise of the Internet. It would be a lot easier now to do what I did—a simple website and a Facebook page can go a long way.) I hoped that the business cards and voice mail would convince whoever needed convincing, if only until I got my papers.

I met another teacher and mentioned to her that I was looking for a passport. She assumed that I wanted to join the Zapatista movement[25] in Chipas, which had gone public at the beginning of 1994. I was so desperate that I went along with it, even going to the library and studying up on their ideology and history. She was so impressed with my pro-Zapatista fervor that she arranged with her brother to try to get me a passport with his name on it. We made the trip to Mexico City, filled out the required papers, and paid the required bribes. Two weeks later, he was notified that he had been denied. They accused him of using a gringo's photo to make it easier for him to enter the United States.

I had been naive in my assumption that I could buy one relatively easy; I couldn't have been more wrong. It was hard enough being on my own in a foreign country, not being able to speak the language, but it was more daunting still that I could be stopped for questioning and asked to show my papers. My California license wasn't going to cut it; neither was my shiny new *Academia Hispano Americano* ID card. Luckily, the residences around the school accepted it, but I knew that most hotels would require me to leave a passport.

And then there was the matter of flying. As much as I was enjoying my time as a student, I knew that I wouldn't be able to stay there forever.

Classes began on June 1, less than two months after I had made my escape. The diverse student body included age-appropriate college students, a U.N. employee, and some older folks (older even than me).

All week I studied day and night, and soon I was making real headway. Almost every weekend, I was invited to a party where I could practice my new language. But it was not all fun and games. I don't think I ever went an hour without noticing someone a bit suspicious: a balding man with the wrong kind of slacks, a woman who asked a few too many questions, a cashier who knew a little too much about Long Beach. I tried my best to keep my paranoia under control, but then my mind would wander back to one of the only things that I had learned in college. When my English professor was teaching us what a paradox was, he used the following example: sometimes the paranoid *are* being followed.

As much as I enjoyed the laid-back atmosphere of student life, the truth was that I was longing terribly to see my wife and stepdaughter. Soon after, I made arrangements with some friends to set up a clandestine meeting. This was a major risk and the first violation of my *Do Not* list.

Through an intermediary, Julie and I managed to set up an elaborate phone system. Dozens of phones in the Las Vegas area (none too close to her house) were labeled on a sheet of paper and given a time and a date. Whenever I could, I would call at one of our assigned times;

whenever Julie could, she would be at the assigned phone. For instance, there was a pay phone at Winco Foods, on Stephanie Street in Henderson. It would be assigned *G3*. *G3* would be given the date and time *Fridays at 3:00 p.m.* If I could get to a phone at that time, and if Julie could get to that phone at that time, we would talk. The pay phone situation in Mexico was erratic at best. As an added precaution, I would not call from any phones in the town where I was staying, which meant that I would take a bus twenty-five miles out of town (three to four hours minimum), hope I found a working phone, that no one was using it, that Julie was able to make it there on that day, and that her phone was free. It is amazing how much we are able to sacrifice just to be able to hear the voice of a person we love. After a few phone conversations, she and I decided to take an enormous risk—she was going to come and visit me.

I gave her specific instructions. She was to keep the garage door closed when she loaded the luggage into her BMW. She and Amber should dress as though they were on their way to soccer practice. She was to drive to the back parking lot of Caesar's Palace, all the while keeping her eyes peeled for anyone who might be following her. I made her promise me that, if anyone looked suspicious, she would abort the mission immediately.

After she parked the car, she was to take Amber and her bags into the hotel through the back entrance and walk through to the front, where she was to hop in a taxi and proceed to McCarran Airport for the hour-long flight to the San Diego Airport. There, she was to take a taxi to the Mexican border. Once she crossed it, she was to take another taxi to the Tijuana Airport.

I had it much easier, but I still almost blew it. I took the four-hour bus ride to the Mexico City Airport. This was before 9/11, back when you could board almost any plane for a domestic flight and not show ID. I was informed that all the flights to Tijuana were booked. Obviously, there was no way to reach Julie. As much as I didn't want to call any attention to myself, I got on standby and waited. And waited.

Luckily, I got put on a flight a few hours later, and I met Julie and Amber just in time—they were ready to go back home.

As I hugged them, I couldn't help but look over their shoulders, almost expecting the agents to rush out after them. I tried to take a deep breath and enjoy the moment, but it wasn't easy.

There were no flights to Mexico City, so we took a bus to Mazatlan and then Puerta Vallarta and finally to Manzanillo, where we stayed at the Las Hadas Resort—the film *10* had been filmed there. There were no Bo Derek sightings, but there were plenty of good times. I will never forget sitting on the beach with my wife, watching Amber play in the black sand.

That was the last time I saw my stepdaughter.

ONCE THE SEMESTER ENDED, I decided to move on. San Miguel de Allende was a nice town, but I didn't want to stay anywhere for too long. I had the bright idea that I would travel around Mexico by bus with no real plan of where I would end up. I would stay in hostels and practice my Spanish with the locals. I would avoid tourist destinations, where, inevitably, I would have to dodge Americans. I was also looking for the perfect place where I could eventually settle down and live my new life.

One of my first stops was in the state of Oaxaca in southern Mexico. The whole town seemed to be a large open-air market where you could buy a small portion of almost anything. Garlic-fried grasshoppers, anyone?

Since I didn't drink, I skipped the local bars, but I had heard rumors about this one no-name *cantina*[26] located in an extremely seedy alleyway not too far from the beach. I had been into some real dives in my forty years, but nothing had prepared me for that place. Two dozen local men sat around drinking cheap beer, playing dominoes, talking to *chancliudas,*[27] and singing folk songs. Since there was so much excitement, no one wanted to waste time walking all the way to the men's room, so the owners had built a urinal right into the bar. That's right. There was a gutter made out of hot water tanks that had been cut in half and welded together into a trough that stretched the length of the bar. They were classy enough to garnish it with buckets of ice and cut-and-squeezed limes. Still, the odor of the urine trumped the smell of fresh vomit, stale beer, and filthy sex.

If you were lucky enough to get a seat at the bar, you could just unzip your fly and piss directly into it without ever leaving your seat. If you sat at one of the tables, you merely nudged your way between the barstools and let it go.

I stayed in Oaxaca for a couple of weeks but, suffice it to say, Oaxaca was not the perfect place to settle down, for a myriad of reasons. After consulting my trusty guidebooks, I decided to give San Cristobal a try.

Situated in the mountains of Chiapas, near Guatemala, San Cristobal had just switched from military rule to democratic -sort of. It was essentially lawless. When I arrived there, the city was awash with international news crews reporting on the Zapatistas overrunning the city and pushing for the rights of the indigenous people. San Cristobal was completely occupied by Mexican Army troops (so much for democracy). The streets were barricaded with sandbags, and military helicopters were monitoring the whole shebang. With the exception of the news crew, I was the only outsider. It was not the best place for *gringo stupido*.

Still, I stayed in a hostel for a few nights, cooking my meals on the roof, watching the whole thing unfold. I ventured out into one of the surrounding villages, where I learned that a coven of witches had been put to death in a pagan church a year earlier. In the town square, candles made of pine needles burned and bottles of tequila and soda were offered to the pagan gods. Several pregnant girls, barely into their teens, roamed the town barefoot with no apparent purpose or direction.

Where the hell *was* I?

My room was infested with roaches and rats, so I spent a lot of time up on the roof. One night I met a guy named Carlos, an American, who was also on the run—for what, I did not know, nor did I care to. He was about my age but looked at least two decades older. He talked in a mish-mash of English and Spanish, and his stories made absolutely no sense. I assumed this was because he had made up so many lies trying to reinvent himself along his journey that he no longer seemed like a real person.

Normally, I would have run away from a guy like this, but when he said that he knew a way out of town, I decided to go with him. We took a bus to an obscure and isolated border crossing in the jungle about a hundred miles east of Tapachula, Mexico. Carlos had promised that all I needed was my birth certificate and driver's license. We said our good-byes at the border. The last image I have of him is walking down a dirt road, carrying his battered duffel bag, muttering to himself in Spanglish. I wondered if this is what I would become if I managed to stay on the run long enough.

Customs on the Mexican–Guatemalan border was a crude affair, a cage-like room with a thatched roof where we were asked if we had any fruits or vegetables that needed fumigating. I answered that I didn't, and just like that, I was handed a ninety-day pass to stay in Guatemala. The pass specifically prohibited me from exchanging dollars for *quetzals*,[28] so I had to do it on the black market, which posed a risk, not to mention I'd be losing money on the exchange. I could not believe, though, how easy it was. I had stayed up the entire night before, my head filled with images of third-world jails where I would try to bribe guards who couldn't understand my Spanish. Eventually they would grow tired of me and call the boys back home, who would be than happy to take me off their hands.

I had assumed that many of the towns that I ventured into during my travels in southern Mexico were decidedly third-world.

I was wrong. I had just entered the *real* third world, and it was appalling.

First, a few words about the bus station—there *was* no bus station. There was just a field, a few hundred meters from the border crossing, in which sat decrepit Blue Bird buses from the early 1970s. There were no bathrooms or trees, so folks just relieved themselves in the adjacent cornfield. (And there sure wasn't much corn growing.) There were no bus schedules, either. I gathered that the bus sitting there was eventually going to go to Guatemala City, my destination. When? I had no idea.

The buses stayed parked until they were full of passengers. And when I say *full*, I am not exaggerating. It seemed to me that the average Mayan was about five feet tall; I am nearly a foot taller, not exactly Shaq but way too tall to sit on those seats. I had to jam myself in sideways because the owners had stuffed in extra rows of seats to increase their profit margin, which couldn't have been great.

My possessions were in two duffel bags, one of which was jammed into the overhead rack and the other on the roof with the chickens, turkeys, and other livestock. Three or four people filled every seat, and the aisle was stuffed with containers of cement and large burlap bags of rice. When it came time for the driver's assistant to collect the fares, he simply hopped up onto the steel rods that ran along the tops of seats and tiptoed through the bus, with the grace of an Olympic gymnast on the balance beam.

When he reached the back of the bus, he crawled out the back window and up a narrow ladder to collect fares from the passengers on the roof, who were guarding their livestock, which included a hog-tied pig. This all transpired as the bus raced down the road, dodging massive potholes and boulders. Cars were few and far between, and there was very little activity of any kind except for the occasional dropping-off and picking-up of a passenger here and there.

At the first three stops, I almost got off the bus. Walking could not be this bad, I was thinking. What's the worst that could happen? But after considering a few answers to that question, I stayed put.

I was in hell. Have you ever been on a roller coaster? Picture that your roller-coaster has not passed any safety regulations, has no seat-belts, and that you honestly believe it is going to come flying off the track at any moment. Now imagine that you're trapped on that roller coaster for four hours and sharing your seat with two others.

After a while, I noticed the trees. I'm from South Dakota, not far from the Deadwood[29] area, so I'm used to weird-looking trees. But this was different. The trees looked healthy but were almost completely devoid of branches. After a long and frustrating conversation with the woman who was sitting on my right thigh, I gleaned the following: tree-cutting was illegal in these parts. As a result, teenage boys would climb up the trees and saw off the branches to use at home for cooking; if they returned without wood, the entire family would go without dinner. Family values, Guatemala-style.

I pondered this for a moment and caught sight of the woman in front of me, who had an obscene amount of dandruff on her head. This also caught the attention of the teenage boy who sat beside me. But it turned out not to be dandruff at all. The boy started yelling, "*Puglas! Puglas!*" until his mom hit him with a backhand. I quickly looked it up in my Spanish-American dictionary. Lice. *Lice!* Sure enough, the dandruff was moving around in the woman's hair like worker ants on a hill. I tried to get away, but there was nowhere to go.

We arrived at another rest stop, another vacant field. Most of the passengers got off to use the rest room. Of course there *were* no rest rooms, so the men did their business on one side of the bus, and the women did theirs on the other. Since some passengers had gotten off, I was able to change seats. My new companion to my right was a woman holding a baby. I couldn't actually see the baby, because she was wrapped up in a pink shawl, but few minutes later I felt her. She started to pee all over the mother and me. I remember thinking that something was off, because the baby kept peeing for nearly a minute, and there is no way that a baby's bladder can hold that much urine. When the woman got off at the next stop, I looked out the window I realized that that she wasn't carrying a baby, she was carrying a piglet. She had disguised the piglet, I later learned, because babies rode for free.

So I sat in pig piss, dreaming I was at the pool in the Mirage in Las Vegas with my wife: We're giggling. . .I'm kissing her neck. . .she rubs against me as I tug on her bikini—

There was a loud bang, and I snapped out of my daydream. A few seats up, a woman was slamming her fist against the window, demanding to be let off.

Two native women followed her to a ditch on the side of the road. My fellow passengers, who seemed so jaded that they very seldom even looked up from their slumber no matter the circumstances, started gazing at them in rapt attention, so I figured this would be good. The bus driver even shut off the engine.

They did not disappoint. The two women spread some old clothes on the ground and laid the woman on top. It was difficult to see exactly what was going on, but I certainly could hear—one of the native women was moaning, and then screaming at the top of her lungs. After about ten minutes, she stopped, and one the native women held up a newborn baby. Everyone on board cheered as the three women and the newborn boarded the bus. It was such a festive atmosphere that they did not charge the new mother for an extra rider.

The bus driver started up the engine, but just as we were beginning to pull out, the new mother started pounding the window again. The bus driver shut off the engine, and the foursome—new mother, newborn, and two helpers—left the bus again and returned to the ditch. A few minutes later, everyone began applauding again as the five of them—yes, she'd had twins—boarded the bus.

We finally reached Guatemala City. I found a cheap hostel and a tutor within a few days, but I really never meshed with the town. The highlight of my time there was training with some local bodybuilders;

I even witnessed a contest. My new friends tried their best to get me a passport, but they came up short. I was beginning to panic—I needed papers, and I was no closer to getting them than I had been when I'd come to Latin America six months earlier.

I headed to Guadalajara, Mexico, in the hope of finding my old friend Maria Rosa. Honestly, I had been hoping to avoid it. I loved Maria Rosa. But she was a gangster, and I did not want to get caught up in anything that might compromise my freedom. Still, I couldn't think of any other way to get my papers, and I certainly could not go on much longer as I had for the past six months.

I wasn't about to take that bus trip back, so I hired a guy I'd met at the gym, Lupe, to drive me back to the border in his 1969 Volkswagen. While the trip glowed in comparison to the bus, it sure had its moments. We had only been on the road for a couple of hours when the sun went down, and of course there were no lights on the road. We hit pothole after pothole until we got a flat tire. Not only did Lupe not have a spare, he didn't even have a jack. But he did have a hammer, which is apparently all you needed in these parts. He simply beat a large hole in the asphalt around the tire (which probably explains why there were so many potholes in the first place) and pulled off the flat tire. Then we waited and waited until a trio of guys came loping up the road. A quick negotiation took place, and a few minutes later they were rolling the flat tire down the road.

"Time to chill, amigo," Lupe said to me as he made himself comfortable and fell asleep. In a while, I followed suit. Hours later, we were awakened by the voices of the three men, who had rolled the newly repaired tire up to the car. I paid them one dollar American, put the tire back on, and drove off.

Lupe explained how they had performed this miracle. They didn't have an air compressor, so after removing the nail, piece of metal or whatever had punctured the tire, they'd set the bottom of it against the rim and swabbed gas-soaked cotton around the rim. Then they had ignited the gas. This had created a vacuum that inflated the tire and sealed it to the rim. It was pretty damn amazing, if you ask me.

When I reached Guadalajara, I checked into a run-down hostel and tried to devise a game plan. I did not have an address or phone number for Maria Rosa. I remembered from our conversations that she had a large family. For a couple of days I tried to track her down by bribing workers at utility companies. They were happy to take my money, and they gave me addresses, but no one at those addresses had ever heard of her.

By the third day, I had all but given up. How could have I thought that I was going to be able to find a woman in a city the size of Philadelphia? *Gringo stupido*. I was drifting around in a daze, really feeling the weight of the situation, when I looked up and saw Maria Rosa driving a black SUV, her arm hanging out the window like a boss. I couldn't believe it. If I read it in a novel, I *wouldn't* believe it. *But there she was!*

"*Maria Rosa!*" I shouted.

She spotted me and made a U-turn. "*Danny?* What the hell are *you* doing here?"

"I came to see you," I said.

"Yeah, sure." She jumped out of the SUV and embraced me. "Danny, it's so good to see you."

"I'm Judson," I said. Maria Rosa knew what was up.

"What's with the truck? I thought you were a *federale*."[30]

"I am," she said.

I laughed.

She explained. She and her crew would dress up in suits and uniforms and drive the SUV right into local police stations, commandeer their computers, and use them for their business. They would check on search warrants, track open cases, and even print out driver's licenses at the DMV. Believing that they were *federales*, everyone would get out of their way.

She invited me back to her home, where she lived with several of her girlfriends whom I knew from Geiger and none other than my old weight-training partner, Manny.

He still looked good. A couple inches shorter than me and probably the same weight, it was obvious that he had still been training. We caught up quickly and it was pretty cool to be hanging out with my old prison pals without any bars or hacks in the picture.

Even though I had worked diligently on my Spanish back at *Academia Hispano Americano*, we all agreed that I would not be able to survive if I didn't learn to communicate much better. It turned out that Maria Rosa had a friend who was a principal at a local school, and she arranged that I could attend classes there. I told her that I was really going to stick out in high school, given that I was more than double the age of the average student. She told me not to worry, that I wasn't going to high school.

She was kind enough to accompany me on my first day. We pulled up, and all of a sudden I was hit with the image of dozens of children. When I say children, I mean little kids, the age of my stepdaughter.

She turned off the ignition as I started to laugh. "You can't be serious," I said.

"Listen to me," Maria Rosa said. "If you want a Mexican passport and live in Mexico, you're going to have to become a Mexican. There's no better way to do this then learning the same way we all learned—in elementary school."

"I'm not sure this is going to work," I said.

"Stop being such a *puto*[31] and get in there with the kids," she said.

Now, I've always considered myself pretty tough. I've walked into prison yards where I was the only gringo. I've had sit-downs[32] with some scary bastards. But the thought of mixing it up with children, hordes of them, terrified me.

Maria Rosa led me to the warden's office, which was disguised as the principal's office. The warden was a well-dressed man in his early forties. As soon as we appeared at his door, he leapt up from behind his desk and greeted Maria Rosa with a big hug, all the while looking me up and down, trying to figure out why I was there.

"My friend here is starting a tequila export business," Maria Rosa told the principal. "He will be working and living here, but his Spanish is horrible. He tried an immersion program and private tutoring, but obviously it hasn't worked."

"What level is he up to?" the principal asked as if I wasn't even in the room.

"Ask him some questions," she said.

The principal asked me three questions. I got two wrong. In my defense, one was not my fault. He had asked, "*Como se llama?*"[33] Since I was using the fake name, I got all tangled up. Anyway, he sent me directly to the third-grade class.

I was wondering if there had ever been a college graduate who had been sent back to the third grade. It was if Maria Rosa had been reading my mind. "It's because you're so special," she said.

"Maybe I should get another tutor," I said.

"No!" she said.

Maria Rosa, playing the role of *la mama*, grabbed me by the wrist and dragged me into the classroom, leaving me standing there in front of the teacher and twenty-four third-graders. They immediately laughed at me, because I couldn't fit into the desk. The teacher was kind enough to get me a large plastic chair and direct me to the back of the room, next to the only other "deskless" student—a fifty-five-year-old, 260-pound American woman who was wearing a school uniform, a light blue skirt, and a sweater combo in an attempt to blend in. The truth was, she looked more like a Miami Dolphin linebacker than a student.

After that first class, I sat on the opposite side of the classroom. The last thing I needed was to be tripped up by an American. And honestly, she scared the hell out of me. I guess I creeped her out too, because she never made an attempt to befriend me.

The first three days, the kids ignored me, except to giggle when I botched up a verb conjugation or a simple math problem. Then, on the fourth day, during recreation, a chubby kid named Carlos, who seemed to be the bully of the class, came up to me and asked me for Chiclets. After five minutes of trying to figure out what he was saying, I did my best to tell him that I didn't have any. He eyeballed me suspiciously and walked away, shaking his head, to the other side of the yard, where he met up with his crew. They all stared me down with contempt. Was I going to have a beef? I wondered. I had made it through sixty months of prison without a problem, and now I had to watch my back in third grade.

On the way home that night, I noticed what only could be described as a sales force of children standing on street corners, holding trays of gum and candy. When the light turned red, they would dash out to the motorists and sell them those items. These children were much poorer than my classmates. They toiled from sunup to sundown, breathing in the fumes of the anti-environmentally sound cars, going home to sleep on their cardboard beds. Very little of the proceeds they earned actually made it to the children or their parents.

I bought all the candy that the kids had, and I made them promise that they would go play the rest of the day. I kept the candy and gum in my bag, and at recess, I doled it out to Carlos, his crew, and the rest of the kids. From that day on I was the king of the class, even supplanting Carlos, who didn't seem thrilled but took the Chiclets anyway.

As the weeks went on, I got into a groove. My day would start when I joined the kids singing the Mexican national anthem. I generally did better with the written work. My pronunciation still elicited giggles, but fewer guffaws. It took me a few weeks, but I managed to earn my first star, which signified a 10/10 on an assignment.

Of course not a day went by when the kids didn't remind me of my stepdaughter. How I missed her and wished that she were among these kids, playing and laughing. Believe me, the thought crossed my mind to move her and her mom out there, but I wouldn't endanger their lives any more than I already had. I knew I was making the right decision, but it hurt.

One day I was in the back, conjugating verbs, when I noticed a woman approach the teacher's desk. I also noticed that the students were attending to their studies much more seriously than usual. A few minutes later, another couple came in, and soon a lined formed. I tapped the shoulder of Maria, who sat in front of me and had hair so long that it traveled almost to the floor, and asked her what was going on.

"*El dia de los padres,*" she whispered. The day of the parents. . .I finally got it: Parents' Day. I could see a couple of the parents glance in my direction, but apparently it wasn't as strange as it seemed. I had come to learn that several adults took classes at elementary schools. I couldn't imagine it going over back in the States.

I had gone back to work on my verbs when my teacher summoned me to the front of the room. "Judson, this is Señora Castro, Carlos's mother," my teacher said. We glanced at Carlos, who was turning red. "She would like to ask you some questions."

We shook hands, and Mrs. Castro, in pretty decent English, hit me with a barrage of questions. Why was I here? Did I want to relive my childhood? Was I a child molester? She didn't actually ask the last one, but I could tell that was her main concern. I guess I passed her quiz, because she smiled and wished me luck. As I returned to my seat, I linked eyes with Carlos, who was giving me the death stare. I smiled at him and winked, which made him even angrier. Hey, you can never show your fear.

Back in the adult world, Maria Rosa was hard at work at getting me Mexican papers. This was proving to be quite difficult. She explained there was an added limitation: I needed documentation for someone forty-plus, because if I were younger, I would face the possibility of conscription into the Mexican Army. That was a chance that I was not willing to take. So I stayed in limbo, a gringo without papers, unable to contact my family back home, always looking over my shoulder, wondering when I would be surrounded by *federales* or Interpol, shoved into a van and onto a plane, whereupon I would be convicted of a crime that I had not committed.

The days crawled by, but I tried not to get down. I was diligent in my studies. And I was training pretty hard. Every morning before school and before the sun appeared, I joined Manny, Maria Rosa, and the other house guests for a ninety-minute power walk through the dark streets, up into trails, and back to the house. Every night at 7:00 p.m., we would meet at the local gym and hit the weights, but the local gym wasn't nearly as plush as Geiger's gym. Plastic water bottles filled with sand were our dumbbells, and the lone barbell was a rusty rod that barely held the mismatched plates. But we made do, and my time in Mexico proved to be one of the healthiest of my life.

One night after school, I came home to find Libby sitting in the kitchen. She was a friend of ours from prison who had come from a wealthy Mexican family. She had just been released from prison, five years after me, having served ten years. After we caught up, she offered to help me get papers. She said that it would involve my taking a trip with her back to her family's house in the state of Michoacán.

We took the four-hour ride on a second-class bus where a porno tape played on the public video monitors. I enjoy an occasional porno as much as the next guy, but this was a grisly affair. From what I could ascertain, the lead woman, who probably rocked the scales at about 220 pounds, was on a job interview with a guy who shared an uncanny resemblance to Cousin It. After a few exchanges, the woman grabbed Cousin It by the hair, threw him onto the desk, and ground herself against him. I was curious to see where this was going to go, but I was getting embarrassed in front of Libby, who was studying my expression. I just shook my head and turned away. She giggled.

I noticed that well-off people in Latin America weren't above traveling or staying in less-than-glamorous situations. They seemed not to forget where they were from, something that cannot always be said for

Americans I knew who often lived beyond their means.

Her brother picked us up in a new Toyota Land Cruiser and drove us to their property, a mansion that covered half a city block. There I met her father, who was in a wheelchair due to paralysis from a shootout. One of Libby's brothers had been kidnapped, one murdered, and one was doing life in prison. Their mother had been driven to such anguish that she abandoned the family and no one knew her whereabouts.

This was Libby's first time home in well over a decade, and the next night they threw a massive homecoming party for her, one that all of the state of Michoacán seemed to crash. I had a fine time, but I couldn't really enjoy myself with the thought of those papers on my mind.

The next day Libby said that her brother had agreed to help me. I thanked the family for their hospitality and traveled back to Maria Rosa's, where I got some decent news.

Maria Rosa had managed to get me a Mexican passport, a voter registration card, a PGR card (the PGR is the Mexican equivalent of our FBI), and a driver's license, all for the bargain-basement price of five hundred American dollars. I jumped at the deal, but whom was I kidding? Even though I had busted my ass studying non-stop since I left the United States, I knew that I would never pass for a Mexican if I got stopped by authorities.

As Maria Rosa and the others prepared our Christmas dinner, I was feeling probably the lowest I had felt in the nine months I'd been on the run. I missed my wife and stepdaughter, my mom and siblings. I missed the snow in South Dakota, the sand in Las Vegas. I was sick and tired of not being able to have a real conversation with someone, of trying to express my feelings in a couple of hundred mispronounced words. I was feeling sorry for myself, so I took a walk along the dusty streets behind our *pueblo*.

Dogs barked at me from the flat rooftops, when I walked by. It had been a particularly dry fall and the dust pooled up to three inches in spots. Most of the cooking and playing was done on the rooftops. I was about three blocks from home when I saw them: On the edge of the street, a family of four was preparing for Christmas dinner. The father was a *campesino*[34] who wore a large sombrero. He was squatting next to his wife and two young children, a boy and a girl. The mother was cooking tortillas on a barely burning fire inside a triangle of wooden chucks. In it were a few twigs and newspaper. Over the firewood sat a grill supported by three legs, topped by an old piece of corrugated tin that had been beaten almost flat for cooking. The kids were playing in a dust pile with their Christmas presents—two plastic toys that you might find in a box of Cracker Jack.

Lost in my thoughts, probably fifteen feet away, I assessed my surroundings and thought about how this family had the audacity to be merry on such a Christmas Day. How were they content with a small quantity of meat, and a couple of chilies and peppers, that lay in small bags next to the fire? I could not believe how the children howled with laughter at whatever adventure they made up with the plastic pieces that they rolled around in the dust bowl.

They must have noticed me standing there, wiping a couple of tears from my eyes, because the father waved me over.

In Spanish, he asked me if I would like to join them for Christmas dinner. They barely had enough food for themselves but would not take no for an answer. It was the most profound Christmas dinner that I ever had, and I even got the gift of gratitude.

A few days into the New Year, Manny's kid brother Julio came into town. He was about ten years younger than I, the youngest of the clan, and he ran things back in Medellín. He, who like his brother Manny, spoke English very well, and had probably been a good-looking guy once, but he was badly disfigured—he had a deformed nose, a long scar across his face, and his right eye would slide lazily to his left.

Manny had told me the story the night before Julio came.

A few years back, someone had ratted out Julio to the authorities—

they'd said that he was sitting on a load of cocaine. On the Mexican border near Texas, members of the Mexican National Police tortured him night and day, working in eight-hour shifts. They bashed him repeatedly with the butt-ends of their rifles (which explained his eye), they electrocuted his testicles, hanged him upside down, and poured Tabasco sauce up his nose, nearly drowning him. They shoved him into a tire and doused him with lighter fluid, threatening to set him on fire, which was a favorite way of killing someone in the War Against Drugs. Just about the time when Julio was begging them for a gun with a single bullet so he could end his misery, Manny showed up with a bag of American hundred-dollar bills and managed to get him out of there.

Even with his less-than-attractive bodily deformities, Julio still walked with an air of confidence, dressed well, and spoke English very impressively. He seemed more like a Ph.D. candidate than the underboss of a Medellín cartel.

"You ever been to Colombia?" Julio asked.

"No," I said.

"Come back with me," he said.

"I have my Spanish classes."

"We speak Spanish there, too. And maybe I can pull some strings and get you into a fourth-grade class."

Maria Rosa snapped, "Hater!"

"You know that ain't true," Julio said, laughing.

"All I have is a fake Mexican passport and a fake California driver's license," I said. "And, oh yeah, I'm a fugitive."

"Yeah, my brother told me about your situation," Julio assured me. "We'll make it work."

I thought about going to Pablo Escobar's Colombia and living out a serious adventure. The way I looked at it, I was going to be on an adventure for the rest of my life because (to paraphrase Escobar) I thought I would rather die in Latin America than live in an American prison, especially for a crime that I had not committed. At the time, Colombia was the Mount Everest of adventures, so why not scale the biggest of them all?

Before we left, I said my goodbyes to the women and thanked them profusely for their hospitality. As we got into the car, Manny came out. He told the driver/bodyguard to take a walk for a minute.

He put his arm around his younger brother and said, "Julio, Dan—"

"Judd," I said.

"Judd is family, and I want you to treat him accordingly."

"So no kidnapping or torture?" Julio said.

Manny playfully slapped him on his cheek. "*Bandito,*"[35] he said, "not unless I give the order." We laughed. "And get him some papers so we don't have to call him by that *maricon*[36] name."

Julio summoned back the driver/bodyguard, and we left. As we drove down the pockmarked roads, I started to consider what I was getting myself into, and I started to sweat—not from the heat and humidity, but from the gravity of the situation. And I would be lying if I said that I did not consider giving them the slip. This wasn't Fonzie or Babe. Julio was running a cartel in the cocaine capital of the world. And I was going to be his guest. What the hell did that even mean? I had known the guy for less than twenty-four hours.

AT THE MEXICO CITY AIRPORT, we met Julio's connection, a small, nondescript man in his early forties who treated Julio with reverence and me with courtesy. He stamped my fake Mexican passport accordingly, and we sailed through Customs and Immigration. I was nervous that my weak Spanish would give me away, but Julio did all the talking, and no one questioned us.

On the plane, I asked him what the main differences were between Colombia and Mexico.

"Well, to begin with, Colombia is my home, and even though I hate the government and the corruption, I'll always love it," he said. "But even the bad can be good. Because the government is so corrupt, some of us have been able to gain some power, a lot of power. Not to sound arrogant, but I can do basically anything I want in Medellín, and no one is going to tell me differently, especially now that there is no extradition to the United States." He paused. "That doesn't mean I act like an asshole. I make a good living, and I try to spread it around Campo Valdez, where I'm from. I do my best to help the people, and I never forget that I was one of them. Some nights, when I was a kid, I went to bed so hungry that I would eat a bug if it crawled on the wall next to my bed. I'll never let myself forget that."

We flew into the Augusto C. Sandino Airport in Managua, Nicaragua. Nicaragua was under the control of the Sandinistas, and the airport was completely militarized. But no one bothered us as we changed planes. I was sure that was because of Julio. I was quite impressed with my new friend.

7

LIFE AFTER PABLO

ON JANUARY 4, 1995, WE LANDED late in the day at the Rio Negro Airport in Medellín, Colombia. When most people heard Medellín back then, they thought of one guy, Pablo Emilio Escobar Gaviria, who was a Colombian drug lord and leader of one of the most powerful criminal organizations ever assembled. During the height of his power in the 1980s, he controlled a vast empire of drugs and murder that spread throughout the world. He made billions of dollars, ordered the murder of thousands of people, and ruled over a personal empire of mansions, airplanes, and a private zoo. His private army of soldiers, criminals, and police officers protected it all.

Escobar's ruthlessness was legendary. Many honest politicians, judges, and policemen who did not like the growing influence of this street thug tried to oppose him. Escobar had a way of dealing with his enemies. He called it "*plata o plomo*."[37] If someone with power got in his way, he would first attempt to bribe them, and if that didn't work, he would order them killed, occasionally including their family in the hit. The exact number of honest men and women killed by Escobar is unknown, but it definitely runs well into the hundreds and perhaps into the thousands. By the mid-1980s, Pablo Escobar was one of the most powerful of men. *Forbes* listed him as the seventh-richest man in the world; his personal wealth was reported to be between twenty-four and thirty billion dollars (which is Bill Gates money today).

Slightly more than a year before I arrived, Colombian security forces using American technology located Escobar hiding in a home in a middle-class section of Medellín. The Search Bloc moved in, triangulating his position, and attempted to bring him into custody. Escobar fought back, however, and there was a shootout. Escobar was eventually gunned down as he attempted to escape on the rooftop. He had been shot in the torso and leg, but the fatal wound had come through his ear, leading many to believe that he had committed suicide (which he had promised he would do if he was backed into a corner). Many others, however, believe that one of the Colombian policemen executed him. With Escobar gone, the Medellín Cartel quickly lost power to its rival, the Cali Cartel.

As we disembarked and entered the airport, I wondered where this left Manny and Julio, who were born and raised in Medellín; and more to the point, where had it left *me*?

Almost immediately, I came to learn just how powerful Julio and Manny were. Members of Julio's crew, at least a dozen deep, were waiting for us at the front of the airport with a five-piece band in tow, which played a kind of salsa version of the Rolling Stones' "Brown Sugar." The crew surrounded Julio, who either hugged or shook hands with everyone. In Spanish, he introduced me as his American brother who would be staying with them in their *barrio* for a while.

In the mid-1990s, Campo Valdez was one of the toughest and most dangerous neighborhoods in the world. I had read that ninety-nine percent of the people who lived there did not attend school past the eighth grade, and I would be damned if I could find the other one percent. If they were fortunate enough to find work, it was usually in factories in the textile or fashion industries, or in the drug trade. Obviously, the latter paid much better—the average monthly income for a factory worker was about fifty American dollars a month. Another way they earned money was to send young boys around to sell coffee from large, round, insulated thermoses, which they carried in hand-held wooden boxes. There were different coffees sold in combinations in plastic cups approximately equal to two shot glasses (four to five ounces); these could include sugar or milk. They lived in small, poorly made houses that were built one on top of another on the steep mountainside where Campo Valdez perched. There were no lawns or parks; the kids played *futbol*[38] on the narrow streets and more often than not on the steepest ones, since it was less likely that a car could make it up the hills and there was less chance that their games would be interrupted.

The entire barrio's economy was based on credit. Can you picture being so poor that you have to buy cigarettes one at a time, or single diapers—when you can afford one? But you probably couldn't afford one, so you bought it on credit and paid when you got work. Stores were merely fifteen-by-fifteen-foot cubicles with goods stacked in boxes. Just the basics: rice, beans, flour to make *areapa* dough, the ever-popular *aguadiente* liquor in half pints, diapers, tampons, toothpaste, and candy. They sold soda in plastic bags—a can of Coke would have been too expensive.

These corner stores served as social gathering spots too, and some of the more prosperous locations would put a plastic table and chairs in front of the store.

Since hardly anyone had a car and practically no one could afford bus fare, weekend nights were spent in the barrio. Young girls would walk up and down the streets in the evening, dolled up with makeup and perfume, which they paid for in weekly installments, showing off for the neighbors, and especially the young men of the barrio. Occasionally, a fashion show would be staged on the narrow main street that ran through Campo Valdez. The folks, after all, lived in Medellín, which was the manufacturing and textile capital of Colombia. I couldn't imagine that they were actually buying the fine garments they wore at the fashion show. I presumed that the material, the cloth, was from the factories, and that the garments were made at home.

The girls would stroll the catwalk (the main street) in their Sunday best, usually a nice dress that was clean and professionally pressed, all of them scented with fake cologne. Their delicate facial features were accented by a surprisingly professional application of cosmetics. The fashion show started at around 4:00 p.m., when the employed residents got home from work. The shows lasted until about 6:15 in the evening.

Just above Campo Valdez was another destitute barrio named Manrrique, which was even more notorious than Campo Valdez. There the young boys worked, not as coffee boys but as *sicarios*,[39] to which trade they had been trained up from an early age. So pervasive was the practice, in fact, that the mothers wouldn't feed their sons. In Medellín, if a mother loved her ten-year-old assassin child who was about to go out and do "some work," she wouldn't feed him. Why? She was looking after him from experience, since she knew that, if he was wounded and rushed to the hospital for surgery, he would not lose valuable blood and time getting his stomach pumped before surgery. This could possibly save the child's life. Even under these circumstances Mother knew best.

The hopelessness and despair in which these people lived made their barrios the perfect recruiting ground for drug dealers and guerrillas who would recruit children as young as ten. Many children were actually born into the lifestyle, with parents or siblings already involved in criminal activities as a way of life and livelihood. When survival is the top priority and family second, it was difficult to see where education fit in.

They also worked as scouts or spies, hired by the guerrillas to report on daily activities of residents, the arrival of new residents, or any abnormal occurrences. Representatives of the guerrillas would assemble groups of young boys and fill their heads with visions of the glory and glamor that could be theirs as members of "the revolution." That meant leaving their barrio for the mosquito-infested jungles to live off minimal rations of green bananas, which were seldom cooked to soften them up because smoke could tip off their location to the enemy (government soldiers).

Poverty of this depth, experienced by a society with knowledge of an outside world of success and plenty, created a vacuum where the desire to acquire the better things in life gave rise to exploitation of every nature. Adolescent revolutionaries were fighting other Colombians who were considered wealthy because their children enjoyed running water. This was compounded by the presence of cheap VHS tapes. These kids got their education from their TVs, and Tony Montana was their professor.

Julio put me up in the house of a family friend named Doña Ruth. The unofficial Godmother of Campo Valdez was in her mid-fifties, dark, and striking. She had been born in the house and raised six kids, three of whom still lived there. She was the one other women went to for words of wisdom or to settle small disputes. Julio loved her like a mother and would often show up unannounced for a quick cup of coffee or a large meal.

The apple of Doña Ruth's eye was her youngest son, Hector, who spent a lot of time at the house with her. I came to learn that she had made him off-limits to Julio, which meant that he was going to lead a straight life. He already had an entry-level job at an engineering company, and there was even talk of his going back to school.

The four-story house was crunched in the middle of a block of about forty similar homes. A moat—a concrete ditch, really—separated the house from the street; you had to cross a bridge to get to it. It was a dark house that saw light only when the sun was directly overhead.

To say that it was modest would be an understatement. I shaved in a concrete sink out back. The path from my room to the sink was littered with boat and plane parts.

I had my own room, but the quarters were pretty cramped—members of the hit team would often show up unannounced and crash in the living room. Because my Spanish was so bad, I never really had an in-depth conversation with anyone but Julio. Hector spoke some English, but all he wanted to talk about was *futbol*, a subject about which I knew very little. When Julio dropped by, he probably thought that I was a maniac, because whenever I saw him I would often go on long-winded diatribes, starving for any real human interaction besides "*¿Como estas, amigo?*" But it was not always easy getting his attention.

Julio was a rock star in the neighborhood. When he drove up on his loud Harley-Davidson in the middle of the night, people would get out of bed just to shake hands with him. Often, this led to an impromptu party that lasted until well after the sun rose.

The residents of Campo Valdez were fiercely loyal to Julio, and for good reason: He provided many of them with jobs—something that the government didn't seem to care about. The kids looked up to him and hoped someday that they would be able to work for him and eventually move to the United States. He was friends with the priest at the neighborhood church, and every so often he dropped by with a big bag of cash, which the priest would dole out to the poor. I know it sounds like a cliché, but I honestly believe that many of the young men in the barrio would have risked their lives for Julio.

On weekends we headed to Julio's *finca*.[40] Almost the total opposite of Campo Valdez, the getaway, about twenty miles out of town, was an oasis. Once you were past the armed guards, guests were treated to a swimming pool, a restaurant, and even a regulation soccer field. Friends and family could sleep in one of the twenty bedrooms and then relax and party on the lush grounds among the mango orchard. But

Julio didn't limit this oasis to just us.

Sometimes, he hauled as many as sixty people from the Campo Valdez out to the *finca* in a ten-foot-wide, twenty-four-foot-long two-axle truck with dual wheels in the back. Normally used for hauling cattle, it had slots on the side that held the wooden side panels that surrounded the flatbed, and it had a neatly rolled-up tarp that he used to keep the passengers dry during a rain.

While this might seem crude, it was a luxury there, and folks were thrilled at the opportunity to escape the tedium of daily life in the concrete jungle, to take their children to the ranch to play soccer on actual grass instead of the asphalt surfaces at home, where traffic and the sloping city streets made normal activities unsafe and impractical. However, any kid who grew up playing in those conditions became a superstar when afforded the opportunity to play on a normal, well-maintained field like the one at Julio's *finca*.

As I said earlier, in the mid-1990s Campo Valdez was one of the most dangerous neighborhoods in the world. It was almost completely lawless. Murders did not, for the most part, get investigated. Only two years earlier, Pablo Escobar had offered a bounty on the head of any policeman, turning the poorest residents of Medellín into an army of *sicarios*. Almost two thousand police officers were murdered. Imagine how this hurt the recruiting efforts of the police force.

One midweek afternoon, after I had been living in Medellín for about six months, I was in the car with Mateo, Julio's driver/bodyguard, waiting at an intersection for the light to change. We were in the heart of downtown in rush-hour traffic, amid an ocean of yellow Renault taxis, diesel commuter buses, and beat-up cars, each of them providing massive quantities of carbon monoxide for our breathing pleasure. It seemed as though half of Medellín supplemented their income by selling rides in the family sedan to the other half of the city.

The monotony of our ten-mph drive was broken up by energetic and colorful street vendors who would dash out into standing traffic and pitch their wares—bootleg Yankees caps, *Buñuels*,[41] mangos, or perhaps a woman's evening gown—to drivers and passengers stuck in traffic. This was the Wild West of free enterprise—no permits or licenses, and certainly no traceable profits to report—just raw, unfettered capitalism. From our Toyota Land Cruiser, which towered over the majority of cars on the roads, I had a bird's-eye view.

And all of a sudden I did not like what I saw.

A rice rocket[42] rumbled in between the lanes of cars to our left. Julio had warned me that many hits in Medellín were carried out via motorcycles. The guy wore a helmet to conceal his identity. Due to the popularity of these hits, the Medellín government had made it *illegal* to wear motorcycle helmets. It was also illegal for two men to ride on a motorcycle at the same time. Even though Escobar was dead and his terror attacks had stopped, there was still plenty of mayhem on the streets because various families were trying to fill the power vacuum that he had left in the lucrative cocaine business.

I double-checked my rear-view mirror and, yes, the men were wearing blue helmets with tinted visors. The moment got even more serious when I noticed that Mateo had taken out his nine-millimeter, cocked it, and held it on his thigh, ready to fire if the men made a move in our direction. I tried to say, "Oh, shit," but nothing came out of my mouth.

Lowering myself a few inches, I peeked out from behind the headrest. They were only a few feet from our car and Mateo began to raise the gun. At that moment I was pretty sure that he was going to try to shoot them preemptively. A few seconds later, the door of a taxi two cars in front of us swung open and a heavy-set barefoot Latino in a shiny silver suit about thirty-five years old, jumped out and begin to run between the cars.

The man on the motorcycle took notice and tried his best to weave through the cars, but it wasn't easy, and he popped a wheelie trying to move through the dense traffic. The barefoot man in the suit made it to the red light, looked both ways, darted to the right, and ran straight into the lane where a backup team was waiting—two men on another motorcycle. Caught in the open of the intersection, he sprinted toward the surrounding block of nondescript brown buildings, hoping that he could find an unlocked entrance, but he couldn't, and he ran back into the traffic.

For a moment I thought he might be able to escape, the two motorcycles caught in the maze of stalled traffic, the cars stopped, passengers ducked down in their seats, but with only twenty yards to go until he reached a sanctuary—an extremely narrow alleyway, not more than a couple of feet wide—he slowed ever so slightly, turning back to check the distance between him and his pursuers, and at that moment the backup team broke free of the traffic and flew toward him as he was turning back to run into the alley, and there was a burst of Uzi fire that sprayed him with half a dozen slugs, and he fell writhing to the sidewalk. In seconds, the other motorcycle had screeched to a halt, and the guy in the back pulled out a Mac 10 and finished him off with a few more spurts, and the two bikes vanished into the obscurity of rush hour traffic and the maze of choked-off streets.

There would be no story in the newspaper, and certainly no investigation—as I said, most murders did not get investigated in Medellín back then. Mateo slipped the nine-millimeter back under the seat as I stared ahead, still stunned. I was jolted back to the moment when a vendor knocked on my window, asking me if I wanted to buy a pretty blue-and-gold scarf with a colorful Inca design embroidered on it.

Even with all the lessons and classes that I had taken since I left the States, my Spanish was still pretty horrible. I could communicate with Julio (mostly because he spoke English pretty well), but I couldn't have a real conversation with anyone else. He agreed that I needed help, but he didn't know any teachers except for a former girlfriend, whom he was reluctant to ask. Messed up as he was by his torture session with the Mexican *federales*, he had no problem getting women. Besides his wife, he had two very attractive girlfriends, but he told me that the teacher had still not gotten over their breakup, and that he didn't want to raise her hopes. But he finally agreed to call on her.

Monica, who had graduated from the university and supposedly spoke English as well as Julio, soon agreed to take me on as a student. The next day Mateo drove Julio and me to her apartment in nearby Envigado, which she shared with her parents and brothers. A gray-barred metal fence surrounded the bright eight-story apartment building, which was a big step up from the squalor of Campo Valdez.

At the front entrance, an armed guard greeted us. He seemed to recognize Julio and must have been expecting us, because he opened the gate and escorted us to the elevator and up to Monica's apartment.

The *señora* of the home, Monica's mother, answered the door and welcomed us in. Julio knew everyone there, and the rest of the family—Monica's parents and her two brothers—all welcomed him in as if he were part of the family.

Monica entered the living room a few minutes later. At twenty-four, she had long, thick light brown hair that she pulled back and tied with a white bow. Her nails seemed to have been professionally manicured, and her Nike workout outfit (legit, not bootleg) highlighted a well-sculpted frame.

After Julio kissed her on both cheeks, he introduced me to them. They invited us to sit down in the living room, where we were treated to freshly brewed Colombian coffee and homemade pastries. Small talk led to Julio's request that Monica begin tutoring me at once in an intense and rigorous manner. She readily accepted the proposal, more for the opportunity to be closer to Julio, I suspected, than for the five dollars an hour that she was going to charge me for the lessons. But I wasn't complaining.

Julio's cell phone had been ringing nonstop the whole time during the visit, which was quite common for him. He told us that he had to get back to Medellín, and since he wanted me to begin my lessons the next morning and he felt that public transportation was too dangerous, he asked if I could stay with them that evening. I thought it was odd, but the family seemed happy to have me. Monica's mother began almost immediately to pull the bed out of the fold-out couch, and Monica brought the bedding.

I spent the first evening with the family, watching *telenovelas* [43] and talking to my new professor. Nearly all our initial conversations were in English due to my weak Spanish, which was depressing since I had been working so damn diligently. We made a plan: We would study for two to three hours every morning and then go jogging, or what I called "dodging." Since there were no parks anywhere in sight, we would jog on the streets, weaving in and out of the bumper-to-bumper traffic that clogged almost every inch of pavement.

Monica usually left immediately after our lessons to go work her second job, and I spent the rest of the day sitting in cafes, trying to strike up conversations with the locals. At night I continued to watch *telenovelas* with Monica's family, and most of the time she would come back and catch a couple with us. I tried to speak Spanish as much as I could, and the family did their best to show patience but I did notice Monica's brothers snicker a few times at my blunders.

Since it was important for me to get myself immersed in the culture as much as possible, Monica sometimes took me along with her on errands.

One morning was particularly memorable. I accompanied her to the funeral of a well-known *sicario* whom she had known from childhood. We joined the mourners—young assassins and *banditos* who surrounded the hearse as it rolled slowly down the street. They popped wheelies on their motorcycles, honked their horns, yelled, drank *aguadiente*, and smoked pot. Behind them, old women in black cried and held their rosaries up to the skies, praying for God to have mercy on his soul.

I noticed that Monica seemed constantly on edge, scoping out the perimeter. The procession stopped at the expansive cemetery's front entrance, several blocks from the actual burial site. From this point, four pallbearers carried the coffin on their shoulders, and at each block replacements tapped their shoulders to take over. All of these young men were friends and associates of the departed, and it was their honor to participate in the duty of transporting him to his final resting place. We followed them as they navigated through the labyrinth of graves and crypts. The crypts were about twenty feet tall and thirty-five feet wide, with three-foot wide compartments.

They set down the coffin in front of the crypt, and soon Monica and all of the other younger mourners were smoking weed and passing around more bottles of *aguadiente*. Since I didn't drink, I stepped back and paid my respects along with the old women, who continued to pray. One of the guys opened the coffin and poured the *aguadiente* down the young *sicario's* throat, much of it splashing on his face. Another guy gave the departed a shotgun hit of weed. They closed the coffin quickly after that, so that the cloud of smoke would linger in there with him as they pushed him into the crypt. I was able to see the smoke because the coffin was equipped with a glass hatch.

Several of the women pulled pistols out of their handbags and handed them to the men. (Women were less likely to be searched by the police.) The men pointed their guns to the sky and began shooting, emptying their chambers and magazines. When they were done, they returned the guns to the women, who dutifully put them back in their handbags for safekeeping.

Once the corpse was securely in the crypt, enjoying his buzz, the men and women got on their motorcycles and sped off in different directions, from what I could gather to evade any police pursuit.

As Monica and I were walking back to the bus, I asked her, "Is this a normal occurrence?"

"I don't know one single *sicario* who died from old age," she said.

I wondered how many *sicarios* she knew.

After about two months of intensive lessons, I got a call from Julio to say that he was picking me up for breakfast, and that Monica wasn't going to be available for tutoring that morning because she had to work her other job. He arrived with Mateo and another bodyguard. They dropped us off at a nearby restaurant. Mateo stayed in the car, and the other bodyguard posted up in the back of the restaurant.

"How's your lessons going?" Julio asked.

"Much *buono*," I said.

Julio started laughing.

"Monica's a great teacher," I said. "But I struggle."

"We all struggle at something," he said.

". . .What do you struggle with?" I asked.

"Shaving," he said, and we shared a laugh. "Things may get a little rough here over the next few days."

He took a few more bites and, after a long pause, broke it down.

Monica had been part of Pablo Escobar's hit squad since she was a teenager. When I made her acquaintance, she was working freelance—as a *sicaria*, that is. Julio explained that she had been hired to put a hit on a particular target who was accompanied by three armed bodyguards at all times. It was not going to be an easy piece of work.

At first I thought Julio was pulling my leg, but I quickly realized that he was dead serious. For the rest of the day I went on a few errands with him. He dropped me off about 5:00 p.m. When Monica's mother answered the door, she seemed a bit frazzled. She led me into the living room, where I found Monica sitting on a chair, her right upper thigh wrapped in a large white bandage. I asked if she was okay. She nodded and said that the doctor was coming any moment.

He arrived about an hour later, and I took a walk while he worked on her. I learned later that he had come to extract a bullet that was lodged there only inches from her femoral artery, which, if it had been hit, would have bled her out if not treated immediately.

I came back a few hours later; Monica was in her room, sleeping. I sat with her mother and watched *telenovelas* until late that night. The *señora* watched the shows more intently than usual, barely blinking, probably trying to get her mind off of what had happened in the last twenty-four hours.

The next morning, I woke early and came in the kitchen, where Monica was hobbling around with the help of a cane.

"Hi, Judd," she said with a smile. "I'm heating up some pastries, and we can begin with our lessons in a few minutes."

"How are you feeling?" I asked.

"Pretty good," she said, as she made her way back to her bedroom.

I noticed a copy of the local newspaper lying on the table—something that I had not seen in the house since I had been there. It was folded open to an article about a businessman and one of his bodyguards who had been assassinated early the previous afternoon. From what I could understand, they were looking for a female assailant who had been shot as she escaped on a motorcycle. This businessman must have been a big shot, because I knew for a fact that the police had long since stopped investigating murders in Medellín. The article reported that the police were questioning the staff at local hospitals and asked that they be on the lookout for a female in her early twenties with a gun wound in the thigh. I was rereading the article, trying to grasp everything in it, when Monica appeared next to me holding a steaming-hot plate of pastries.

"Practicing your reading?" she asked as she sat down slowly, wincing in pain.

I put the article to the side. "It's over my head," I said.

"I am aware that Julio told you about my other job," she said.

I nodded.

"If he trusts you, so do I," she said. "Okay, let's work on past participles."

Over the next few days, Monica began to confide in me. I guess it was a relief to talk about her secret life with someone whom she could trust. She went into detail about the hit on the businessman. She was the designated assassin, which meant that she was to pull the trigger on the main target. Since the target was traveling with three armed bodyguards, there had been a real possibility that she could have been killed.

She and the rest of the hit team—four motorcycle drivers and three other shooters—planned the attack midday, at a major intersection, where they would blend in with the rest of the traffic. Every afternoon for the past couple of weeks, the shooters had set themselves up as street vendors. They took this precaution so that they would not stick out and attract suspicion from the target's security team on the day of the hit. The motorcycle drivers sat on their bikes, feigning boredom; one pretended that he was working on an engine problem. Monica sold candy from a rectangular box that was big enough to obscure the Uzi that she would carry.

That day, she was supposed to approach the car, tap on the back window, where the target sat, and offer to sell him candy. She was then to whip out her mini-Uzi and kill him at point-blank range. After she was sure he was dead, she was to focus on her own safety and get away—the rest of the hit team would deal with the bodyguards.

Backup #1, who posed as a newspaper vendor, was to take out the bodyguard seated directly next to the target if he tried to interfere with the hit or leave the car to fire on Monica. It was crucial that she execute the target quickly and efficiently, because the bodyguards would be less likely to risk their lives if their boss was already dead.

Backup #2 waited on the opposite corner, selling coffee out of a thermos, ready to take out the bodyguard, if necessary, who sat in the passenger seat up front. Backup #3 sat at the opposite corner—he would take out the driver if he didn't mind his own business.

As the businessman and his security team waited at the red light, Monica strolled up from the sidewalk and tapped the businessman's window. He looked at her for a moment and quickly waved her away without even rolling down the window, but she was already pulling the

Uzi from under the box of candy and fired into the car, shattering the window and hitting her target with a barrage of slugs in the face and torso.

Certain he was dead, she tossed the box of candy off to the side and ran the few feet to the motorcycle idling under its driver. As she was sliding onto it, the bodyguard in the back jumped out of the car and begun to fire at her. *Where the fuck is Backup #1?* Monica thought. It turned out he'd been smoking weed on the sidewalk and missed his cue.

One of the other backups had taken out the bodyguard, but not before my tutor caught a bullet in the leg. Wisely, the other bodyguards dove on the ground and lived another day.

The second Monica's ass hit the seat of the motorcycle, the team dispersed on designated routes and, after traveling eight to ten blocks, pulled off their colorful shirts and gave them to the motorcycle drivers, along with their guns. They were left wearing plain white T-shirts and free to travel on public transportation.

Monica wasn't as lucky. She was forced to stay on the bike until they got far enough away, when the driver did his best to tie a tourniquet using her outer shirt. She ordered him to drive her back to her house, where her mother re-bandaged her until one of her boss's doctors came. That was when I had appeared.

A couple of days later it was reported in the news that there was a huge reward for information leading to the arrest of the woman who had killed the businessman, who, as I had surmised, was a big shot. Monica and her employer agreed that it would be better if she moved to Bogota for a while. My lessons were officially suspended.

Julio told me that he had a cousin who taught English at a local private university, and that he'd see if he could get me enrolled there without ID. When I asked him why it had to be a private university, he said that the FARC frequently probed the student bodies of national universities to find anti-government or pro-revolutionary individuals and tried to recruit them to become higher-ups in their organization, to be sent to Russia or Cuba to be trained in the use of weapons, bombs, military strategies, and communist ideology. After this training, they would return to Colombia to initiate their careers in kidnapping, extortion, drug dealing, and murder. Julio predicted that, if I went to a national university, I'd be kidnapped inside of three weeks.

Within a week I was enrolled in the *Universidad de Bolivarina,* and I have to admit I was proud that, somehow, I was going to be studying at such a prestigious college. But make no mistake, this was Medellín, not Cambridge, and there were certainly differences. The place had a chain link fence ten feet high with barbed wire at the top, and every entrance had a walk-through metal detector with security personnel checking bags and pocketbooks, and other personnel checking the trunks and engine compartments of the cars. They even checked underneath the frame with mirrors attached to long sticks.

You cannot imagine the looks that I received from the students my first week on campus. Though I tried to limit my interactions exclusively to Spanish, it was quite obvious to everyone on the campus that I was not Latin American. The students and professors were polite, but I could tell that they could not believe that an American was living in Medellín and attending college, no less. The only modern-day comparison that I can come up would be if an American just showed up one day at a university in, say, Bagdad and started taking classes. But even Bagdad has American troops stationed there. In all my time in Medellín, I don't recall ever seeing an American—certainly not one strolling around campus. But there I was. And I don't know whether it was because everyone else was polite or in shock, but no one ever asked me why I had chosen Medellín as the place to restart my college education.

The university was quite pleasant and offered an abundance of attractive coeds. I was, however, drowning in loneliness. I kept reminding myself that I wasn't there to socialize but to learn Spanish and not get kidnapped.

My classes, in the morning, lasted three hours. During lunch, I would smile or say *hola* to the students who surrounded me. Out of what I assumed was morbid curiosity, some even engaged in short conversations. But for the most part, I sat alone and tried to read the newspaper. Julio had warned me against making moves on ladies, young or old, since they could be girlfriends, mistresses, or wives of powerful *narcotrafficantes*[44] who would get jealous and have "a *pinchie*[45] gringo rubbed out." I took his advice and made no romantic advances on any other woman at the college. (Rule #7—Don't make any emotional decisions.)

The highlight of my day came after lunch, when I played tennis on the university's clay courts with Andreas, the twenty-five-year-old grounds keeper, who was just beginning to learn the game. He proved to be a tough opponent, because he was quite an athlete—he'd almost made it onto Colombia's national *futbal* team.

I usually stayed on campus from about 7:00 a.m. until about 7:00 p.m. I worked diligently on my Spanish and tried my best to blend in. On the surface, I probably appeared to be like any other guy entering his forties and going through the first pangs of a midlife crisis, but the truth was that there wasn't a day that passed—hell, not even an hour—when I did not break out into a sweat because a security guard looked me up and down or a professor asked me one too many questions.

When I got home at night, Doña Ruth would have a plate of whatever she had cooked waiting for me, and she was more than happy to let me bounce off her a few of the new words that I had picked up. Her son Hector, the only high school graduate I met in Medellín besides Julio, was by far the most educated resident of the house. He sometimes helped me with my homework, between rants about the Colombian *futbol* team, which had made a poor showing in the previous year's World Cup. Even the guys from the hit squad would throw in their two cents. It takes a village. . .

On weekends I usually accompanied Julio and his crew to his *finca*, where we partied the weekend away. I tried my best not to be a party-pooper but I have to admit it wasn't easy socializing when everyone in the room had a buzz on but me. I did not want to seem ungrateful for Julio's hospitality, but the truth was I wouldn't be able to breathe easy until I got my papers, and even then I knew that I would be looking over my shoulder the rest of my life. I missed my wife dearly and still managed to speak to her about once a week. She would fill me in on details about our daughter but I could hear the frustration in her voice. She wanted to leave Las Vegas and bring Amber to join me. It was tempting, but I knew it would be the most selfish thing that I could possibly do. As much as I was dying to see them, I would not expose them to the dangers of Medellín. Maybe I would reunite with them once I acquired my papers and was set up in a more family friendly location than the slums of Campo Valdez.

Even though I had been hanging out with a wide array of women—from Mexican drug traffickers to American students—I hadn't hooked up with anyone but my wife since we married. I felt too much guilt for what I was putting her through, and anytime we spoke she never failed to mention that she was being faithful to me. So I remained faithful to her, so much so that I raised suspicion with the guys in Julio's crew.

After a few beers and shots of *aguadiente*, one of them would invariably start to bust my balls. "Judd," one of them would say. "I've got to ask you a question."

"Go ahead."

"How come you don't ever go on dates with a lady. You a *maricon*?"

The guys would howl in laughter.

"I'm a married man," I'd say, which produced even louder fits of laughter. I think they would have been more understanding if I were gay than monogamous.

But this all changed one hot steamy night in April.

It was another rocking party on Saturday night at Julio's *finca*.

Along with his regulars, Julio had invited about a dozen well-to-do folks from El Poblado, an affluent suburb of Medellín. A local rock band was doing its best to reproduce the sounds of Led Zeppelin, the Rolling Stones, and a band I had not yet heard of at that point, Nirvana. Julio was practically obsessed with Nirvana and their lead singer, Kurt Cobain, who had committed suicide a short time before. He told the band to play "Lithium" at least ten times that night. I was sipping on a Coke, talking to Julio's driver, Mateo, when I spotted quite possibly the most exquisite woman in all of Latin America.

She was the kind of woman women loved to hate. She carried herself with the confidence of a forty-year-old, but she still had the exuberance of a teenager. And while she had long, lush chestnut hair framing wide, dark eyes, she didn't look like a model but more like an action star. Her muscle definition was perfect, but she would probably tell you that she didn't work out and you would want to believe her.

We made eye contact, and I just froze. Hector giggled as he walked by and made the heart sign. Mateo wasn't as sweet when he too noticed the exchange and my subsequent inaction—he whispered into my ear that he would shoot me on the spot if I didn't go talk to her, even stuck his nine-millimeter into my ribs to make his point.

So I made my way over to her and struck up a conversation. Her name was Lucy. She was, as I had guessed, from El Poblado. She had been to Julio's parties on several occasions. I mentioned that Julio was a close friend who had been sponsoring me in Medellín while I studied at the university and worked on setting up a business exporting *aguadiente.*

She had a daughter enrolled in the university, too. Recently, she had also taken in a ten-year-old girl who had been living on the street.

As I stared into Lucy's eyes, I noticed that she had two small scars on her cheek. She must have noticed that I'd noticed and almost matter-of-factly mentioned there had been a bombing in her town courtesy of Pablo Escobar; she had lost her baby sister in another bombing. She did not romanticize the drug lord.

If a beautiful woman had told me this story in the States, I would have assumed that she was practicing for a movie role that she was up for, or that she was delusional. But in Medellín in the 1990s, it was extremely rare to find anyone who *hadn't* been touched by the war.

I told her that I was living in Campo Valdez, which shocked her because, as she put it, Campo Valdez was an "off-limits zone" where even Colombians knew not to go, a very unsettling thought for a gringo with poor Spanish. Somewhere in our conversation, I wove in an invitation to have dinner together the following weekend, which she accepted on the condition that we met in El Poblado. I confessed that I didn't have a car, but that I could get a ride to her place. She suggested that we meet at a nearby gas station. My kind of lady.

The next day, when I told Julio that I had landed a date with Lucy, he smiled. I didn't want to know if he had gotten with her, but if I had to guess I'd say yes because there weren't too many beautiful women in Medellín that Julio hadn't hooked up with. Either way, he seemed happy for me. I asked him if I could get Mateo to drive me out there. He needed him that night, so he introduced me to a former cop named Orlando, who lived across the street from Doña Ruth.

Orlando was the proud owner and operator of an older-model heavily armored and bulletproof yellow Renault taxi. The car was faded and underpowered. Its thin cloth seats let the springs in the cushioning poke passengers in the back. The bulletproof glass was so thick that the factory-model electric power-window motors couldn't move it, so the windows remained closed permanently. There was no air conditioning. I assume that most of his passengers cared more about safety than comfort.

Since I was an American and a prime target for kidnappers, who were known to prowl in affluent communities like El Poblado, I hired him for the night. He charged me a hundred dollars American, a discount price because of my friendship with Julio but still about twenty-five times the price of a regular taxi.

We showed up at the gas station a few minutes early the following Saturday night, and Lucy was right on time, driving an old and faded Renault with bald tires and a leaky exhaust. We followed her to one of Medellín's upscale restaurants, the one she had suggested. Orlando said that he would be nearby and gave me the number to his car phone, which was still pretty rare in Colombia back then.

At dinner, Lucy and I made small talk, and soon our legs began to rest against one another under the table. Between her tragically poor English and my Spanish, we were unable to converse about much. My Spanish was improving, but none of lessons thus far had prepared me to couch my romantic overtures in delicate innuendos. I did my best to not say that I wanted to give her rug burn or something crude like that, but I tried to make it clear that I wanted to get it on.

"*Quiero hacer amor contigo,*"[46] I said, as if I was translating a phrase at school.

"This is possible," she replied. "Or should I say probable?"

That was easy. Our options included her place, where her kids were waiting for her, or the basement apartment I shared with Julio's hit team. I was embarrassed, but she wasn't dissuaded in the least, and half way through dessert she suggested that we get a room at a Love Hotel. I called Orlando and told him that I was going to continue on with Lucy, that he was done for the night, and that I would pay him tomorrow. He tried to talk me out of this—he had promised Julio that he would make sure that I was safe. I assured him I would be fine.

On the way, Lucy told me that a Love Hotel was for couples that wanted a part-time room, not an all-nighter, where the price was cut-rate and where extramarital affairs were encouraged. When we arrived, there was a line of cars waiting to get in. Apparently, indiscretion was a booming business in Medellín.

When it was our turn at the drive-through window, we put our three-hour rental fee in the sliding steel drawer, like the banks have at their drive-through windows, and the clerk returned with a map to our room, a key, and a receipt, all of which Lucy fished out of the drawer in a single move.

We drove across the lot and found our designated room number above a one-car garage where we parked. Immediately, a handsome teenaged boy pulled down the door, which privatized our arrival from the view of the pantheon of lovers seeking rendezvous quarters. We climbed the stairs to our room directly above the garage, where we found a king-size bed with a full-size mirror on the ceiling above it and a four-person Jacuzzi. We passed on the room menu's many offerings, from lubricants to condoms, adult toys and porn movies, and made out on the bed while we waited for the Jacuzzi to fill.

Lucy, however, was not in the mood to wait. I kissed her, but it felt like she was barely tolerating our make-out session, and sure enough, as soon as I paused to take a breath, she broke away from my embrace, lowered herself onto her knees, and went to work. She went at it with such passion and exuberance that I had to do everything in my power to hold out and not be labeled a three-minute man.

She knew what she was doing; she was a master at the art of edging, expertly stopping and starting at the precise moment. When I could not take it anymore, I pulled her back up on the bed and ripped off her panties (white with purple polka dots). I returned the favor and then got on top and put in some work. I had never seen a woman orgasm so many times and so ferociously as Lucy did that night. The only negative was that we forgot all about the Jacuzzi, which flooded the bathroom.

Due to the intensity of this interlude, Lucy insisted upon subsequent encounters, and after our fourth or fifth tryst, we were awarded a VIP card. From then on we needed only to flash the card at the desk to get a personal garage door opener to escort us to our room, where we completed the required paperwork and simply pushed it through the slot in the room.

As beautiful as Lucy was, both inside and out, I didn't fall in love with her. I like to think it was because I was still married, and that I still had feelings for my wife. But it was also because I didn't want to drag a nice woman like Lucy into my dilemma.

Spring break was coming up, and I decided that I wanted take the opportunity to travel out of Medellín for a few weeks. As much as I appreciated the hospitality that Julio provided me, the truth was that I was no closer to getting my papers than I had been when I arrived. Plus, I had gotten spooked several times in town. Even though I was under Julio's protection, I couldn't help but think that someone might mention to the authorities that there was a gringo living with Julio's hit team—in exchange for, say, a lighter sentence, or a few pesos.

Spring break fell during *Semana Santa,*[47] and caravans of buses, and some private automobiles, would leave for Cartagena every twenty minutes or so with military escorts behind and in front of them. The streets were jammed with people headed for the bus station who finally had the chance to leave the city under this new level of security.

At this time, the guerrillas' control of the countryside made bus travel sporadic at best in Colombia. Murders and kidnappings will do that. The guerrillas had been setting up roadblocks and kidnapping travelers, burning buses, and committing armed robberies of passengers, and they were raking in the cash. It was reported that in 1994 alone they made a two-hundred-million-dollar profit from kidnappings. You would think that this knowledge would have dissuaded me from taking the bus. Nope. *Gringo stupido.*

Air travel was better but was not a sure thing, either. During the fight to have the nation's constitution amended to prohibit extradition of drug cartel members to the United States, a young boy who worked for Pablo Escobar's Medellín drug cartel inadvertently set off a bomb on a commercial domestic flight, killing 107 passengers and the crew. The target was a certain government minister who, at the last minute, had decided not to board the flight, which saved his life.

Julio's trusty driver, Mateo, drove me to the bus terminal. As we stopped at a traffic light, we noticed a motorcycle coming up the side carrying a guy on the back. We simultaneously glanced at one another, and I asked, "Are you thinking what I'm thinking?"

"The motorcycle hit men usually take *Semana Santa* off," Mateo said. "Don't worry."

Manny dropped me at the bus station and wished me luck, half-jokingly making the sign of the cross. I bought a ticket to Cartagena and proceeded to the security checkpoint. Before entering the bus, passengers were searched and asked for ID. When my turn came, I was sure to repulse the guard with my poor Spanish, telling him that I was an exchange student while I displayed my university identification. I was waved through without incident.

During the journey, we passed several military checkpoints. As they boarded the bus and looked us over, I was sure that, at any moment, they would invite me to step off the bus. They would cuff and frisk me and throw me in the back of one of their Jeeps, maybe blindfolding me for good measure. They would drive me to a nearby jail. If I was lucky, they would try to blackmail me. I would be given permission to try to contact my people and come up with, say, a million dollars American. If I was *really* lucky, they would take the money and let me go. Then I would have to get out of Colombia immediately, because they would still contact the American authorities, who would hunt me down.

If I wasn't so lucky, they would call the DEA, and forty-eight hours later I would be on a plane, handcuffed, sitting between two DEA agents heading for the United States. I would go through the humiliation of a trial, my mother and wife tearing up in the courtroom. I would get sentenced to thirty to forty years in federal prison for a crime I had not committed and be eligible for parole at the age of seventy-five. Maybe I would hire someone to whack my old pal Marvin Schumacher. And then maybe I'd get the chair.

The soldiers who boarded the bus looked me over but didn't pause. Luckily, I didn't seem too impressive.

About three hours into our drive, a boulder tumbled down a slope to the right of the bus and struck the front wheel, disabling the bus. Had we been sixty meters farther down the road, the avalanche of rocks and soil would have broadsided the bus. The road was officially closed. The head of the caravan radioed for mechanics and heavy equipment to clear it. The mechanics never ceased to amaze me, meeting timetables under stringent conditions with their ingenuity and their work ethic.

It seemed Colombians never let a good crisis go to waste—it becomes time to party. Behind the buses, a crowd began to form. Soon most of the passengers were dancing, drinking *aguadiente*, and then some local capitalists from a nearby village showed up carrying cases of beer and even some sodas for the children. This fiesta served as the inaugural celebration to kick off the holiday, and as the first chance to let go of all the pent-up tension from being trapped in the city for as long as they had been. We were on to Cartagena.

A few hours after we left the landslide area, the caravan again came to a halt. The police who stopped us said that, about forty kilometers[48] ahead, a skirmish was taking place between guerrillas and the national police and military, and that we'd have to wait until the fighting was over.

It was very hot outside, and again we were stuck on a road in the middle of nowhere. The passengers were exiting the buses and mingling on the highway. Forty-five minutes later, some young men on motorcycles drove up carrying beer, sodas, liquor, food, water, and mosquito repellent. They warned us that, when evening came, the mosquitoes would be out in full force. A couple traveling in their own car brought out a radio and cranked up the merengue and salsa music. Suddenly, almost everyone was dancing and drinking: the clashing of the army and the guerrillas was another excuse to party.

Three hours later, we were again given the green light to proceed—but not for long. After an hour, we came to a roadblock where men in military fatigues, carrying AK-47s, grenades, and mini-Uzis, stopped our bus and three other vehicles. One of the soldiers boarded, telling all of us to wait there, inside the bus, and the other three vehicles were allowed to leave. Eight more uniformed soldiers with long rubber boots then boarded, and one of them sat in the driver's seat, started the bus, and took us down a dirt road, stopping ten minutes later. I mention the boots because they just didn't seem right. The one good thing about not being able to rely on the spoken word for most of your information is that it forces you to pay attention to details that you might have missed if you were blabbering away. Not that this information did me much good. Bad boots or not, I was at their mercy, and I doubted that they gave a damn what I thought. Even though I had been in some dangerous situations in the past year and a half, something in me said that this was going to be different.

We were ordered to leave the bus with our possessions in hand. I had my small backpack in my hand and fanny pack around my waist as I did. The soldiers broke us up into two groups—men on the right, and women on the left. Five of the soldiers guarded the men, and one male and two female soldiers guarded the women. I kept my head down. One of the soldiers was standing in front of me. I took note of his footwear. He, too, was wearing long rubber boots like the ones that fishermen wear, not standard military boots. I raised my eyes furtively and noticed that his uniform was old and faded. There was no way these guys were legitimate Colombian military personnel. Still, when they shone their flashlights on us, they told us that we would be shot if we tried to escape. I believed them.

Whoever they were, I was pretty sure that I would have a better time escaping them than the authorities. As I stood there, I wondered how the hell I was going to get out of it. If they were kidnappers, as I suspected, and they pressed me, would I be forced to call my family to get money? I certainly couldn't do that. I then reasoned how terrible an idea calling the States was. My only choice would be to call Julio. As one who lived on the edge of Colombia, he was certainly knowledgeable about the lay of the land and likely had experience in how to deal with people like these. But I didn't think he'd be too happy about it. He had warned me not to leave Medellín but I'd had to play tourist. *Gringo stupido.*

In shorts and a T-shirt, I was easy pickings for the mosquitoes that now flocked and stalked their prey. Where were the locals with the mosquito repellent when you needed them? Eventually, people in our party started asking if they would be permitted to go to the bathroom. They were denied. But after reconsideration and possible fear of a mutiny, the female guards took the women, one by one, to use the rest room. The men were treated in kind, escorted only fifteen feet away from the group and held at gunpoint while we relieved ourselves.

Hours later, our bus reappeared, lights on, creeping toward us down the dirt road. This made me wonder if this group was working with the army. We never had a clue what their next move would be. I had concluded that if I was going to escape, it would have to be on the trail they would use to walk us to their camp or facility. Once at that destination, my chances would diminish immensely.

Fortunately, I didn't have to put any of that into motion, because shortly after the bus arrived we were permitted to board, and the bus driver was ordered into the driver's seat and told to continue on to our destination.

Once the bus reached the paved road, the guy next to me, a Colombian, told me that our captors were a group that worked to protect an organization led by a *narcotrafficante* named Rodrigo Cadena. He pointed at the blood stains on the floor and on some of the seats, telling me that they had used the bus to transport their wounded, and probably their dead, to a hospital after their battle over a roadblock the guerrillas had set up on the highway, and the kidnapping and murder of people, burning cars and trucks, and so on. I had been truly terrified, but I was enormously relieved to be free, and thankful for having missed out on all of that.

Sure enough, fifteen minutes down the highway, we had to slow down and weave through burned-out cars, buses, and trucks in what looked like a war zone.

It was shaping up to be quite a spring break.

As I looked out the window during my taxi ride to the Cartagena Hilton, it hit me that the *Semana Santa* celebration was a big deal in Colombia. The city was packed with people, dressed in bright, festive colors, carrying a wide range of religious artifacts. I had chosen the Hilton because of the good name it had throughout the world, presuming it to be one of the best hotels in the city. Once there, the receptionist told me that there were no vacancies, and that no openings were expected due to the festival. The fact that this was the busy season didn't help matters, but it didn't dissuade me from asking to see the manager either. His name was Francisco—a charismatic, well-groomed man about my age who spoke decent English, which was proven by his pronunciation of the word "impossible."

Nothing was impossible in Colombia, I had learned, as long as you were willing to part with some greenbacks. After some haggling, and a payment of a hundred and fifty American dollars, the impossible became possible, and I was allowed to pay the daily rate for three nights' lodging.

From the speed with which Francisco tucked my bribe into his pocket, I could tell he had done so before, for other gringos, probably. He told me to go back to the receptionist to register, but that posed yet another problem: I had no passport. The hotels in Colombia were required to fax a list of all hotel guests to the local police daily, so they could perform background checks on them to find terrorists, criminals, and anyone else who they might deem a threat or at least a person that they could shake down for a few bucks.

"We cannot break the rules and register anyone without a passport," said the attractive young woman at the front desk. Despite my charm, she said that she would be jeopardizing her employment if she registered me without a passport.

When Francisco saw me entering his office, he appeared anxious, probably because he did not want to part with the cash in his pocket. I explained the situation, and he immediately began to thumb through his Rolodex, making phone calls to friends. But no one came up with what he needed to register me—passport number and expiration date.

Initially, he thought of simply making up a number and date, but he was cautioned that there remained a slight possibility the police might happen to punch those numbers into their database and a red flag come up. I told him that I would not take that chance. I thought he was ready to give up when, all of a sudden he said, "I have the solution, amigo!"

How much is this going to cost me? I wondered. However, without asking for another dime, he said that he would put the room under his own name and use his own passport.

I waited in his office while he went to the front desk, and upon returning, he sat down, handing me a card-key with holes in it to open the door to the room, and promised to make my *Semana Santa* a memorable one. He reached into his desk drawer and pulled out a VIP pass to his amigo's strip club, El Mitote, which according to my dictionary meant "the brawl." That certainly sounded sexy, didn't it? But according to Francisco, El Mitote was the "best strip club in all of Cartagena—hell, all of Colombia!"

After a long nap I jumped into a taxi. "El Mitote," I said.

"Amigo," the driver said, smiling widely, "El Mitote is the best strip club in Colombia!"

I was shocked that he spoke English. I tried to converse with him, you know, to get a few pointers from a local about Cartagena, but apparently those were the only nine words he knew.

He dropped me off at the club and even high-fived me after I paid him. I walked up to the door, past the surprisingly long line, and presented my VIP card to the bouncer, who gave me one of those looks, up and down, with doubt and contempt in his eyes, as if I was lying about owing him money.

"I'm a guest of Francisco's, at the Hilton. He wanted me to tell you that he couldn't make it tonight," I said.

"Oh, Francisco. *Si, hombre. Donde esta?*" he asked.

But the card worked—the bouncer unhooked the red velvet rope and opened the door. Once inside the maître d' greeted me graciously and escorted me to a stage-side seat, for which I tipped him handsomely. He told me that I was just in time for the featured dancer, Alicia, whose life-sized posters graced the front doors of the club.

My goodness. She had blonde hair down to her waist, in sharp contrast to her tanned and incredibly maintained body. I was taking eyefuls of her and the several girls who flanked the main stage, gyrating and dancing against strategically placed and heavily polished brass firehouse poles. All of them were attractive, but Alicia was in a league of her own.

As I looked around at the heavy-breathing hordes of spectators, I concluded that competition was stiff—as I determined by adding up the volume of peso notes that landed on the stage.

A few tunes into their sets, the choreography dictated that the girls discard, high into the air and onto the ceiling fans, their minuscule G-strings. This move, which they carried out simultaneously, nearly killed every man in the place and was the prelim gesture to mark a dance-off lasting the duration of the final two tunes.

I played it cool, sipping on my Coke, smiling at Alicia, and I decided after the set to take advantage of her break. I knew I had to act quickly to beat anyone else in the crowd who had designs on her. I signaled the maître d' over and tipped him to get the dancer to join me at my table for a cocktail.

In only a couple of minutes, she showed up in a skimpy powder blue slip that obscured her finer points. We made some small talk and exchanged names. I wondered how many times the customer was the one to give a fake name to a dancer. I sensed that her time was at a premium, so I asked her what it would cost to spend the evening with her.

"I'm sorry," she said. "I'm busy tonight."

I guess she could sense my heartbreak and reminded me that she was the most popular girl in the club and was therefore the most desirable and the highest-paid. The maître d' told me that her popularity doubled the price over what the other dancers at the club got for such an interlude. She charged two hundred American. I asked her about the following day's schedule, just for kicks, and she said I could call her in the afternoon to see if we could possibly have "a date." We didn't discuss money, so I presumed she was financially stable, and I fantasized that she was actually attracted to me. Only at strip clubs do men get a license to become so delusional.

The next day I played it cool and waited until a minute past noon to call her. A woman answered and handed the phone to Alicia, who sounded well-rested, fresh, and vibrant. She told me how to get to her place, where she told me to ask the guard to ring her apartment. She lived in a tall white apartment building with the standard guard shack in front of a steel fence. She answered the guard's call and told him to send me up right away.

On the way to her floor, I kept thinking that I should be ready for anything—an enraged boyfriend, a pushy pimp, or both. I was relieved when a woman of about sixty answered my knock on the door and warmly told me, "*Adelante*."[49] I entered a pleasantly decorated and furnished home that immediately put me at ease. I sat on the couch, accepted the woman's offer of a cup of coffee, and after only a minute Alicia appeared in the main salon, dressed in comfortable, loose-fitting casual pants and a blouse, as though she were ready to go grocery shopping. She leaned over and kissed me on both cheeks, and then introduced me to the woman as her aunt, and to the teenage boy watching TV as her nephew.

Just as I wondered if we were going to make it in the bedroom down the hall, she said that she had some things she needed to pick up at Boca Grande, an upper-class suburb, and asked if I would like to tag along.

Immediately, she was in control. Her casual nature, coupled with her laid-back demeanor, left me without a clue. In the short time I was with her, up to that point, her phone rang constantly, including two calls from Italian club owners in Europe where she had previously performed who were trying to get her back to their stage. This was at the dawn of the cellular communication age, when calls cost a dollar per minute.

We drove to a store in Boca Grande in her flashy red sports car, where she bought some writing supplies. I asked Alicia if she was working that night. She nodded. So I asked her if she'd like to go back to my hotel before she returned home, and she nodded again. I felt like dancing in the street.

"But we must stop at the clinic and both get AIDS tests," she said.

I wasn't expecting that, but I had no problem with undergoing a test for the AIDS virus. I was confident that I was fine. I had used condoms with Lucy, the only woman I had been with besides my wife since I got married. And I have to say that it was even more of a turn-on that Alicia acted so responsibly.

Back in my room, we made love like a real couple. At the time I thought it was because she really dug me; I would later learn that this was called the Girlfriend Experience. I can honestly say that it was one of the greatest times I have ever had in bed. But as I waited for her to shower, my mood changed as I came to the realization that I could not continue to lead on my wife. It was not fair, and I felt terrible about it. We had been talking less and less frequently. I could say I had trouble finding working pay phones, but the truth was that I wasn't trying nearly as diligently as I had during my first year on the run. I had to stop being so selfish and cut it off.

I would like to report that I arranged to meet my wife somewhere in South America and broke the news to her like a man, or at least that

I had sent word with Paul Holt, the one friend with whom I kept in contact in the States. But I didn't. I just stopped calling her, and eventually she got on with her life. In time, the feds stopped harassing her, and her daughter stopped asking for me. She remarried; I have not spoken to her again.

As Alicia and I sat in the restaurant, I noticed Francisco making his rounds, inspecting the hotel's amenities. When he glanced in our direction, I waved to get his attention. The double-take he did was a classic, as if to say, "How the hell is the *gringo stupido* with such a vision? And with no passport to boot."

He pulled a quick U-turn and sped over to our table, almost panting.

"Hi, Francisco," I said. "This is Alicia."

He wasn't there to see me. He did his best to put together a few coherent sentences. She handled it well; I assumed she was used to such behavior.

When he finally got the hint and left, we finished our lunch. She said she had things to do before she went to work. I returned to my room to recover. I lay down and reflected on how different the day would have been if I hadn't left the States: prison food, prison guards, cold cement to sit on, and hairy cell mates to avoid. But I also knew that I couldn't get cocky or comfortable. At any moment I could be found out and spend the rest of my life in prison. And the odds would continue to be against me if I didn't get papers.

I hadn't been back in my room for more than a half-hour when Francisco knocked on my door. The room was in his name, so I didn't hesitate to let him in. His hospitality and the way things had worked out had put him at or near the top of the list of my most preferred connections.

He wanted to hear all of the details, but I don't kiss and tell. I merely said that Alicia was a wonderful person or some shit like that. He told me that he hadn't had the pleasure of spending any quality time with her yet because he was trying to get out of a relationship with one of the dancers, so he had been avoiding the club for the past couple of weeks. He confided that, despite his having a wife of more than fifteen years, he had gone on "dates" with several dancers. But like a fool he'd begun to see one of them several times in a row, and soon she'd started to reduce her fee for her "dates" and ultimately stopped charging him altogether because she was in love with him, despite her knowledge of his marital status.

Francisco was miserable, because he wanted to get back to "playing the field" among the other dancers. "I already got a wife. I don't need another," he said, head in hands, as though he was going to cry.

I asked if there was anything that I could do to help.

He looked up. "Maybe we can go to the club," he said.

"I can do that," I said.

Once we were seated, the dancers flocked to Francisco as if he was an old friend, but the fact was that he was an executive client, which was one step above a VIP. I'm pretty sure that they would not have dared to do this if the possessive dancer had been at work that night; it would have been considered a *faux pas* in that industry. It turned out that she was away to take care of some "family business," though, so it was open season on Francisco, whom the dancers clearly deemed very good-looking (and probably more importantly, a big spender).

After watching the grand finale, he told me that if shit was going to hit the fan with his possessive wannabe girlfriend, he wanted to have a good time doing it. Watching Alicia on stage solidified his resolve to approach her for a date, which was as easy as asking the maître d' to inform her that Francisco would like to speak to her at our table. She came over and kissed me on both cheeks, remaining professional and understanding, even as Francisco was slobbering all over the place. As they made a date for the following day, she did glance over at me a couple of times and smiled, but that's all I got.

Francisco's behavior in the restaurant with me had convinced Alicia that he was all hers, and she was going to make the most of it. Being a married man didn't save him from having to get an AIDS exam. The next morning he was to take the exam on a solo trip to the clinic, then meet Alicia at 4:00 p.m. in the hotel room with his name on it, where I was staying. And I wasn't to return until the drapes were open and the light was on. "You better go take a tour of the city or something, amigo," he said with a gleam in his eye. "Because once she gets a piece of me, she's not going to want to leave." I couldn't knock his confidence.

Even the best-laid plans. . . I was sitting by the pool, getting a tan, when I heard a commotion coming from the front desk. I lost a lot of it in translation, but the name Francisco, followed by the words "*esposo bastardo enganador,*"[50] rang out loud and clear. From what I could piece together, Francisco's wife's brother, a police officer, had told her that Francisco had a room under his name on the Hilton's registry during the *Semana Santa* festival, at the peak of the high season. At first the front-desk clerk refused to tell her where the room was. But after she yelled down the halls of the hotel, a well-meaning maid not only led her to the room but also unlocked the door.

I tried to get there to warn him, but she beat me by about five seconds. As I reached the door, she was standing at it, staring at her husband climbing off Alicia. She grabbed the desk lamp and threw it at the lovebirds, narrowly missing Alicia's face; it flew by and slammed into the sliding glass door, sending shards of glass onto the sunbathers a floor below. I stood there dumbfounded as Francisco started screaming at his wife—until she whipped out a .38-caliber pistol from her purse. Luckily for the lovebirds, she accidentally flung the gun under a nearby lounge chair. I momentarily thought about trying to jump on it, but the last thing I needed was to get involved in a domestic dispute. As it was, I wasn't looking forward to the arrival of the police and questions about my involvement. As wifey crawled under the chair to retrieve her pistol, I ran back to the pool.

Francisco and Alicia, for some reason, had crawled onto the balcony, butt-naked. Francisco stood there stupidly while Alicia climbed over the railing, clinging to it with just one hand. The poolside guests, who were still in shock over getting doused with shards of glass, froze in wonder. Just as wifey made it out onto the balcony, gun in hand, Alicia jumped off the balcony and into the pool. Francisco followed her, his chubby gut barely clearing the railing as he jumped.

"*Voy a matarte, tu hijo de puta! Tu maricon!*"[51] she screamed at Francisco. This caused the guests to break out of their trance and into a mad dash away from the couple.

Wifey ran back in the room. I tossed Alicia and Francisco towels as they leaped out of the water. They ran to the lobby just as wifey got off the elevator. She was holding the results of the AIDS test and continued to call her husband a *maricon*, in earnest. She was about to fire at them when the hotel's security guards, who had drawn their own guns, interceded. After a fifteen-second standoff, she dropped the .38.

If that wasn't enough excitement for one day, I only then recalled having stashed two thousand American dollars in the hem of the drapes by the shattered window. As the police took wifey to the cop shop, I realized that I had a very small window of opportunity to go to my room and grab my stuff, especially my money. I took the stairs to the second floor and streaked down the hallway. My adrenaline was pumping as I ran into the room, dug my cash out of the drapes, and stuck it in my pants pocket, then stuffed my clothes into my unzipped bag. With just a few quick steps I was breathing easy, out in the hallway in front of the closed door to somebody else's room. But I had forgotten my AIDS exam receipt in the bathroom, beside the sink! It had my fake name on it, the one I'd spent over a year building, the one I had bank accounts and all kinds of other stuff in; if it was found, it could be used to track me down. If anybody started an investigation, I'd have to get out of Medellín and away from Julio, which would be a *catastrophe*.

I was shaking so badly I could barely stick the key-card in the slot to open the door again. After bolting in and out of the bathroom I booked out of the room and sprinted back down the stairs with my bag, my cash, and my receipt that proved to the world that I was AIDS-free, and unceremoniously joined a line of others who were waiting for a cab.

Armed with the lessons learned from that sticky situation at Francisco's expense, I moved on to another location. How could I possibly stay at the Hilton after that? It wasn't hard to imagine that, through the interrogation of hotel staff, the brother-in-law would learn that I was the actual occupant of the room, which would result in my own trip to the cop shop. If they discovered that I had no passport then, well, you can guess what would transpire.

Fear and adrenaline fueled me to hastily seek a bus ride out of town. I reached the bus station and stood in line, only to be asked for a passport I didn't have, so I left and inquired of a woman selling shaved mangos (with salt) how somebody might reach Santa Marta without a bus.

According to her, I could take a short taxi ride to a nearby barrio that had a taxi pool that served Barranquilla, and from there I could take a taxi to Santa Marta. I did as she instructed and, after a fifteen-minute wait, was in a cab speeding to Barranquilla, from which I had no problem catching another taxi to Santa Marta, where anything was possible, or so I had heard.

I recalled from reading my guidebooks that Santa Marta was a transit point for many travelers leaving or entering South America. As I was making my way from the taxi station to my hotel a few blocks away, I noticed other travelers looking at their guidebooks, which confirmed this.

I found that every single hotel had no-vacancy signs out. The town was packed—there were people sleeping on the balconies, in tents pitched on the flat concrete roofs, and on the floors of the hotel lobbies. I finally found a hotel that had a room, which should have been a warning to stay the hell out of there. *Gringo stupido.*

It was by far the worst place I have ever stayed in, filled with the nastiest degenerates that I have had the pleasure of meeting. This is saying something, considering I've spent over a third of my adult life in prison. Zombies hastened up and down the halls without uttering a word. Most of the doors to the rooms were either missing or off their hinges. In some rooms, wide-eyed faces peered at me, coarsely laughing faces that sucked on cigarette butts or beer bottles. In other rooms, couples or threesomes engaged in sexual acts that are not fit to describe in print, often while an audience of up to six men masturbated near-by. I barricaded myself in my tiny, filthy room and sat in the corner, trying not to weep. I escaped the next morning, but I still haven't recovered from that night.

I wandered into a theater, where I viewed three movies for three American bucks. After that, I was walking down a pedestrian passway, very bored, when I overheard a guy touting a strip club. It was Sunday, so everything else was closed, and I learned that this strip club was nearby, only a few blocks off the main street.

As I opened the door to the club two drunks stumbled out, cursing at one another so ferociously that they didn't even notice that one of them had slammed into me. Why didn't I heed that warning and turn back around? The club was poorly lit, which I soon realized was probably intentional, given who was under the lights. My visions of Shakira quickly faded, and I realized that I had made a huge mistake. There were five or six guys sitting at the bar and an empty stage, which sat elevated about three feet in front of several empty booths, where they seated me. A few minutes later, two drinks arrived along with two linebackers for the Green Bay Packers wearing G-strings. I was positive that the drinks were spiked to knock me out, and I certainly did not want a table dance from either of these . . . ladies.

I repeatedly asked when the show was going to start, and they kept telling me, "In a few minutes, amigo."

I got up to leave but was stopped by two of the men sitting at the bar. "Where are you going, amigo?" they asked.

"To my hotel."

"You need to stay and watch the show, amigo," one of them said.

I was telling them that I had to go when another guy approached and demanded that I pay for the drinks that I hadn't ordered. I refused. That was when I got punched in the stomach and struck until I hit the floor. They held me down and rifled my pockets, where they found only a few dollars in local currency and one of my college IDs. I had approximately a thousand bucks in a slit I had cut in the waist of my Levi jeans, which they missed.

They started screaming at each other about having scammed a tourist with no money and a plastic watch, and then they kicked *"el tecaño cabron"*[52] in the stomach a few times, which hurt more than I would have imagined. Then they threw the cheap bastard out onto the sidewalk.

I got up and staggered toward the street with my bloody nose, my bulging lip, and my wounded pride, but with my naiveté intact, gathered my wits, and looked up and down the street to get my bearings. If I hadn't been in my present situation, I would have handled it differently, but that option wasn't available to me. If I continued taking chances like this, I wouldn't have to worry about the quality of dancers that I met. I wouldn't be coming in contact with any women for the rest of my life.

The next day as I sat in the courtyard, trying to figure out what my next move would be, I overheard a couple of fellow travelers talking about the Fruit Lady, who was located catty-corner from the courtyard, across the dusty street.

The Fruit Lady was about forty-five years old and had the deepest wrinkles I had ever seen on a human forehead. She was wearing what could best be described a discarded prom dress from the 1970s. By contrast, her hands were immaculately manicured and featured long artificial nails. I soon discerned that fruit was the last thing on the menu, which explained her departure from the norm.

"I saw you walking down to the other Five-Star hotel, yesterday. How was your stay?" she asked.

"I've been in jails that were better than that place," I said.

"Me, too."

I have to admit she was the most outgoing and gregarious vendor I'd ever met. We laughed, and she wondered if I needed anything to make my stay more enjoyable.

"What's on your menu?" I asked.

She handed me an actual menu, which listed such items as cocaine, women, Colombian bootleg moonshine, and a tour of *La Ciudad Perdida,*[53] in that order.

"Well, *cariño,*"[54] she said, "I have some pretty young ladies who'd love to spend some time with a handsome foreigner."

The truth is, I couldn't picture getting it on with anyone but Alicia, but out of morbid curiosity I asked, "Do you have any pictures?"

"No, I don't," she said. "But it's early in the day. I can gather up fifteen of my girls that you can choose from."

"Only fifteen?"

"Hey, it's *Semana Santa,*" she said.

I explained that I had checked out of that fleabag hotel, and that there was no way that I was going to step back into it, no matter how hot the girls were.

"*No problema*," she said with confidence. "I know the owner of the Hotel Miramar."

"It's full," I said.

"Leave it to the Fruit Lady," she said. "I send him girls all the time. He's one of my best customers." (So much for the supposed anonymity of the prostitution industry.)

She wrote a note asking the hotel to give me a room and told me that, if I had any problems, to call the owner, Don Marcos, and say I was a personal friend of hers, and to return to the fruit stand once I had secured lodging. She turned to her assistant, a young errand boy, to go and round up the girls.

The Hotel Miramar had no office to speak of. Registration was handled at a large wooden desk that faced the courtyard, where the manager was sitting with her back against the wall. She had a glamorous view of the courtyard and the roof with the rebar sticking up through the concrete, and of the vividly colored tents of the travelers who lodged on the roof. The humidity and open-air exposure was peeling the varnish off the manager's desk, and the sun was turning the rooftop tents into saunas, which forced the roof-toppers into the shade of the central courtyard to rest in the comparatively cool breeze created by cheap plastic fans mounted on the concrete ceiling.

The Fruit Lady's note was written in a fine calligraphic hand, which probably meant that she'd had a formal education that she was employing to dominate the local black market economy with the help of hotel owners and management. I walked in and handed the manager the note, and she told me I was out of luck—it was *Semana Santa, gringo*. But she would see what she could do.

She placed a call to someone I presumed was Don Marcos, because when she was through she turned to me and told me two backpackers were going to leave their room to take a tour of Tayrona National Park and wouldn't be back until the evening, adding that she'd put me on a waiting list for the room. I walked across the street to the Fruit Lady and told her how the matter had been handled, and she said that she would delay the girls' arrival. It wasn't long thereafter that the room was vacated by the nice couple who had paid for it and who had every right to expect that their room not be used as a tryst-o-rama in their absence. Enjoy the national park, gringos!

The maid had barely finished changing the bedding when I was taken to somebody else's room, where I sat alone for about an hour, and no bevy of beauties appeared—until, finally, a bad-smelling, potbellied, chubby, dark-skinned, pear-shaped reject from a Saddam Hussein look-alike contest entered the room, twisting the ends of a thick black mustache.

"*Me llamo Don Marcos*," said he. Apparently, the Fruit Lady had run into a delay because the girls had put in a tough shift the night before.

He went on to say that he seldom visited the hotel, but that he wanted to see if the Fruit Lady had any new talent among her troupe. He claimed to have taken her entire pit crew around the track any number of times. I thought, *Bullshit*. He pulled out a long, thin bottle of cologne called Siete Machos and practically bathed himself in it, which was when it hit me: The stink wasn't body odor at all; it was his ghastly cologne.

I waited another hour, with Don Marcos, and saw that the sun was going down. The cologne had given me a migraine, and to be honest, Don Marcos was an extremely creepy guy, not to mention that I just couldn't get comfortable in a room that belonged to the two unsuspecting hikers.

The Fruit Lady finally arrived. Don Marcos sprang to his feet and rushed out to the lobby, where she paraded in five proposed partners for me (and, I assumed, Don Marco) to assess. The first four were each about fifty pounds overweight and sported hairy legs and armpits. The fifth one was anorexic, with excess skin sagging from her upper arms and the sunken face of a crack head.

Don Marcos looked on in awe. I, on the other hand, shook my head, which was my way of staving off the urge to bring up my last three meals.

"I'm going to pass," I said.

The only live one in the crowd was Don Marcos, who ended up paying the Fruit Lady for the services of two of the girls. I had sat and listened to his stories of sexual conquest and prowess with the Fruit Lady's girls for an hour, viewed the opposite of good-time possibilities for another ten minutes, and worst of all, been forced to inhale the essence of Siete Machos.

I wondered how the hell the hotel was going to explain to the people who really owned the room that their belongings smelled as they surely would after Don Marcos's presence had scented their things with the odor of Siete Machos. But that wasn't my concern. All I wanted was to rest for a while and think pure thoughts. I stepped outside in front of the hotel and felt I owed the Fruit Lady an apology. I waited several minutes to assure the nice girls had left the fruit stand, cleared my head, and then strolled back across the street.

"*No te gusta las chicas?*"[55] she asked.

"They weren't really my type," I said.

"I can't believe that you didn't like my girls," she said.

I could tell that I had hurt her feelings, so I bought a tour of La Ciudad Perdida, which began with a ride to the beach in a van with six other foreigners. Among them were two couples from England, along with a driver and a guide with poor English, both Colombian. We left Santa Marta at 7:30 a.m. and reached Tayrona National Park a little while later, where we were dropped off to spend the day exploring the park and hanging out at the beach. The driver took the van back to Santa Marta.

As the sun set, we put up our tents and settled in for the night, sacking out plenty early for our 6:30 a.m. departure and hike from the beach up to La Ciudad Perdida.

In the morning, we set out through the hills in terrain that was, at times, so steep that it was more like climbing than walking. The air became noticeably cooler. We encountered some rocks that had spring water flowing heavily out of them through cracks—water the guide claimed was safe to drink. At about 4:30 p.m., we stopped for the night and made a meal from the canned goods we had brought with us.

As we were pitching our tents and unrolling our sleeping bags, about fifteen guerrillas, dressed in army fatigues and carrying AK-47s, emerged from the trees. The first thought that entered my mind was that they were there for me. I had to do everything I could to stop myself from making a run for it, which would have meant suicide. The guerrillas pointed their rifles and shouted orders. My command of Spanish was limited at best, but at that moment I forgot almost everything that I had learned; they might as well have been speaking Swahili. Our guide translated for us. They weren't there for me, apparently.

The women were led to a spot behind some trees and were told to strip to their underwear. The rest of us were made to strip right there. Our clothes and baggage were searched, our supplies gone through, and our tents emptied before we were allowed to get dressed again. We scrambled into our shirts and pants. The women were reunited with their husbands, who hugged them as though they had been gone for months and not minutes. One of the guerrillas found a GPS device belonging to one of the British couples. Again, I couldn't understand what they were saying, but very quickly the owner of the device, a well-mannered gentleman from Nottingham, was ordered into the brush by *El Comandante,*[56] who sported some stripes on the shoulder of his camouflaged shirt.

El Comandante and two soldiers dragged the Englishman behind the trees, out of our view. After about ten minutes, one of the soldiers appeared from that direction. He looked us over and began to question the woman, who turned out to be the Englishman's fiancée. When one of them asked if her man was, by chance, an American policeman, she assured them that they were only British tourists. She was then asked why her Spanish was so good; she replied that she had been raised in Spain and had moved to England as a teenager.

"*No le creo!*" the guerrilla snapped. I was proud that I understood that it meant: "I don't believe you."

The guerrilla went back to the direction of where the Englishman had been brought. About five minutes later we heard a gunshot, then everything in the jungle went silent. The fiancée began to scream. One of the guerrillas comforted her by sticking the barrel of his AK into her cheek. The guerrillas muttered something and our guide told us to be calm; these men were just investigating. Well, who were we to doubt the word of a man who would lead foreigners into the heart of guerrilla-infested Colombia, right?

El Comandante and one of the guerrillas then returned to our group. Except for the fact that they just stood there and stared at us with their hands on their triggers, everything seemed fine. They were reading our faces, and from what I could tell they did not like what they were reading. Then, all of a sudden, one of the guerrillas grabbed the fiancée by the arm and led her away in the same direction they had taken the Englishman. Five minutes later we heard another shot.

The fugitive lifestyle had been very good to me, I thought, as I recited the Lord's Prayer to myself. The guide remained silent. The other British couple clutched each other and tried to remain strong. They asked us for our identification, and I turned over my student ID card. *El Comandante* looked at it and snickered, as would a bouncer at a fake ID. He began by accusing me of being a DEA agent or a spy for the United States, telling me that if I didn't come clean I would meet the same fate as the English couple.

What was I going to say? My mother had always advised me to tell the truth. How's this sound, Mom? "Hi, I'm a fugitive from America. I've been staying in Medellín under the protection of one of the heads of the local cartel. I learned some Spanish in a third-grade class in Mexico and from my tutor, a hit woman. I almost fell in love with a stripper. And, oh yeah, I don't have AIDS, I have a receipt!"

Sorry, Mom. I just kept my mouth shut. These guys were well-armed, in uniforms resembling those of the Colombian army, but their boots were different from the boots worn by the guys who hijacked my Cartagena bus to take their wounded to the hospital. These appeared to be U.S. military issue.

They seemed convinced that I was DEA. I repeated to them, with the help of the guide, that I was just a tourist who wanted to see La Ciudad Perdida, and that my passport had been lost when I was robbed of my fanny pack in the bus station in Cartagena. I explained that I was or had been taking Spanish lessons in Medellín, and that I never carried my student ID anywhere but in my pants pocket.

El Comandante gave the order to take me into the brush in the same direction they'd taken the others who had been shot to death. Two guerrillas grabbed me by the arms and hauled me off. When we got to the spot, the scene of the crimes, I saw the British couple tied with military-style belts at the wrists, the ankles, and the knees. I was quickly restrained in the same way.

El Comandante then drew his pistol from his holster and strode toward me in a posture likely to evoke urination on my part, because I had nothing else to tell him and had given him nothing of use. I was a dead end. In hyper-speed I pictured the bullet going into my head, my blood splattering on the British couple. I envisioned two of the guerrillas taking my body and dumping it into a pit. I flashed to South Dakota, to my mother, who was sitting on her rocking chair looking at my high school wrestling picture. She would never know what happened to her son.

El Comandante raised his gun slowly, past my face, whereupon he pointed it into the air and fired a shot. Then he put the pistol back in its holster and walked away. I took the deepest breath of my life. I still thought about the possibility of being sent back to the States, but at that moment I was more concerned with the possibility of being shot in the back of the head, and I had to do everything I could to try to remain calm.

We were immediately left alone while the men returned to the tour group. I asked the English couple if they were all right, telling them that everyone thought they were dead. They said they had been accused of being agents for the American government, DEA, CIA, or something, and that they had denied everything, claiming truthfully to be mere tourists. They asked me if I thought the men would kill us.

"No. If they were going to kill us they'd have done it by now," I assured them—not that any assurance from *gringo stupido*, who'd had the bright idea of securing a tour from a fruit-lady pimp, inspired confidence.

The truth is that I did, in fact, have a feeling that the men were just mining information via this bluff. About two hours after the guerrillas had arrived, three new guerrillas came over and untied us. One of them, who spoke decent English, asked us if we were all right, revealing sort of a *Candid Camera* (or *Punk'd,* for you younger readers) element to their mission. We said that we were fine but scared, fearing that now we'd be kidnapped and held for ransom.

We were taken to the other tourists, who were astonished and relieved to see us alive, and we were told by *El Comandante* that we had been questioned to see if any of us was an agent of the Colombian or American governments, which were trying to infiltrate the zone they controlled. He explained that they were the AUC (*Auto Defensas Unidas de Colombia*), paramilitaries comprising ex-military and ex-police, that they were protecting their area, and that they were not murderers or kidnappers.

He added that his main adversaries were the FARC guerrillas, with whom they regularly engaged in up to three shootouts a day. We were asked not to mention this episode when we got back to town, and *El Comandante* kept the GPS unit to prevent the location from being discovered or disclosed. We, of course, agreed.

El Comandante ordered us to go straight back to Santa Marta and suggested we would be more likely to remain undetected if we stayed out of the higher terrain on the way back. Who were we to argue? We hurriedly broke down our tents, stowed our stuff, donned our packs, and headed back down the trail in an outwardly deliberate procession, motivated by our newfound absence of confidence and safety.

El Comandante had also told us not to use our flashlights because the other paramilitaries in the area might take us for somebody who should be shot and killed. All of us had been scared shitless and were thinking that we had been colossally lucky we hadn't fallen into the hands of another group, such as the FARC. At the hands of another group we definitely would have been kidnapped or maybe even killed, although I doubt the latter, since we were worth much more to them alive than dead. Their main goal was to kidnap for ransom money to support their cause.

After walking all night with just the moon to illuminate our path, we arrived at Tayrona National Park and hitched a return ride to Santa Marta, during which there was little if any conversation.

There was no need to stop in Cartagena, so I bought an express ticket straight out of Santa Marta and direct to Medellín.

When I told Julio of my close encounter near the lost city, he said that I was lucky the paramilitaries hadn't shot us, and instructed me to call him when I arrived in Medellín.

Somewhere back at Santa Marta, somebody was laughing and telling others, "I told the *gringo stupido* that the bus would not stop in Cartagena, and he believed me!" We stopped in Cartagena only four hours into the trip, and a fat, sweaty, newspaper salesman boarded the bus and sold me a paper. A police official boarded the bus too and began walking down the aisle as if searching for a particular person, maybe the gringo with a college student ID card, I thought. I pretended to be asleep but I kept one eye open. He reached the back and started back toward the front, walking slowly, checking from seat to seat.

Just before he left he faced the passengers and inquired whether anyone had seen anything or anyone suspicious lately, asking also if "all was well." He didn't wait for us to answer.

As the bus sped along I noticed I was on the same highway where the armed conflict had taken place just a few days before, the one featuring burning cars, trucks, and buses, and I thought, "A sequel—this ought to be good." The security checkpoints were only fifty miles apart, so I sensed that all systems were at Defcon One, that opposing forces were competing for the first chance to take somebody out into the brush and fire their weapons into the air to scare all of the others in the bus. At these checkpoints, there'd always be an official who boarded the bus and quizzed the driver, and sometimes the passengers, about any sightings of armed and suspicious-looking hombres, in uniform, wielding AK-47s. It was becoming almost commonplace, which wasn't a good thing. I couldn't pretend that I fit in or that my situation was a safe one. But what could I do?

For one thing, I could get my ass back to Medellín and focus on the mission at hand—getting a damn passport. But that did not seem as though it was going to happen so easily.

Even though my bus was supposed to be an express right to Medellín, the bus driver apparently had other ideas. He decided to make a detour to San Antero, a small, slow, culturally stagnant, commercially stunted town that required all motorized vehicles to remain hidden from sight. Picture Venice without the beautiful buildings, water, and gondolas—actually, it was nothing like Venice except for the fact that neither had cars. And that San Antero had burros, lots of burros, instead of gondolas.

Why? The Burro Festival. We pulled into town about 11:00 in the morning. The festival was supposed to start about one o'clock and last about three hours. A five-hour detour. Not bad. I walked down to the beach, where I bumped into some fishermen readying their fishing nets for a day of fishing, one in his mid-forties and two boys in their early teens. After speaking with them for only a short while, I learned a great deal about the town's history, and about local customs and practices, which are likely those that gave rise to the festival.

Their Spanish was heavily laced with slang, so I'm afraid I probably frustrated them with all of my insistence that they repeat their statements from time to time. I learned that the Burro Festival gave every burro owner the opportunity to dress his up in a miniskirt, perhaps a teddy or a bikini, a bra, earrings, red-painted lips, and a mane styled into elegant spectacles of femininity, and to have them judged by a distinguished panel from San Antero, who would crown a "King and Queen of the Burros."

I asked them why, of all things, the town had a burro pageant.

"In this town," one fisherman explained, "the burro is like the second woman to each married man. Without them we'd have to screw our ugly wives all the time."

I asked him to repeat what he had just said because I did not get the joke that he was telling me.

The man said slowly and clearly that boys aged eleven and older usually had their first sexual experience with a burro, that that area of Colombia was renowned for this style of sex education. I nodded, figuring he was just pulling a gringo's leg. He continued to tell me that burro "sex" was juicier, hotter, and tighter than that with a woman, and that the animal had internal movements that gave men more pleasure during intercourse. He went on to clarify an important point: If a woman did this with a male burro, it would be considered "unfaithful." Also, the burro action most often lasted well beyond one's wedding day, for human male-on-burro action was not considered "cheating" by the women. Are you still with me?

I decided to press the envelope to gauge their veracity. "What if there are no female burros available? What do you do then?"

I thought, as I'm certain you would, that the guy would answer, "Then we have to fuck our ugly wives, *gringo stupido!*" and laugh their asses off at me. Among the sleazy slang terms they used in their reply, however, I was certain I that I had heard a reference to a male burro, with matching hand gestures.

The older fisherman got tied up with a customer, so the fourteen-year-old took over. He told me about *burro chancletiado*[57], which he described as something he would do to the burro, the male burro that was standing right in front of us. The plan was to tie the upper part of his burro's testicles with a piece of string, and attach the end of the string that hung down to the end of a small stick of wood that would hang just above the ground. By stepping on the stick, like a gas pedal, and by releasing the stick, one could open and close the burro's sphincter, which emulated the female burro's contractions that occurred during intercourse.

They called this feat *chancletiado* because when they had no board available they would tie the string off on their left side three-pointed sandal. I also learned that if I were to stroke the burro's back—I mean, if someone were to stroke the burro's back—with a broomstick during intercourse, it made it even more pleasurable. Good to know.

They must have sensed that I wasn't buying it. The twelve-year-old said, "If you want to see this live, then give us some money, then we'll give you a live performance."

"How much?" I asked, out of curiosity.

"Ten dollars," he said. "American."

Now I am all for respecting cultural diversity, and I never wanted to be one of those Americans who travel abroad to feel superior, that our way of living is more morally correct than that of others. I'm sure that this kid could have used the ten bucks. Hell, I could have just given it to him. But who was I to judge? I told him that I would pay him ten bucks after he did the deed because, even up to this point, I didn't believe it was going to happen; I still couldn't quite embrace as truth the claim that burros held a place of such high regard in Colombian society as to serve as surrogate first loves to boys coming of age.

They told me that they could really use some booze to get warmed up for the main event and told me to give them the money for it. *No problema.* I gave the money to the man, who, in turn, gave it to the older of the boys, who ran off to get the booze. In his absence, the other boy was busy tying a string to the burro's balls and to the end of a half-inch-thick stick that lay on the ground.

Once the boy with the booze arrived, the entertainment began without hesitation or contemplation. Immediately after he took a couple of swigs of the *aguadiente*, the younger of the two boys jumped the burro's bones. What impressed me most was the almost ambidextrous abilities of the boy, humping and pumping the stick up and down at the same time, for all the world like an organist playing a tune while using his feet to play a bass line.

His brother did not want to be shown up. As soon as the first adolescent finished, the other followed suit, eager to prove that he, too, was dexterous enough to satisfy the burro's libido, as it were.

"You're not in Kansas anymore," was all I could think as I watched in horror. I wasn't sure if I should ask what else wasn't taboo around there, or perhaps I should call the ASPCA's[58] Colombian office. As an obvious precaution against infection, the two boys jumped into the ocean to freshen up, while the man stroked the male burro's head and congratulated him on another stunning performance.

The boys left the water and immediately began making passes at the female burro. She pointed her posterior up toward the morning sun as one boy stroked her back with the broomstick, which was so exciting to the other boy that he rapidly crossed the finish line.

"It's okay to come inside the female burro," said the man, "but it's homosexual to do it inside the male burro."

The younger boy finished his performance, and then it was the older brother's turn—he clearly had more experience, as proven by his confidence and Elvis Presley-like moves, and by the fact that now the burro's ass pointed nearly straight up—he was a true master. As the two brothers again bathed in the sea, the man told me that the brothers came from a poor family, that their father was a fisherman and was only able to afford a single female burro for his two sons.

I walked back to the center of town in a daze just in time for the main event. Judging by the turnout, the Burro Festival was celebrated throughout the region. Farmers and fishermen from far and wide, some with burros and some without, were streaming into town, along with a smattering of tourists. On this, the "Saturday of Glory," a doll of Judas Iscariot was paraded around on a burro and was burned at the end of the procession as a gesture of revulsion at Judas's ratting-out of Jesus. The burros seemed to be posing, dare I say, in provocative guises.

Burros that normally worked days toting goods and wares were on the job, accompanying their owners, who had them loaded down with items usually needed in their work. One might carry coconuts, another bottles of water, and they all followed the lead burro, ridden by the Judas doll. But they were dressed to the nines. Additionally, bands and singers led the crowd in animal sounds as the procession made its way down the street. The burros were named after family members, friends, or neighbors. A few members of the press were there, reporting on the festivities.

The moment that we had all been waiting for—the crowning of the Burro King and Queen—started promptly at 3:00 p.m., a mere two hours late. Contestants were judged in three categories: dress, formal gown parade, and swimsuit competition. Judges awarded points in each of three categories as the burros were displayed in all their elegance and beauty.

My favorite, and the apple of her owner's eye, Rosa, took first prize in the female side of the contest. Dressed in a multicolored linen summer gown and a pink-and-green bikini, she was a show-stopper. Upon the announcement that she had won the competition, her owner rushed the podium on the stage to accept his prize and to kiss Rosa several times on the lips. I thoroughly expected him to turn and announce that he wanted to thank all of the little people who had made it all possible.

The show that I had been offered at the beach didn't appear to be tied to the festival, not officially, but to see an entire parade of burros dolled up in sexy feminine attire says to me that there's an underpinning to the festival that only those of us tourists with ten bucks would have been aware of. Strangely humorous and politely staged, the festival offered an outrageously hilarious good time that was well-publicized and enjoyed by all who attended.

We left San Antero at 6:00 p.m., and I have to say that the seven-hour detour was well worth it. It meant that we would have to ride all night, but if everything went smoothly, I would arrive early on the morning of Mother's Day.

AT THE BUS STATION, JULIO'S DRIVER, Manny, and Monica, my tutor who also shot people in the face, greeted me warmly. While the streets of Medellín were likely the most dangerous in the entire world, I felt safe. This was home, where I had friends and members of Julio's family to look out for me.

I told Julio about the Burro Festival. I think he got a bit defensive and assured me that only in rural areas, impoverished isolated villages, did things like burro abuse occur. He did not want to talk about the Burro Festival because he was focused on Mother's Day, one of his favorite holidays of the year.

It was an incredible affair. Earlier that week, he had handed out raffle tickets to all the mothers in the *barrio*. I accompanied him on a big truck that carried, not only the prizes (big-ticket items such as washer-and-dryers and refrigerators), but also a 250-pound hog. The women had teamed up and built fires along the main street. The hog must have figured out what was going on, because he started screaming piercingly, that is, until one of the men in the town deftly stabbed him in the heart with a long ice pick, dropping the boar onto the ground without a drop of blood leaking out. The hog was butchered right there on the street, and the women prepared everything from blood sausages to pork chops for the Mother's Day celebration for the entire neighborhood.

Julio gave out about ten prizes, and each bestowal precipitated a mini-celebration that ended with the winner crying tears of joy, embracing him, and thanking him profusely. At the end of the raffle, he called up Doña Ruth and gave her the biggest prize of the night—a large television and living room set. Her son Hector, and her daughter Ana, jumped for joy as she cried and thanked God and Julio—not in that order.

The next morning, Julio came by at about 7:30 for a cup of coffee and asked me to accompany him downtown while he visited several banks to make payments on credit cards he used. He promised Doña Ruth that we would be back by noon. She promised that she would prepare a special lunch for us. We left with his two bodyguards at returned at 11:30 a.m., eager to dig into the meal that Doña Ruth had prepared. Julio said he hoped that she had made *puchero santafereno;*[59] I was craving her *mondongo,*[60] which was the best I'd ever had.

As we came to a stop, I noticed that a couple of Julio's guys were standing in front of the house, and that their expressions were not cheerful. As soon as they saw us, they practically ran to the car. The elder of the two told Julio that Doña Ruth's son, Hector, had been abducted by armed men who had forced him into a taxi and sped away, accompanied by others on two motorcycles.

We rushed inside to find Doña Ruth crying and shaking uncontrollably. Julio, ever in control, immediately called a doctor, who arrived only minutes later—the same doctor who had tended to Monica's leg wound. He checked Doña Ruth's blood pressure and listened to her heart, then gave her a few yellow tablets he'd pulled from his black medicine bag.

It wasn't until she calmed down that we able to get details about the abduction from her and Ana. They said that, about twenty minutes after we left that morning, five men had rushed into the house armed with machine guns and pistols, asking where "the Americano" was. Doña Ruth had told them that no Americano lived there, which caused the men to curse and to insult her, and to search the home. While one man kept a gun trained on her and Ana, the others had swept through the house swiftly and efficiently, searching room to room. The only other person in the home had been Hector, who was in the upstairs shower.

"They were very professional," Ana said.

During the search, the men had found Hector's work ID card. A few minutes later they'd caught him in the shower and told him to put a towel around his waist. One man had put a gun to Hector's nose and demanded to know where the Americano was, but Hector had denied knowing any Americano, so they'd taken him downstairs.

When Doña Ruth saw that the men had Hector, she had sprung up, shouting, *"No llevas mi hijo, por favor, no llevas mi hijo!"*[61] Then Ana had jumped in to defend Hector but been pushed back into her seat on the couch at gunpoint. They'd shuffled Hector, wearing only his boxers, out of the house and into the taxi.

Before leaving the house, the last of the kidnappers had turned to Doña Ruth and informed her that they would be in touch, and that she was not to contact the authorities in any way if she wanted to avoid severe consequences—this last while dragging an index finger across his own throat. She had been so distraught and intimidated by this threat that she even abstained from calling Julio.

She said the kidnappers would call in about eight hours. Julio pulled me aside. "She's hopeful, but only amateurs would call any time soon. If these guys are professionals, they will take their time."

He was right. Eight days passed before the kidnappers called, claiming to be affiliated with E.L.N.[62] We were to negotiate with Senior Alejandro, who was in charge of the operation. Julio was to conduct the negotiations, and due to his absence the call lasted only three minutes, but before hanging up the man on the phone told Doña Ruth, who did not speak during the call, to remember the name Senior Alejandro because that was the name that would be used when they called in *another* eight days to negotiate the ransom for Hector's return.

The waiting game caused Doña Ruth to become severely stressed, which favored the kidnappers, who didn't call until the fourteenth day after the phone call. They told her that her son was in fine condition and that his ransom was two and a half million dollars American. She thought they meant pesos and told them, "I'll just take a second mortgage on my home."

Even the best house in Campo Valdez would have been worth no more than five thousand American, and the man on the phone knew this, so he asked, "Is Julio or the Americano there?"

She told him that she knew of no Americano, and that Julio was not there. After hanging up, she said there had to be a family meeting with Julio right away.

When he came, she told him that the caller had asked for us both, which convinced Julio that I needed to be moved to another part of the city right away where nobody knew who I was.

He motioned for me to follow him outside onto the patio and said, "If you don't leave the house immediately, I can't protect you."

I was just a *gringo stupido,* and now I had kidnappers asking where I was. Julio was thinking in high gear and had lived much of his life in circles and situations that made him well aware of angles and possibilities I could never imagine, so I certainly was not about to question his judgment or advice.

As we left the house, he called out to Doña Ruth, in a voice loud enough for the neighbors to hear, that he was taking me out of Medellín. When we got into his shiny-new bulletproof Toyota Land Cruiser (the vehicle of choice for *narcotrafficantes* at the time), he told me that he was going to put me in a safe place.

We drove to the pool hall where he had an office in the back. As we sat in the office waiting for the call, an absurdly tall, skinny fifty-year-old man approached Julio and asked him who I was.

"This is the gringo I told you about," he told him.

It made me think for a fleeting moment that I would indeed be handed over in exchange for Hector. I was sitting near a bookcase and was asked to move over by the man who had asked about me. He reached between a couple of books and unlatched something, pulled a lever, and then pushed the bookcase aside a couple of feet, revealing a staircase that descended into the basement.

He waved Julio and me to follow him downstairs into what turned out to be an social club with a full liquor bar, card tables, dart boards, a stripper pole, and three separate offices Julio said belonged to him and his partners. The thin man, named Sergio, was the manager of the underground social club.

From there we took another hidden staircase into the subterranean office beneath the underground club, which I figured was a hiding place for Julio and his crew when they needed to stay out of sight. He and I sat in the small apartment there, sort of a presidential suite, professionally decorated and extremely comfortable, while Sergio brought us snacks and Julio a couple of beers. Sergio couldn't quite figure out why I didn't drink alcohol, and he kept grilling me about it until Julio finally told him to mind his own business.

"Are you thinking of giving me up to the kidnappers?" I asked Julio.

"I can't believe you're even *asking* me that question," he replied.

That was not exactly a "no," but I trusted him. Anyway, did I really have a choice? He seemed serious and resolute about finding a solution to the problem. He told me that I would have to stay there until we got Hector back.

"How long will that be?" I asked.

Julio stood up. "Sergio will get you whatever you need, but don't even think about leaving. It's too dangerous."

He gave me a hug and left before I could say anything.

Sergio was available via intercom from the basement suite. I looked around the place and discovered camera surveillance, but I had no idea where the signal went—until I noticed the video stream on Julio's computer showing the front of the pool hall on the street.

I lay down to relax, but my mind was churning at high speed, poring over facts and questions. While I hadn't officially been kidnapped, I was staying in a secret underground apartment, and I couldn't leave. If I screamed, nobody would hear me, and I couldn't convince myself that Julio would not just hand me over to Hector's kidnappers. Would prison be better or worse? Was this safekeeping for my health or for easy transfer of my person to others? I tried to calm down and even thought about grabbing the bottle of *aguadiente* and drowning my fears. But I knew that would only make things worse.

Then another thought crossed my mind—was this an inside job? I had been under Julio's care. Maybe he figured it was time to pay up. I know that his brother would not sanction anything like that, but how would he find out whether the kidnapping was legit or an easy and nonviolent way to get a few million dollars for a rich American?

At 9:30 a.m., after I spent a night tossing and turning, Sergio appeared with my breakfast. He didn't speak much English but cheerfully asked me for a list of what I would like to eat. I also noticed that he had a nine-millimeter tucked into his waist. I wrote down hamburgers from Presto, Coke, bottled water, and ripe king mangoes . I also wrote down dishes I had eaten at Doña Ruth's and at other homes I had stayed in, such as *morcilla rellena, sancocho,* and my favorite dessert, *arroz con coco*. Sergio had told me that there was a restaurant next door, and to name any particular Colombian dishes I had a yen for, so I made the most of it. I also asked him if he could get me some Spanish grammar books. For some reason he found this hysterical and couldn't stop laughing as he left the room. I was glad that I could be such a source of entertainment.

At 1:00 p.m., he returned with lunch, and came back at 6:00 with dinner, just like in prison. At 9:30, he came back and told me that I should use the number taped to the refrigerator if I had an emergency. I presumed that he was closing the pool hall for the night.

I had all of the essentials—even a small kitchen where I could cook eggs and prepare coffee. It was a perfect hideout, and though I was on lockdown, I tried to be grateful, knowing that it had to be better than where Hector was spending the night.

After about a week, Julio said the kidnappers had proposed giving me up in exchange for Hector, but that he had assured them I was not on the trading block. He also said that the kidnappers had refused to let Hector speak on the phone to prove he was all right, and told Julio that they wanted to negotiate with him face to face. He'd told them it was out of the question, that he was just a friend of the family and a middlemen in this situation. He'd also told them that he was staying to help Doña Ruth, and that he would send someone to verify Hector's pulse and condition.

The kidnappers agreed to this proposal and said that they would call in three days to make the arrangements with Julio. He suggested that I be there for the call, since he had a call transfer system that would forward their call from Doña Ruth's house to his office phone.

Three days later, we got the call. The kidnapper's voice was raspy, but I could tell from the words that he used that he was educated. He asked Julio if he planned to meet them. Julio assured him that there was no way he would, but that he'd have the priest make the trip. The kidnapper said that whoever came would have to wear a red handkerchief around his wrist, pack enough clothes to last five days, go to the central park in San Carlos, Antioquia, sit on a bench, and wait.

The kidnapper cautioned Julio to make sure that he chose someone he could trust. Julio told him that he was sending *El Chura.*[63]

El Chura was to wear the handkerchief on his wrist throughout his bus ride from Medellín, because he would be under the watchful eye of the guerrillas, and was to bring cold-weather clothing. If he failed to show by 11:00 a.m., the guerrillas would presume him to be a "no-show." The man cautioned Julio that it would be wiser to be a half-hour early, and he stressed that there had better not be any tricks, and no sign of the authorities, because they knew where Julio lived. He asked again about "the gringo."

"Let's suppose I *did* have a gringo under my care. What would happen if I brought him to the negotiations?" Julio asked.

"We will take the gringo in trade for Hector, because his family will pay faster, in U.S. dollars," the guy replied.

"Well, there's no gringo with me, so you're just wasting time with that fantasy."

"Okay, when will you have the two and a half million dollars for the boy?"

"I'm just helping my friend Doña Ruth," Julio said. "When you're ready to ask for a reasonable ransom, call me. Until then, please don't waste any more of my time. It's too valuable."

Before he could answer, Julio hung up. Then he leaned over to me, and said, "I wanted you to hear from their mouths what their real intentions were—to kidnap you, not Hector."

"If they want two and a half million for Hector, what do you think they'd ask for me?" I wanted to know.

"Probably five."

"That's all?" I said.

He laughed. "I think I'm in the wrong business," he said.

I nodded, hoping that he stayed out of the kidnapping business.

"These guys are pros, and we have to pay them," Julio said. "We're going to try to negotiate for the lowest price possible. The truth is that you need to help me pay, because there are two people responsible for this situation. Number one is me, because I brought you to live at Doña Ruth's in that barrio full of criminals. The other problem is you, because you're an American."

I nodded.

"And don't think of running off before we get out of this," Julio said. "You have to come up with half."

"Where the hell would I go?" I said.

Julio nodded.

"Look," I said. "I realize that if it weren't for me Hector wouldn't be where he is. Not to mention that I would never fuck you over."

"I know," he said as he pulled me in for a hug.

"Who's *El Chura*," I asked

After Julio hung up he explained that *El Chura* was the sixty-year-old priest who served at the church in Campo Valdez where Julio had donated a great deal of money.

"A priest is going to be able to handle this?" I asked.

"A priest in Medellín can handle anything," he said.

On the following Sunday, Julio came with a big pan of *bandeja paisa* that Doña Ruth had prepared for me. She knew that the dish was my favorite. I would be lying if I said the thought of poison never entered my mind.

After lunch, Julio brought me up to speed. He said that *El Chura* had left for San Carlos. After sitting on a bench for under half an hour, he had been approached by a farmer who told him to go to a store down the street, where he met some men waiting for him who told him to get into the *carro*.[64] When they had driven only a block or so, they'd stopped to pick up a twenty-year-old man, obviously a lookout who was watching for any possible tails the priest might have.

El Chura had then been blindfolded for the entire four-hour drive up a dirt road into the mountains. When the road turned into a trail, the blindfold had been removed, and they'd all hiked on foot for two hours while it got colder, until they reached a farmhouse shrouded in fog. They'd offered him a hot coffee to take the edge off the cold. Fifteen minutes or so later, *El Chura* had seen four men approaching the house, one of them Hector.

The one who had introduced himself as *El Comandante* brought Hector into the house, and he and Hector had sat down to talk to *El Chura*. Hector had clearly been scared, but there had been no physical signs of abuse. Immediately, Hector had asked how his mother and sister were doing. When *El Chura* relayed the fact that they were fine but worried about him, *El Comandante* turned to Hector and said, "I told you we didn't hurt him. And we won't unless your friends try something stupid like getting the corrupt police involved." Hector had implored *El Chura* to ask Julio to please get him home as soon as possible. He'd said that he would pay Julio back the money, which got laughs from *El Comandante* and the three guerrillas standing guard.

The conversation had lasted maybe twenty minutes, *El Chura* said, and then they'd taken Hector out of the house and back into the mountains. Hector had had tears in his eyes as they led him away. *El Comandante* had followed up with a message to Julio to act quickly now that he had proof that Hector was well, that he knew where Julio was living, and that he knew of Julio's student girlfriend in Medellín, Litia.

El Comandante had left then, and the men who'd brought *El Chura* to the house had blindfolded him for the return to the park in San Carlos.

They'd recommended that he stay in a nearby hotel and catch a bus back to Medellín the next day.

When *El Chura* returned, Julio told me that he had been very worried about him for fear that he, too, might be kidnapped or worse. Julio said he was going to try to resolve things quickly. He had done some research, and word on the street was that the ELN was holding Hector hostage. Even though Julio was one of the top members of one of the strongest cartels in Medellín, he was no match for the ELN. Even Pablo Escobar had had to cut a deal with them, and Julio was not in Escobar's league.

The kidnappers called that very night, when Julio and I were playing pool. He put his phone on speaker. From what I could gather, Julio told them that he was only cooperating because Doña Ruth was a friend, but the truth was that she had very little money. He also told them that he had moved his favorite girlfriend Litia to another apartment, and that, although he cared a great deal for Hector, the problem wasn't his.

They said that they understood, but that it was going to be on his conscience if something wasn't worked out. Julio didn't respond. I thought they were going to hang up, and I even made a motion to say something. Julio immediately cut me off by raising a finger. A moment later, they asked how much Julio was going to offer for Hector's release.

"All I can get is a hundred and fifty thousand," Julio said. "I'm going to try to get a friend of mine, a *comandante* in the ELN, to handle the rest of the negotiations with you, because I'm leaving for Miami with my wife and family for business, and I don't know how long I'll be gone."

"What is the name of *El Comandante*?" he asked.

"You will find out soon enough," Julio said.

There was a moment of silence. Julio gave me the thumbs-up sign. The other man told Julio that they wouldn't accept a middleman, especially one of their own.

Julio told them that it would be better if he got out of the negotiations altogether and let Doña Ruth handle it. "Doña Ruth told me that she could come up with thirty thousand dollars," Julio said. "I don't know how this is possible, but God bless her."

"That is an insult," said the guy on the phone.

"I'm just telling you what she told me," Julio said. He suggested they think it over and call him in two days, because he couldn't delay his trip to Miami under any circumstances.

"*¡Que se jode!*[65] We'll call you in two days and tell you where you can find the *maricon's* body!"

Julio smiled as the kidnapper slammed the phone down in his ear. When he saw that I was not getting his source of amusement, he told me that he was getting hostage negotiation tips from a contact in VNASE.[66] He said that the negotiations were progressing exactly as they had hoped. I asked him how he was going to get a *comandante* from the ELN to negotiate if the kidnappers were ELN.

"It's a huge organization. I'm sure they'll try to avoid this, because my guy is going to take a kickback from them." He also said that he would not go higher than three hundred grand, and that I should make arrangements right away for my half of the ransom. He handed me his satellite phone, which he said could not be tapped, and told me that I could use it for the next twenty-four hours, but that under no circumstances should I answer if it rang.

I made a call to my personal banker, Carlos, in Mexico City. I called him several times. There was no answer. Finally, I reached his secretary, who informed me that Carlos was on his honeymoon and would be unreachable for the next ten days. Congrats.

I was really in a bind. Where was I going to get a hundred a fifty thousand dollars while I was stuck in a basement in Colombia?

Rule #5 of my Don't Do list: Do not socialize with anyone from my first life.

Rule #5 was pretty straightforward. I had broken it when I saw my wife and daughter. But who was going to let me borrow a hundred and fifty thousand dollars and move it to *Colombia?* Not only was there the matter of trust, there was also the matter of brains. Even if the courier did everything perfectly, there were still twenty-five things that could go wrong. Then it wasn't so much about the money, it became about whether the courier was going to be able to take the pressure of whoever was torturing him for information. There was only one person I knew I could trust and who had the moxie to take the chance and pull it off: Paul Holt.

I was pretty confident that he would help me out, mostly because that's what friends did. I had helped him out of a jam in prison, and he was not the type of guy who would forget. But that was only part of why I thought of him. Paul loved adventure as much I did. The difference was that I was doing what I was doing because I had to. He took bold chances because he liked the rush—and I was about to hand one to him.

When I reached him on the satellite phone, Paul immediately agreed to come to Colombia with the money, but for reasons of security, and because he didn't want to declare the currency because of the tax ramifications, he couldn't fly directly to me. I would reimburse him as soon as Carlos got back to Mexico City.

Instead, he came up with the following: he would fly from Florida to Seattle, then proceed to the Canadian border in Blaine through Bellingham, and carry the cash on foot across the border into Canada. Once there, he would fly from Vancouver, British Columbia, to Toronto, and then take a direct flight to Medellín on Avianca Airlines.

He left forty-eight hours after I first reached him, and everything went according to plan until he landed in Toronto, where he had to pass through a United States Customs substation. Yes, the long arm of the U.S. Department of Justice had reached into Canada. As one who had purchased a multi-flight, multinational ticket with cash, he thought it was best to just declare the cash on the appropriate currency forms to avoid revisions and problems. So I had to reimburse him for the taxes, but aside from that it turned out fine.

When he touched down at Rio Negro International Airport, outside Medellín, Paul was wearing a T-shirt that read *AJ's Bar, Destin, Florida,* and a Toronto Blue Jays cap, so Julio's security team could pick him out of a crowd as arranged and escort him to where I was waiting at a *finca* several miles from town, which would provide the necessary cover to spot and avoid any tail he might have picked up along the way.

Even with all these precautions, it was still nearly impossible to detect a tail. But Julio's security detail were experts, and after driving Paul around in circles for three hours, they had determined that he had arrived clean. They'd called Julio and me to let us know, and, in turn, Julio had ordered them to bring Paul to the *finca,* where I was eagerly awaiting my good buddy.

Julio left, wishing me good luck and reminding me that my friend and I should enjoy the *finca*. He said that he had arranged for a cook, a maid, and two bodyguards to stay there with us. He also said that he would be back in three days to get the money and me. Though he did not communicate it directly, I knew that that was when he wanted Paul to head out.

About a half-hour after Julio had left, I heard voices coming up the driveway. They were speaking Spanish. One belonged to Paul, who was speaking Spanish much better than me, which really pissed me off. Sure enough, he walked in and rattled off a long Spanish greeting, which I was sure that he had practiced on the plane. The cook prepared a feast for us, and we got to catch up.

Paul confirmed what I had suspected about Marvin Schumacher. After he framed me on the meth charge, he had been able to weasel out of serving any time and had entered the witness protection program. Paul had spoken to my brother on a couple of occasions and assured me that my family was doing well. However, he hadn't been in touch with my wife.

I had asked him to bring two hundred thousand. I wanted fifty extra just in case Julio couldn't negotiate the captors down to a hundred and half. Besides, I was going to need more cash to live.

But when I began to move the stacks, I realized Paul had brought much more. He had the money from my final weed deal, the one he had salvaged when I got arrested. I thanked him profusely, but I wondered out loud what I was going to do with all that money. It wasn't as if I could open a bank account.

"Well, buddy, I thought of that," he said, after a few glasses of wine. "I have a business opportunity in Mexico, so it won't be a big deal to figure out how to get it to you as long as you're around here."

"Well, that's great," I said, feeling extremely blessed that I was going to have a friend living in Latin America.

I told him that I had set up VIP service at the best strip club in Medellín, which I was sure that he would pounce on.

But Paul surprised me. "I'm going to pass, my friend," he said. "I have an early flight out in the morning."

"Really?" I asked. "Since when did you ever need sleep, and why the hell aren't you going to stay a few more days?"

After more wine, the truth came out: he had convinced his new girlfriend, Heather, to move to Mexico with him, and he had promised that he would be back to get her the following day. He went on and on the rest of the night about how great she was, and that she was the woman that he had always dreamed of, how he could not wait for me to meet her, and so forth. By the time we went to bed, I could not believe that this was really my friend the wild man.

When I woke up the next morning, he had already left.

Four days later, I happened to be with Julio when the kidnappers called back, and I could see that Julio was very nervous because, as he said, one slip-up and Hector would be killed. When the call came, they demanded half a million American. Julio told them it was impossible to pay that much, and that they were wasting valuable time, because his trip to Miami was in only six days, that they could check it out with Avianca Airlines if they wanted.

On the next call, the following day, Julio negotiated a three-hundred-thousand-dollar payment for Hector. They asked Julio if the money was in fifties and hundreds; he said that it was, that the money was ready and waiting. He also insisted on hearing Hector's voice to confirm his well-being before making the payment. Then he asked if he could use a friend of a friend, who worked as *comandante* of the militia of ELN in Medellín, to act as a guarantor that Hector was safe and that he'd be delivered to us as promised. The kidnappers asked for one more day to respond to that request, and asked for the name of *El Comandante.* Julio asked them to call back in twenty minutes to see if he could divulge *El Comandante's* full name.

They called back in an hour. He gave them the name "Alejandro." There was a pause before they asked for the name of the friend of *El Comandante*; he said, "Diego," and added that he was the owner of Diego's Auto Service Center in Medellín.

The voice on the other end said, "*Esta bien,*"[67] that Comandante Alejandro could serve as the guarantor that Hector would make it back to us safely. Then he told Julio to hold while they passed the phone to

Hector, who began to cry the moment he heard Julio's voice and upon hearing that his ordeal would soon be over. When Julio asked his impression of his captors, whether he felt they'd hold up their end of the deal, Hector told him that they appeared to be very well-organized politically and militarily, and that they had treated him well.

He handed the phone to the kidnapper, who said that they wanted the money delivered by the same person who had been sent to check on Hector—*El Chura*. This time *El Chura* was to wear a red cap and have a white handkerchief tied around the right mirror of the car. They recommended that he drive a Toyota *campero*[68] because the priest would have to do some challenging driving on dirt roads.

We were to bear responsibility for the money until it reached San Carlos. Once there, they would assume responsibility, as the town was controlled by the ELN. They were to free Hector three days after payment was made, for he had been moved from the spot where the priest had originally seen him.

Julio told them that he had borrowed a Toyota *campero,* and that it had to be returned with the priest because Julio had borrowed it from the car lot. They asked if the *campero* was blue, which surprised Julio—but he only said that they'd have the money within two days.

When Julio called Diego and asked how these people knew the color of the *campero,* Diego told him that he was going to say something he was not authorized to—that Comandante Alejandro and the voice on the phone had been the same person when the kidnappers said they'd call back in twenty minutes. *El Comandante* had called Diego and asked him about Julio, and Diego had told him that Julio was a serious businessman who did what he promised to do. Diego told Julio not to worry about anything, because Alejandro kept his promises, too; Hector would be fine. After the call, Julio and I decided to go down to the car lot and speak with Diego in person.

He was there to greet us, and I just kept my mouth shut while Julio spoke with him.

On the way back, Julio told me that the ransom could not be reduced because the amount had been called in to the ELN's highest-ranking official. The next day Julio picked up his portion of the payment from the safe at his office and drove me to the *finca*, where I had stashed my money.

The *campero* had a secret compartment, a sort of double floor, accessible by raising the body of the truck to get below the first floor. When we closed everything up, the compartment was undetectable. Then Julio called *El Chura* and told him that he needed to drive to San Carlos, to the same park, and call Julio when he was with Alejandro because Julio wanted to talk to him.

The priest was to leave no later than 5:00 a.m. because delivery was set for noon. Julio was at the house to give *El Chura* full instructions about what was expected of him. He was told nothing about the money or its location, so he'd have nothing to get nervous about if the police stopped him. Julio handed the keys to him, turned to me, and told me that he was sending two more cars to follow him from a distance to watch over him.

Five hours after *El Chura* reached San Carlos, he called Julio, saying that the kidnappers were demanding the money from him, but that he didn't know what they were talking about. Julio asked for Alejandro but was told that he would not arrive for another thirty minutes. Julio told the priest to have Alejandro call him when he got there, and hung up.

When Alejandro called a half hour later, Julio started to explain that the money was hidden beneath the floor, but Alejandro cut him off and told him not to worry, that he had already taken the money out, and that the total was confirmed as having been delivered. He knew where the compartment was located because it was the car that Diego had lent him to transport ammunition, weapons, and communication equipment up into the mountains, and on occasion to bring cocaine down from the mountains and drive it into Medellín.

Alejandro told Julio that, in a short time, he would be hearing from Hector. Julio told *El Chura* to drive to the church. Mateo would be waiting for him and then would drive him to the pool hall where we'd be waiting no matter what time he arrived, because Julio wanted all of the details while they were fresh in the priest's mind.

At nine the next morning, Mateo led *El Chura* into the pool hall. Hector looked older than twenty-five. He had long hair and a beard, and smelled of sweat. But he was fine.

When he saw Julio, he began to cry and gave him a big hug, and gave me a hug, too. As the very reason he had been kidnapped in the first place, I felt undeserving, to say the least. Julio sent Hector to the shower and got him some fresh clothes. We shared our breakfast with *El Chura*, who dug into the food while Hector had the first hot shower he'd enjoyed in more than two months.

It was hard to believe, and two days earlier than Alejandro had said to expect to hear from Hector. As we left, Julio, Hector, and the bodyguards hopped into Julio's SUV, while *El Chura* and I took the *campero*; we drove to Doña Ruth's for the reunion.

When we got to Campo Valdez, we found Doña Ruth and Ana, along with other neighbors, making banners and drawing hearts and smiling faces on big sheets of paper to welcome Hector home, which they all thought would happen sometime in the next several days. Since Doña Ruth's health had deteriorated during the ordeal, Julio told Hector to stay in the car until he could warm her up for his appearance, because he suspected that a sudden shock might cause her to suffer cardiac arrest or something.

He and I went into the house together, and Doña Ruth seemed a bit disgusted to see me because, though I had told her I was leaving town, there I still was, hanging around, and of course because I was the cause of Hector's kidnapping. Julio told her that he had very good news, that he'd gone half and half on the ransom with me, and that Hector was outside in the car. She screamed and literally got down on her hands and knees to thank God for her good fortune.

A few minutes later, Hector and Doña Ruth embraced. She looked him up and down to confirm his good health while everybody was jumping for joy. Hector was crying like the rest of them. The unfinished banners were thrown into the air to shower Hector, and he looked around as if lost, stunned that he was finally home. Doña Ruth then gave Julio, *El Chura,* and me a great big hug for bringing her son home to her.

After this reunion and the ensuing celebration, things in Campo Valdez returned to normal—as normal as Campo Valdez would ever be. For me there was nothing normal about Colombia, and I needed Julio to come through with a passport, so I could be on my way. I appreciated everything that he and his extended *familia* had done for me, but I knew that I could not settle there. I still needed to find a home country—a base where I could begin to rebuild a life.

Julio told me to be patient. "I promise that you will graduate very soon," he said.

"Graduate?"

He smiled.

Two weeks later, I was summoned to Julio's *finca,* where I joined about thirty people—hit-men and their wives and children—to prepare for our graduation ceremony. Over the course of about three days, a photographer and a passport-forger worked painstakingly to match a passport for each of us. Everybody but me would be graduating from Colombia to the United States, where they would work as mules and then eventually run operations in major American cities. Julio's crew was being dispersed to different parts of the United States, depending on the job he needed them to perform for his operation. His people of Afro-Colombian descent were typically sent to Atlanta, while others went to Miami or New York. I guessed that the wives and children accompanied them, either to lend legitimacy to their relocation to the States, or because the men wouldn't leave without them.

Not only did a passport have to match the approximate age of its recipient; it could not expire within the next year, because some countries would refuse entry to a person with a short window of travel eligibility rather than risk admitting somebody who might end up overstaying his visa. Most of Latin America issued passports that expired in five years.

The *carte blanche* was a passport from Spain, which did not require a visa to enter the United States. In fact, when traveling around the world, you needed fewer visas if you had a Spanish passport than an American one. Argentina and Uruguay were second on the list because, at that time, they also did not require a visa to enter the United States.

Julio managed to get me two British passports, a Swiss passport, and a Canadian passport, all of which had been stolen. He also acquired several Spanish passports for his top people. We all went to a photographer's studio, where it was like a high school graduation photo op, with wives, children, husbands, and me, the token gringo.

One of the British passports was a nearly perfect match. It had lots of space for stamps, and it was not going to expire for another eight years. The only problem was that it was for someone nine years younger than me. Luckily, I'd flown to Bogota the previous week and gotten a hair transplant. My reasoning was that, if I were matched with a younger man's passport (like the British one), I would fit it better. If I was matched with an older guy's passport, I could always cut my hair.

At the photo shoot everyone was quite jovial and likely oblivious to the danger of doing in America what Julio was asking them to do, especially prison time. If any of them did know, they didn't care, as long as they got the chance to move to the States.

Then the time came to graduate—our passports were ready.

We gathered in the enormous living room. My fellow graduates had done their best, on their respective budgets, to dress as sharply as possible. If the men did not have a suit and tie, Julio provided ones for them. He passed from family to family, displaying their newly acquired passports with their professionally inserted likenesses, giving each a short lecture about their responsibilities and the trip ahead of them.

He again reviewed the ranks to be certain that all were familiar with the responsibilities they would soon have, and that all the wives and children fit the part he had them playing. He made certain that the men had debit cards and business cards, as well as a bit of money to keep in their wallets. Lastly, Julio's girlfriend, Litia, went to her university and enlisted the help of a young man in her acting class to come to the *finca* to play the role of U.S. Customs and Immigration agent.

The actor was a handsome nineteen-year-old with long, curly hair. Julio sat him down and walked him through a faded, wrinkled, and expired U.S. Immigration and Customs manual. He was told to tie his hair back, sit at the desk, and pose as a suspicious and determined immigration official whose job was to quiz the folks entering the United States, taking his questions and allegations from the manual's contents.

The actor did an excellent job but maintained that he should have been provided a bona fide uniform from the United States to visually intimidate the clan from the barrio. I thought it was kind of poignant—only an actor would take a job acting in a production put on by a drug lord and risk getting arrested or possibly worse. Think about it: this was a soft college kid, an artist, not some thug. Only the acting profession could create that kind of desperation for work. It was funny to see, from a particular perspective, a neophyte pretending to be a United States Customs official, with Colombians pretending to be businessmen.

The official U.S. Customs uniform was about all Julio did *not* provide for that part of the operation, but probably only because he hadn't thought of it. The drill by the actor was drawn-out and difficult, just as Julio wanted it, and lasted as long as it took to get his people into shape to satisfy most any agent who happened to screen his people.

I could see why they wanted to leave, regardless of the conditions and danger they might ultimately face once they reached America. Virtually anyone in the barrio would have rolled the dice this way, with their families in tow. To them, anything would be better than Campo Valdez. It was quite touching to see them say their goodbyes as they boarded a bus to the airport, where they would wait in nearby motels for the call. One little girl began to cry as they boarded. She said that she didn't want to go to the United States, that she wanted to stay in Colombia with her friends. Her mother assured her that she would come back and see her friends soon, and that, when they came back, they would be rich and she could bring all her friends toys that she would buy in America. The little girl finally cheered up and hugged her mother.

8

MOVING ON

MY SITUATION WAS A BIT MORE COMPLICATED. Getting an entry stamp on my passport reached my front burner as a priority again, and I thought that I should go to the airport at Turbo, on the Gulf of Uraba, rather than to the airport at Rio Negro. In Turbo, I could, for a price, get an official Colombian entry stamp. After receiving this stamp, I would be in the country legally for the first time. Julio had somebody checking to see whether my passport showed up in the DAS (Colombian FBI) database as having been stolen.

Under a black light, one could see the various security seals that were embedded and embossed in or onto the paper. Some of them incorporated a seal in addition to the visible print. In the case of the British passport, the seals were an invisible crown that filled the entire first page, and identical little crowns at each of the four corners of the passport holder's picture, under the sealed plastic that encased the page. If these smaller crowns weren't perfectly aligned, customs and immigration personnel would presume the photo had been replaced.

I had no use for a document that couldn't survive at least a typical and basic scrutiny, such as a black light test, so I examined my new wares very carefully. The forger was not going to be at the gate with me to say, "Oh, my mistake—stay right there, and I'll fix it and get right back to you." One mistake and I'd be done.

The seals on the British passport lined up perfectly, the plastic seal was pristine, and the expiration date was nine years out. The British passport was the best of the forger's work, but I felt that I could still use the others in a situation not likely to include formal or in-depth examination. The only problem that I could see was that the passport gave my age as thirty-two when in fact I was a decade older. *No bueno.* I knew at some point that I was going to have to get a face lift, and the prospect of getting one in Latin America was not something I looked forward to.

Julio gave me the phone number of one of his men, Edwin, and said I needed to fly there to meet him and he would get me across the Darien Gap. He said I would definitely get kidnapped if I attempted to get there by bus, and that the road ended at Turbo. Edwin, he said, was a serious guy who would take good care of me; Julio would call him to make sure of it.

When I called Edwin to arrange for my visit and asked him how he was getting along, he immediately started complaining about his situation. From what I could gather, the President of Panama had recently signed a treaty with Japan that allowed the Japanese to fish in Panamanian coastal waters, and this had decimated the native fisheries, making it nearly impossible for the locals to feed their families or earn their meager living by fishing. He explained that they did their best to live off the fruit they picked in the jungle, and how he occasionally poached a cow from a local rancher's herd, which often wasn't enough. He said that he had been forced to resort to skills developed in the military just to get by, making two hundred dollars American from the drug cartels for each hit he conducted. It wasn't nearly the money that he had earned killing cops for Pablo, but it was better than nothing.

Edwin was all business on the phone. "*Tu necesitas que mate alguien?*" he asked. "*Te doy un desquento.*"[69]

"No," I replied. "*Estoy bien.*"

I went shopping before I left Medellín and bought a huge box full of groceries for Edwin and his family, which I then placed in a second backpack—rice, beans, *arepa* mix, cooking oil, meat, sugar, candy, and toiletries.

I left the central airport in Medellín, Aero Puerta Olaya Herrera, as morning broke, and flew to the airport in Turbo on the Gulf of Uraba. From there I took a cargo flight to Acandi in a big single-engine, fat-bellied, tail-dragger plane with dual wings that barely had enough room to land on the grass airstrip carved out at the base of a hill. Acandi wasn't exactly a tourist destination. It sat smack-dab in the middle of one of the world's most notorious passageways.

As the plane made its landing approach, Acandi seemed to me to be home to five hundred or so people, judging by the size of what's best described as a field of ramshackle structures pieced together out of scrap steel and plywood, obviously lacking in indoor plumbing and electricity.

What exactly is the Darien Gap? It's a break in the Pan-American Highway consisting of a large swath of undeveloped swampland and forest within Panama's Darién Province in Central America and the northern portion of Colombia's Chocó Department in South America. It an area almost a hundred miles long and about thirty wide. Road-building through the area is expensive, and the environmental cost is high. A political consensus in favor of road construction has not emerged. Consequently, there is no road connection through the Darién Gap connecting North America with South America. It is the missing link of the Pan-American Highway.

If you think I am exaggerating, here are some of the accounts that I have found:

> *This area is a forbidding mountainous jungle on the Panama side; full of swamps, guerrillas, drug traffickers and kidnappers on the Colombian side, making travel through the area not just a struggle against a hostile environment but also a maze of bribing the right people for passage and ducking bullets.*
>
> *The Darien Gap is one of the last—not only unexplored—but one of the last places people really hesitate to venture to. . . It's also one of the most rugged places. The basic problem of the Darien Gap is that it's one of the toughest hikes there is. It's an absolute pristine jungle but it's got some nasty sections with thorns, wasps, snakes, thieves, criminals, you name it. Everything that's bad for you is in there.*

In case you forget these dangers and are still thinking of putting *Crossing the Darien Gap* on your bucket list, here is an easy list to remember:

- *Tough nasty jungle with plenty of disagreeable wildlife*
- *Impenetrable swamps*
- *Crazed drug traffickers*
- *Pissed-off guerrillas*
- *Greedy kidnappers*
- *Paranoid government police*
- *No marked trails*

When the plane touched down and rolled to a stop in front of the one-room terminal shack, Edwin ran out and greeted me on the runway as I came down the portable stairs. He was smiling and hurried to help me with my backpack and the second backpack of food I dragged out of the cargo hold. He was a well-built man and pretty intimidating. The former Colombian Marine had been in charge of a small gang of hit men and thieves in Manrique, the neighborhood just above Campo Valdez. Manrique was the only place in Colombia that I had ever heard was more dangerous than Campo Valdez. I had no idea what Edwin was doing in Acandi, and I certainly was not going to ask.

The propeller was still spinning and pushing a lot of air past us, so I can't say I understood what he said there, at the plane, but he seemed to be happy enough to see me. When Edwin motioned me to follow him to his house, I got the sneaking suspicion that the plane's engine was the only one in miles.

He led me toward the end of a straight, narrow dirt street that was nearest the runway and lined with shanty-style homes, if you could call them that. There were no cars, and transportation was limited to a motorcycle or two, starving horses, some emaciated donkeys, and mosquitoes big enough to fly out on. Only a couple of streets over, I could see a hand-painted sign above the general store, which doubled as the gathering spot or watering hole. As we passed maybe a dozen homes, through open doors and windows I met the gaze of the residents of Acandi, who peered at me with little or no expression. I wasn't uncomfortable, but I wished I could have gotten some idea from their stare of the welcome I would or wouldn't get there, in the jungle.

Something in the air was burning my eyes and lungs. Through an alley running between a couple of homes, I caught a glimpse of a government health department employee who had an insecticide dispenser strapped to his back that belched out a diesel-smelling fog of mosquito-killing chemicals. This was in the wake of a malaria outbreak that had occurred in several towns in this region, including Turbo. It explained the carpet of dead mosquitoes that covered the street.

Edwin's home was at the other end of the row, on the right, at the high end of a very slight grade, which meant that the raw sewage drainage trenches beside the road were narrow and shallow in front of his house. The house was distinguished from the others by the presence of a derelict canoe on sawhorses and a rusty outboard boat motor that looked as though it had been sitting there, in the front yard, since the Spanish-American War.

As we approached the house, a skinny old black dog came out of the house, wagging its tail at Edwin, who uttered some term of endearment as he reached down and scratched the dog on top of the head.

Edwin's "house" was basically a tin shack, dimly lit by the sun that shone through the many small holes in the rusty steel roof, with a very hard-packed dirt floor throughout. A large, empty cable spool cloaked in a white sheet would serve as a dinner table after the dead mosquitoes were brushed away.

There was a common area that served as a kitchen and living room, measuring ten by fourteen feet, with a small window above the stove that provided a view so dismal that you would keep the curtains closed, if you had curtains. A makeshift plywood wall separated two sleeping areas that had no doors, each of which contained a mattress on a wooden door, with door knobs and hinges still attached, that spanned two sawhorses. One of these served as a bedroom for Edwin and his wife; his sister and brother-in-law slept in the other.

He gestured to the floor beside his bed and told me to sleep there, in the dirt. He set down my pack, propping it up alongside the baby's cradle.

Though I was desperate to get to Panama, so I could straighten out my passport stamps, I couldn't refuse Edwin's offer to spend a few days at his home. (I doubt that he had many visitors.) Besides, he wanted to take me fishing in the jungle. I had about two thousand bucks in crisp Franklins on me but felt anxious about carrying it around, so I asked Edwin to hold onto it for safekeeping while I was in town. His idea of "safe" was to tuck the bills under his mattress.

The next day, when he took me fishing, I noticed something troubling: every time he turned my direction, I could see a few tightly rolled, newer American hundred-dollar bills dangling from the string that held up his red board shorts, in plain sight, about eight inches below his waist. I knew that there was only one place he could possibly get such bills way out there—out of the stash that I had given him to secure. My first impulse was to confront him, but I kept my cool and decided to wait for a better time and place, when I wasn't all alone, in the jungle, with a hit man, on his own turf.

When we got back, I told him that Julio had told me to be certain to call when I had arrived in Acandi, before we began the next leg to Panama to begin the process of getting my passport entry-stamped, but that, in all the excitement, I had forgotten. The only phone in town was in the Telecom de Colombia office at the edge of the jungle. Edwin took me there.

A couple of tries later, I managed to get Julio on his satellite phone. I didn't mention the hundred-dollar bills, but I did say that I was eager to get to Panama. He told me to put Edwin on the phone. When I handed the phone to him, Edwin asked me to give him some privacy, so I stepped outside and tried to talk to a ten-year-old boy who had been looking at me as if I were made out of vanilla. I felt the same way that young black man must have felt in Pierre when I was a kid.

Edwin came out, told me we would be leaving for Panama the next morning, marched back to his house, and barely spoke to me that night. It was obvious that Julio had said something to put him on edge, and I was not about to ask what it was.

A few months later, I learned from Julio's brother that my host had planned to kill me during our hike so that he could steal the rest of the two grand I had given him for safekeeping. He would chop me up and feed me to the scavengers in the water: clean, no traces. He had offered to split the profits with Julio. Julio had been good enough to caution him against harming me in any way, warning that, if anything bad happened to me, he would not only kill Edwin but his wife, his parents, his grandparents, his brothers and sisters, his baby, his friends, and his friends' friends as well.

I needed a shower after all that hiking, so I went just behind the shack, where there was a pigpen and a shower stall with artesian well water that rose up through a makeshift pipe into a cracked blue plastic bowl. I had to scoop quickly to get the water I needed before it spilled onto the floor of the shower, which had been fashioned from a wooden shipping pallet resting on several bricks. The walls of the stall were rotting wooden doors nailed up horizontally, which rustically left my head, shoulders, and shins in plain view of Edwin's neighbors.

As I was drying off, I heard a terrifying female scream from inside the house—not just once, as if someone had been startled, but persistently, as if she desperately needed help. I jumped into my cut-offs and hopped quickly through the pig-mess and the mud into the house to see what the problem was and what I could do—and there was Edwin's wife, Adriana, running around the living room and into the bedrooms, yelling and reciting shrill incantations as she dipped her right hand into a box of white powder of some kind and hurled it onto the floor and into the air.

When I tried to ask her what was going on, she pointed to the baby's cradle and then to a snake, smaller than most in the area, a mere five feet long, that was writhing and pinned under a brick to the floor in the main room. I surmised that she had reached into the cradle to pick up her baby, found the snake wrapped around the child, wrestled it away, and smashed it with the brick; the powder was something the local witch doctor had told her to use to keep serpents, evil spirits, and demons out of the house.

I grabbed the snake by the tail and ran into the front yard to convince the neighbors, who were also investigating the commotion, that all was well.

Later, as a direct result of having given those groceries to Edwin that I bought before getting on the plane, I learned that dogs like snake for dinner: had I not stocked Edwin's cupboards, there wouldn't have been enough snake left over to feed to the dog. The baby, praise the

Lord, had survived the attack. Edwin came home after the excitement was over and went straight to sleep. He never mentioned the incident to me.

The next day we left for Panama. It was the most difficult thing that I have ever done. We wove our way through the stifling humidity on the rivers and creeks. Although it was just a small, hollowed-out log, his canoe was the equivalent of a sports car with shallow water on the floor in a modern city. Edwin's mastery of his surroundings, and the two-horsepower engine, did surprisingly well at getting us from place to place.

The dry season was past, so visiting much of the hiking terrain now required a canoe. After making our way upstream and into a couple of tributaries, he gracefully steered the canoe into a depression in the bank, where we disembarked to do some hiking in the labyrinth of overgrown quasi-trails that wound through the Darien jungle.

I had never thought of swinging a machete as an endurance sport until that day, when I broke the blisters on my right hand. Edwin gripped the machete handle with a brown rag he had brought with him, but all I had was my bare hands, and I did as much swinging at the mosquitoes as I did at the underbrush that he missed as he cleared a trail ahead of me. My thirst was killing me, but I knew I couldn't drink the water at our feet, and not just because of Edwin's body odor and sweat, which would have been enough for me; you never drink stagnant water.

At the border, we boarded the canoe and crossed over into Panama, where he paid the customs agent twenty dollars American, and, *bingo*, we both got exit and entry stamps in only a matter of minutes. When I reimbursed Edwin, he explained that, had he failed to give the agent this gratuity, the agent would simply have kept telling us there was something wrong or incomplete that prevented him from "being able to provide a stamp at this time."

We had planned to return to Colombia to get its entry stamp at

Turbo, on the Gulf of Uraba. We first went back to Acandi, via canoe, where I got a stamp at the local police station signifying that I could spend time in Acandi. The stamp took up an entire page of my passport, unlike typical stamps, which fit four to a page. This irritated me to the point of shutting my mouth, because when a passport was full of stamps I'd lose that name and identity and have to get new ones. However, I was just concentrating on getting the stamps, my primary goal at the moment, and I had to accept the time, money, and risk associated with the endeavor. Due to the FARC guerrillas' control of the countryside, we traveled exclusively by canoe.

I made it back to Medellín without incident. Julio talked me into staying there for the last two months of 1996. I continued to work on my Spanish and, after an incredible New Year's celebration at Julio's *finca,* I said my goodbyes to Julio, Doña Ruth, and the rest of my Colombian *familia.*

On the second day of 1997, I boarded a plane to Cali, Colombia, en route to Mexico City. First I had to stop in nearby Pasto, to drop off five thousand dollars American to one of Julio's girlfriends, who worked in a bank. I would also get some money from the ATM there. Julio let me deposit my money in a former business worker's account. I say *former* because the guy had apparently been caught stealing from Julio. He would not need the account any more. I chose that ATM because I avoided ATMs at airports, and Medellín's ATMs were a nightmare.

The whole community of Pasto was in a festive mood, to put it mildly. Drunken revelers poured out of the bars and restaurants, most of them clutching their personal bottles of liquor. As I wandered farther into the city, I saw more and more people near the central plaza partying and dancing to salsa/cambia music, and I began to realize that many of them were covered from head to toe in white powder. Passing one of the bars, I came upon a stunningly beautiful woman about thirty years old, with long black hair, who was sitting on a table drinking from a nearly drained bottle of *aguadiente*. I asked her what was going on.

She started laughing hysterically. "*Tu no sabes?*"[70] she asked?

I shook my head.

"Es el Carnival de Negros y Blancos,"[71] she said, as she jumped into my arms, almost knocking me down, and kissed me on the lips.

A couple of moments later a fairly large fellow wearing a sombrero with the legend *Texas Longhorns* on it appeared. I assumed that he was her boyfriend or husband. He didn't say a word, just lifted the woman off me, swung her over his shoulder, and walked down the street.

I headed deeper into town; up ahead, I noticed a stage of sorts where a beauty pageant appeared to be under way. Each young woman had a number taped to her swimsuit and was covered from top to bottom with baking flour. Each contestant (some of whom had very nice shapes) would take center stage, do a little dance to the live music, and then strut off. Before allowing myself a closer look, I thought I should take care of the business of dropping off the five thousand with Julio's girlfriend and going to the ATM machine.

When the partygoers spotted me crossing the plaza without any paint, they surrounded me before I could enter the bank. I thought I was about to get rolled but wondered why I'd be robbed going into the bank instead of when leaving the bank. They tackled me and to covered me with flour (or maybe powdered sugar) from head to toe, until I was as entirely white as the driven snow. While I began to cough up clouds of whatever they had coated me with, I was relieved to see that I wasn't going to be mugged.

They dragged me up and onto the stage at the Plaza Bolivar with the band to dance with a dozen or so partiers. They laughed at the gringo who had no rhythm. And don't forget, I was completely sober, almost certainly the only person over seven years old who could make that claim. They yanked me off the stage and seated me next to a tall, skinny guy about my age who taught English in Bogota. He explained what was going on.

The Black and White Festival had its origins during Spanish rule, when slaves were allowed to celebrate on January 5, and their owners would paint their own faces black in approval. The next day the slaves would paint their faces white, copying their owners.

I made a move to rejoin the crowd unobserved, but even those people wanted to dance with me. To escape the intoxication of the crowd before they thought of something else to coat me in, I figured I'd better make my way to the bus station. I still struggle to see the humor in a sugar-coated foreign gringo, with a backpack and no rhythm, trying to dance to a live band in front of a crowd at a street festival. *Adios*, Colombia. I was ready to see the world.

9

MARGARITAVILLE

FOR THREE YEARS AFTER I LEFT COLOMBIA, I lived like a newly minted college graduate, backpacking around the world. I'd had some great experiences, and I'd managed to stay off the grid and out of prison, but it was time to start acting like an adult again and to start earning some money.

Two days into the third millennium, I made my way to Margarita, Venezuela. Paul had promised that it was worth my going there—that the guy that I was meeting was a serious guy, and that he had a business deal in which I might be interested. I tried to get more out of Paul, but that is all he would say.

So there I was, sitting in a comfortable café on the main drag of Margarita, called Cinco de Mayo, while I waited for Paul's guy, Nick. I was enjoying my second piece of pizza when a new friend reached over and grabbed a slice. Actually he wasn't really my friend. He had sat at my table, uninvited, a few minutes earlier, smiling and amiable, wearing beach clothes and bootleg Gucci sunglasses. I consider myself to be a pretty generous guy, and if somebody says he has no money to buy some food I will likely help him out, but eating right off my plate without asking? Were we family or something?

"Hey, man," I said. "If you want some pizza, go and order your own."

His dumb grin grew even wider, and he nodded and patted me on the back, mumbling a few things in Spanish. Then he flagged down the waitress who came to our table—check that, *my* table —who took his order for a medium-size pie. I noticed that he did not say to put it on his tab, and I should have said something right there and then, but I was in a bad mood, so I sat there almost hoping for trouble.

When his pizza came, two of his *compadres* joined him at the table. I continued to check my watch. Where the hell was this Nick?

My three dining buddies began ordering beer and more food. They kept asking me if I wanted a beer, but I explained that I didn't drink and that I was expecting a business acquaintance to meet me any minute. They laughed; soon my table had turned into a full-blown tailgate party with these guys ordering appetizers, *patacones con queso de mano,*[72] and beer after beer.

By four o'clock, the crowd had begun to disperse, and the waitress arrived with the bill—just one. I hadn't asked for it, she'd brought it on her own. Sure enough, all the food and drinks were on there—over a hundred and twenty bucks American, in a country where the average worker might earn that in six months.

I told her that I wanted my individual bill, and that I wasn't going to pay for everybody's lunch. Upon hearing this, the owner emerged from the kitchen with a stained white apron draped over his bulging stomach, which caught the beads of sweat from his forehead all day long, and approached my table.

The first of the three amigos told the owner that I had promised to pay for their meals, while the other two nodded in agreement. The owner then told me that I had to pay the tab because I had invited them over to eat, that I was responsible.

"Fuck that," I said. "I'm *not* responsible!"

"Why would you invite these guys over if you didn't intend to pay?" he asked.

"I *didn't* invite them over. They invited themselves," I said. I may have been born in South Dakota, but I hadn't been born on the back of a turnip truck. I knew a hustle when I saw one.

I also thought about this:

Rule #2: Don't break any local laws.

I realize I should have just dropped the hundred and twenty on the table and shaken their hands for teaching me a valuable lesson. But that day in Margarita, I drew the line in the sand. *Gringo stupido.*

The police pulled up on Yamaha 250cc motorcycles. One of them was actually yawning as he approached. The owner began to go into a tirade, much of which was lost on me, but I heard the words *gringo* and *Americano*. I jumped in.

"I'm *not* an American. I'm from England!" I went off on a tirade, mostly in English, rambling on about being hustled and how people like me came there and put a lot of money in their "bloody" country's economy, and that they should be grateful. I think I even threw in a couple of "mates."

The cops must have been in on it, or maybe they were just in the mood to bust some gringo balls. One of them gave me the command that I dreaded most: "Let me see your papers."

At this moment, two guys who had also been eating in the restaurant made their way over. One of them, who looked like a cross between Elvis and Rocky, put his arm around the owner and started speaking what I assumed was some kind of Spanglish. The other one, a white guy who looked like he might have been an athlete a long time before, began speaking, too. It seemed pretty obvious that the cops knew both of them, as they began nodding.

After a couple of minutes one of the cops said, "*No problema,*" and the two of them walked out and drove off on their bikes. The cross between Elvis and Rocky whipped out some cash, stuffed it in the owner's breast pocket, and turned to me, and said, "Let's get the hell out of here, buddy."

We walked outside.

"Hey, thanks, guys," I said. "But I wasn't gonna—"

"You do what you want," the guy said. "Just be careful out here. This isn't the USA."

"I'm British," I said.

"Yeah, and I'm Yiddish," the white guy said.

They turned out to be the first American friends that I had made since I went on the lam. Both had moved to Margarita from Vegas when Peter Jacoby, the white guy, had noticed an article in *GQ* announcing one of the craziest new things on the Internet—online gambling. The other guy, Mike Nichols, had done a few movie roles out in Hollywood, but he was itching to start making real money. They came out and opened an online gambling operation, in which people in the United States could bet on whatever sport they liked and not have to deal with bookies.

The two had been in Margarita for three years running the operation, and they were doing very well. I asked them where I could find an internet café—I needed to find out what'd happened to Nick. They said that I could use one of their computers. Their business was right around the corner.

About a dozen men and women, mostly well-spoken Latinos, manned the phones, answering questions about upcoming sporting events. Mike and Peter's gambling room was pretty high-tech—I would say space age for Latin America. The lighting was easy on the eyes, unlike the fluorescents that I had been exposed to since 1994. The computers were about five hundred times faster than the ones that I had been using in the Internet cafes.

It was the first time that I got a chance to explore the Internet. Mike showed me Ask Jeeves, on which I was able to ask a question like: *How many people live in Pierre, South Dakota?* and, within a second or two, I got the answer. Amazing.

It turned out that Nick had been expecting me to arrive the following day. We ended up meeting that morning in El Yaque, a beach town in the south of Margarita. As I got out of my taxi, I noticed a pretty steady wind coming in from the water. And everywhere I looked there were surfers. But on closer examination I realized that the surfboards had sails attached to them. It turned out that El Yaque was known as one of the seven best locations in the world for windsurfing, attracting enthusiasts from around the globe, especially Europe.

It was quite a scene. The most physically fit human beings that I had ever laid eyes on were cruising along the water, which was warm enough so that they didn't need wetsuits, just bathing trunks or bikinis. The bodily energy was palpable, and I began to understand why Paul had thought I should meet this guy Nick Judge.

Nick was a transplanted Australian. He looked as though he belonged on the cover of *Muscle and Fitness*—six feet tall, about a hundred and eighty pounds of lean muscle. He had been living on the mainland before moving to Margarita, making his living, at first, by going from gold mining camp to gold mining camp, buying gold at a discount directly from the miners who accepted Bolivars[73] as payment, which he then sold for U.S. dollars or Euros.

In this trade Nick had been robbed on numerous occasions by gun-toting *banditos* who would sneak up on him while he slept in his hammock, lying on top of his valuables. But he hadn't given up, and after he was able to save some money he had decided that he would try to discover his own gold, investing in a self-built barge that he traveled in, cruising the waterways, extracting gold from the river bottom. On occasion, Nick's mining crew had used high-pressure pumps to break loose gold-bearing ore from the banks of rivers and streams. That crew consisted of about twenty Guyanans who worked for him 24/7. After slightly more than a year—a lifetime's worth of adventures, being thrown in jail, being robbed, and living in perpetual threat of injury or death—he'd decided to retire from the gold-mining trade.

When he reached Margarita, he'd had just over a million Euros in cash, and when he first set his eyes on El Yaque, he had been confident it would become the world's top windsurfing spot. A consistent record of side-shore tropical wind over 350 days per year, shallow and warm tropical waters, eternal sunshine, and located only ten minutes from an international airport that could handle 747s, it was the almost-perfect spot. Nick had set about building luxury townhouses, which he'd just completed when I met him. Those townhouses were by far the most luxurious accommodations in El Yaque, and some of the swankest in all of Venezuela.

The problem was that the windsurfing crowd came mainly from Europe and stayed in El Yaque to practice their sport, typically for one month each year, before moving on; they had no desire to live there and definitely lacked the three hundred thousand American in cash to purchase a townhouse, even if they wanted one, and nobody was going to pay the forty-percent interest for a real estate loan.

"So, mate," Nick told me, "Paul said that if anyone could help me with my dilemma, it would be you."

"That's very nice of Paul," I said, more pissed-off than flattered. Yes, El Yaque was incredible, but I needed to start earning some money. I told him that I would think about it and get back to him in a few days.

That night I was sitting on the beach, looking out into the water, when it came to me.

I met Nick the next morning and I told him that, in my opinion, he should start up a topnotch international escort service, where clients would fly into the adjacent airport and come to Nick's property to spend, not an hour or a day, but an entire week, paying a flat fee for the woman or women. I told him that he should include lodging in a five-star townhouse, a private chef, food, and all they could drink. Margarita was a tax-free port, so liquor, beer, and wine were less expensive than at other locations.

A day later, he asked me to be his partner. I thought about it for about a day, maybe a day and a half, and concluded that life was an adventure, and this would just be another chapter. So, I said, "Yes."

At the time, my pal Paul was living nearby. I visited him and told him the news. He replied that he thought I was nuts for doing it, lecturing me about being an international fugitive, telling me that I couldn't go breaking any laws or do business in any gray areas. But Margarita was wide-open. If you wanted a casino, you opened one; if you had the money for liquor, you opened a discotheque. Everybody was taking advantage of the free-market atmosphere—not to mention that here were numerous places featuring "ladies of the evening."

After Paul's reality check, I reevaluated my situation and my location, observing that most people in Latin America were not opposed to prostitution and gambling, but that drugs carried a stigma with the average person. I made an appointment with one of the local attorneys, who had a reputation for being in the know, and described my concerns about possible arrests or confrontations, and about the operation of an escort service.

"Here, there's no risk being arrested for running an escort service," he said. "If you aren't smuggling drugs or petroleum, *no problema.*"

Upon hearing this I told Nick that I was in.

He decided to plant some coconut palms around the townhouses to add some tropical flavor. He bought several saplings about four feet tall and set them beside ditches he had dug to irrigate them, cordoning them off with yellow plastic crime-scene tape.

He and I were sitting in a parking lot one day at about two o'clock in the afternoon when a guy from the mainland, in a brand-new white Jeep Cherokee, drove through the tape and set up a picnic for his wife and kids.

When Nick saw this, he stood up, approached the guy, and demanded to know what the hell he thought he was doing.

Nick was fluent in Spanish and listened as the driver of the Jeep told him, *"Tu eres un maldito gringo, nada mas esto. No es tu tierra, maricon!"*[74] When Nick heard the word "*maricon,*" he told him he was going to beat the shit out of him.

This caused the driver to retreat to his Cherokee to get his pistol, which he proceeded to point directly at Nick's face. It was a bad situation. I certainly did not want to lose my new partner or, worse, get shot myself, which was a very real possibility considering that I was standing right beside him.

It turned out that Nick had been in similar situations many times when he was in the gold business, and he saw fit to escalate the situation, not flinching one bit. He strolled right up to the "loco native" and told him that, if he didn't put the gun down, he was going to shove it up his "*culo*." The driver turned right around and bolted out of there with his family. I have to say that I was pretty impressed. Crocodile Dundee had nothing on this guy.

"The guy had his wife and kids with him," Nick said. "It was broad daylight, and his vehicle was brand-new. When I added it up, I was pretty certain that this wanker wasn't likely to open fire." From that moment on I felt quite comfortable that my new partner was going to protect the women we were going to hire.

Nick and I determined that we needed a website to promote Paradise Vacations. For an establishment like ours, there would be very little competition. The internet was still in its infancy, only a few people on the island even knew about it (much less used it), and the performance was profoundly slow. However, we needed to stay out of gray areas and litigation, so we decided to limit our services to non-Venezuelans, so as not to compete with the locals and to prevent problems like getting strong-armed by local or national governments.

We offered luxury, five-star-quality townhouses, but we still lacked the dimes[75] that we needed to staff the entertainment department. To get around this we put photos from *Playboy* on our website and told anyone who asked for one of those girls that she was unavailable—and then try to find a Venezuelan angel to assign to the guest instead. I later learned that, in our business, this was called the bait-and-switch. We must have done pretty well in our selection of staff, which was largely attributable to our madam on the mainland who did all of the screening, and who did manage occasionally to send us a bona fide beauty queen.

Our fee was thirty-five hundred dollars American, which included a woman for the entire week, food and drink, and a furnished luxury townhouse. Even the horniest of guys would only put in so much work with his date. After the first day or two, they would hit the local casinos, shopping malls, strip clubs, beaches, and other gourmet restaurants. We facilitated all of this with a Paradise Vacation driver and shuttle van that made the entire island accessible to our guests.

As if that wasn't enough, I also adopted a business strategy I had learned from my old friend Francisco. I contacted the local strip clubs and got them to acknowledge our guests as VIP members, roping off sections of their seating as "executive members only" areas and reserving them for our guests and their "dates." Our international guests threw so much money around that the clubs eventually began calling us to ask when more of our "high rollers" would be arriving. This evolved into us actually getting a ten-percent kickback on all of the money our guests lost in the island's casinos or spent in the strip bars. We treated our guests, their dates, and their personal hosts like royalty, as did the pre-selected establishments they patronized. After several content clients gave us glowing testimonials and their referrals, Paradise Vacations started to blow some gold dust our way.

In a short time we replaced the pictures we had borrowed from *Playboy* with pictures of our own women. I realize that prostitution is a volatile subject, and I know that there are horrible injustices in the global human trafficking market, but I can honestly say that our employees fought for their positions, and that most of them seemed to have a pretty great time. In a perfect world, they would have been escorted by the men of their dreams—their husbands or boyfriends. But they weren't complaining. Most of them were college students who spoke very little English, and the tales they told their fellow students made many of them eager to get in line for the air travel (most had never been on a plane), the paychecks, and the gifts and good times our clients shared with them. The Paradise Vacation women's own satisfaction kept us well stocked with new and very pretty talent.

Another amenity that we were very proud to provide was the availability of personal bilingual hosts to bridge communication gaps between our guests, our women, and local businesses and establishments.

Our most popular was a young man named Rafael.

I met him right there, in El Yaque, during a vacation with his girlfriend, Viviana, a curvy, good-looking Brazilian-Venezuelan. She and the six-foot-two former pro basketball player were the best-looking couple in town.

Rafael was extremely proud of his accomplishments on the basketball hardwood. He showed me his scrapbook, which went back as far as his play in a peewee league, to when he averaged twenty-seven points a game at the legendary Rucker Park in Harlem. He told me of certain trips through the airport in the Dominican Republic when he had been asked by immigration officials for his autograph and permission to take a picture with their kids. He eventually played pro basketball for the Caracas Crocodiles, and he had played in Germany, Amsterdam, the Dominican Republic, Tijuana, and in the CBA in Worcester, Massachusetts.

After his pro career fizzled out, he had found another endeavor. Europe was where the ecstasy craze had originated, and in Holland there were many small labs manufacturing the tablets. It wasn't long before

Rafael returned to New York, then to Tijuana, and revved up a lab to produce X-pills for New York and Miami synthetic-drug enthusiasts. Everything went great until Rafael got busted over a call he made about cocaine to an old friend in New York.

The next time we met up for drinks (shots of scotch for him, Diet Coke for me) he divulged even more sensitive information. (You wonder why I vowed never to drink?) Facing a mandatory four-year prison sentence, Rafael knew that there was only one thing to do—bail out and flee to Tijuana. Bail was set at twenty grand and airfare was negligible; once in Tijuana, Rafael obtained a Mexican passport, birth certificate, and Mexican Army ID, and did so in only two months. I never told him how that made me feel, when it had taken me over two years just to get some stolen passports. Obviously, it was a stupendous advantage that he was Latin instead of a gringo from South Dakota. So our best host turned out to be a fugitive, just like his boss, except he was able to pose as a Mexican.

As much as I enjoyed Rafael's drunken stories, and as much as I respected his work ethic and admired how much our Spanish-speaking guests took to him, I knew that I had to get rid of him. If he had babbled to me, his boss, about his fugitive status, I could imagine that he had probably told others. And no good could come of that. Eventually the authorities would show up, and it would only be a matter of time before they began to investigate Paradise Vacations and its two owners—an Australian who had been raping Venezuela of its most valuable resources, and Charles Livingston III, a British land developer or whatever the hell I was telling people at the time. They wouldn't have to dig very far to find out that I didn't speak very good British.

Of course, Nick didn't want me to let Rafael go—as I said, he was a valuable asset to our business. When I told him about the young man's fugitive status and how I thought it might bring heat onto us, he told me, "Stop acting like such a pussy." He figured that he was taking more of a chance than I was, and that I should man up. But I wouldn't—

check that, *couldn't*—budge. He finally gave in.

Then I had to get rid of Rafael. I told him that, given his fugitive status, we couldn't keep him on. He did not take this too well. As a matter of fact, he got quite indignant as he stormed out. I assumed that I was done with him, but one night I got a call from our bartender saying that Rafael was in the bar, drunk and belligerent.

I really felt bad that I was being such a hypocrite, but no one was going to jeopardize my freedom—not after what I had gone through for six years.

I walked into the bar. It wasn't open to the public, only our guests and their dates, so Rafael and the bartender were the only ones there.

"Oh, here comes the boss," Rafael said. "The nigga who fired me for no fucking reason."

I told the bartender that Rafael was done for the night, and that I would lock up. He got the hint and left very quickly.

"Yo," Rafael said to the bartender. "Get me another glass of Johnnie Walker Blue." At least the kid had good taste.

"I'll get it for him," I told the bartender, who was already halfway out the door.

"Make it a double," said Rafael.

I went behind the bar, grabbed the bottle, approached him, and poured him another drink.

"Rafael," I said, "I explained why I had to let you go. I didn't want to, but, given your fugitive status, I have no choice. It's nothing personal."

He sipped on his scotch, not saying anything but obviously not ready to call it a night.

"I'm going to say this once," I said. "This is your last drink here, and from now on you're not allowed at Paradise Vacations or in El Yaque."

"Why? You own the beach now, gringo?"

I really hated doing it but I knew that he was at the end of his rope, that he'd had just too much bad luck and wasn't going to go quietly.

I had the urge to go behind the bar, grab the baseball bat we kept there, and hit him in his head with it. But then he would almost surely retaliate, and there is no easier way to do that than by calling the police. No, I was living in a gray area; I could not break a law and risk everything.

Luckily, at that moment, my partner walked through the door with a couple of blokes that I hadn't seen. Apparently the bartender had alerted him to the situation. Old Nick wasn't having it. He walked right up to Rafael and punched him as hard as he could in the side of head, knocking him unconscious. The other guys quickly carried him out the door.

Nick turned to me, rather disgusted, and said, "I don't know if you're tough enough for this business, mate. You don't seem to want to get your hands dirty, do you?" With that, he left.

I cannot describe how badly I wanted to put him on record about exactly who the hell he was talking to. But that option wasn't available to me.

Right after this fiasco, I got more bad news. My FedEx package came from Paul Holt, the usual stuff—coloring books, art supplies, and, most importantly, ten thousand-dollar magic markers.

I started pulling the bottoms off the markers, opening them, looking for my stash of cash. In those days we would roll ten hundred-dollar bills tightly into each magic marker. But to my horror, there was nothing in them—until I opened the last marker, which *did* contain the thousand. The other nine markers should have had the same.

Whoever hit the package had nine grand from me, and as a gesture of kindness or carelessness had left me one. I was pissed off for about eight seconds. . . and then I got very scared. I knew that if U.S. Customs had found the money, they would have taken it all. They would also have put a tail on the package, which would have led to me. Game over.

I had just lost nine thousand bucks because the person sending it had apparently been in a rush and unaware of the potential ramifications for both of us. If the person was in that much of a rush, they probably hadn't used plastic gloves when he was handling the markers, so their fingerprints would be all over the package and its contents. I did not know the person in question. He worked for Paul Holt, though, who had sworn that the guy was extremely reliable.

After fully analyzing the situation I tried to remain positive. I had in fact received a thousand dollars and been neither arrested nor questioned, and neither had Paul or his worker. This breach of our method amounted only to an important nine-grand wakeup call. There was no way of knowing who'd gotten away with my cash, but given my circumstances, I was all right with that.

It was a few weeks before Christmas and, while Paradise Vacations was beginning to get some customers, I was feeling on edge since the Rafael incident and the markers. Not only that, my partner now thought that I was a pussy, and that is never a good thing.

And there was something more as well: for the first time in my life, I felt completely and utterly alone in the world. I had learned through Paul that my father passed away the previous summer. I had heard someone say once that, no matter how old you are, when one of your parents dies, you revert to feeling like a child.

Ronny, a mutual friend of Paul's and mine, who obviously did not know that Paul was in contact with me, had attended my father's funeral. He'd said that it was packed, not only with friends and family, but with armed federal agents and local police officers who had staked out the funeral. My brother had told Ronny that he thought for sure that I was dead, or I would have found a way to attend the funeral.

I was thinking about 9/11 too, which had happened a few months earlier. When I heard about it, I had gotten very upset. But the internet was not as ubiquitous as it was in the United States and practically nonexistent in most of the places that I had been traveling to. So while I mourned the nation's loss, in my own way, it wasn't on my mind as it would have been if I were still in the States or even had I been watching it on my computer screen or television set.

Still, it made me pause and reflect about my feelings for the United States. They were of course colored by the fact that the U.S. government wanted me to go to prison for thirty years for a crime that I had not committed. Still, as much as I pretended I wasn't, I was an American, and America was where my family lived. For all its faults, I did not want to see any harm come to it.

I took a couple of days off and flew to Caracas to buy a Jeep Cherokee. I needed a one-owner vehicle, so I could investigate the title to confirm that it was clear and that the vehicle hadn't been stolen. I intended to take what I bought to the PTJ office (the Venezuelan equivalent of the FBI)to have the vehicle's numbers run through a database of stolen vehicles, which was how most Venezuelans treated their vehicle purchases.

When I got there, I encountered an extremely long line and figured that the process would take more than a single day. I would then have the Jeep shipped to Margarita.

Before I left, I had contacted Jose Rojas, aka Jose Gesteria, a guy whom Mike Nichols and Peter Jacoby, the online gambling guys, had introduced me to when I first moved to Venezuela. Jose was based out of Caracas but visited Margarita quite often. He had given me his business card and said to call him if I ever needed anything fixed.

Jose was a licensed *gesteria.*[75] I had told him I needed a Venezuelan *cedula*[76] and had given him a copy of my stolen British passport, so he could do this for me. Once again, I was praying that nobody would contact the British Embassy to see if the passport was stolen.

I accompanied Jose to the local DIEX office, where he had various contacts. I went to the front of the line, they took my picture, and I left with a Venezuelan *cedula* number issued in the name on my British passport.

This was a transit *cedula,* which meant you could be in the country for one year but you could not work. But I needed a national registration number to apply for a Venezuelan driver's license. In all the years that I had lived in Venezuela, I had never been asked for my driver's license, nor had I met anyone who had one, but my American mentality had convinced me that I needed one.

Since Jose had acquired the *cedula* so quickly, I introduced him to several other travelers who needed a transient stamp in their passports (the seal they put in a passport that confirms your permission to remain for an entire year without having to exit every ninety days, as you must if you lack it).

By remaining inside the country I wouldn't needlessly take up room on the pages of my passport with stamp after stamp for exit and entry. As I have already pointed out, since my passport was a stolen one, I could hardly go to the embassy and apply for an updated one; I would have to get another stolen passport and live as "someone else." Just how I would eventually deal with this was a mystery I avoided thinking about—how I would deal with friends and associates who knew me as Charles Livingston III. All I could do was to forestall that personal doom and pray for a solution. I could conceivably be forced to leave Venezuela only to have to start from square one in another jurisdiction.

Long-term, this would not do. If I was going to achieve my goal of beginning a completely new life as an entirely legitimate businessman, I'd have to acquire a name I could use forever.

Jose told me to go to the DIEX (Direction of Foreign Immigration) office in the center of the city, which was in charge of passports, visas, and other paperwork. He told me to pick up a couple of other passports and titles of cars he had asked for as part of his *gesteria* work too, explaining that those documents should be waiting for pickup.

He had been working on getting a Venezuelan passport for me in a name different from the one on the stolen British passport I had been using. He didn't know that it was stolen and that the name on it wasn't my real name, and he certainly didn't know or suspect that I was a fugitive.

On that note, I had contacted an investigator and asked him to look up the name and passport number on my stolen document, and when I called him back he'd said that the guy it actually belonged to was wanted for murder. So I didn't need much convincing at all when Jose told me to contact the DIEX office, because it was past high time to get another passport.

Jose took me over to an apartment that was filled with men and women who apparently worked in the field of getting people papers. They were a cheerful lot, mostly in their twenties, and a few children were scattered about. The women were unbelievably hot, by the way, but seemed quite apt at handling the technological aspects of the business.

I was a loner on the mission there, asking the questions I thought were of the greatest importance, viewing the blank passports they showed me, going down a list of names of people my own age, and so forth. I posed for passport photos, which a blond bombshell named Exis took with an extremely professional-looking camera. We selected one that would go on the document that was already in the computer; they said that it would be ready in two or three days. It was almost too easy, compared with what I had gone through in Mexico and Colombia.

They were even kind enough to let me stay with them until the process was completed. It turned out that the apartment not only served as a passport-forging facility, they also ran a prostitution ring out of there, which explained why the women looked the way they did.

Picture it—I was a fugitive with a stolen fake passport, but Jose knew nothing about that. I was getting fake documents from a guy who used his license as a *gesteria* to run a fake documents business (along with a prostitution ring), and he was doing exactly that for me, but he thought that the new fake passport was for tax purposes. In other words, I was trying to con a con.

As I waited, I got restless and naturally slipped into my *gringo stupido* mode: without even considering the possible consequences, I decided to take a walk around the neighborhood, about which I knew absolutely nothing. As I strolled up to the first intersection, I noticed the military base on the other side of the street. What a great reference point, a landmark, a location I'd never have any problem finding if I happened to get lost, I thought. I had taken out my note pad and begun writing what I needed to know to explain my location when a car driven by military MPs pulled up in front of me.

As I mentioned, 9/11 was not as big a part of my life as it would have been had I been living in the United States or had the access to the media we have today. Still, that was no excuse for the stupidity of standing in front of a military installation, taking notes, writing down street names and addresses.

The two military policemen approached me. "Excuse me," one of them said. "What are you doing?"

Any damn thing I could have said would have translated to, "I'm a foreigner on a covert mission to spy on the Venezuelan military."

Understand—it's one thing to have to talk your way out of just making notes, but it is altogether different when you face deportation and imprisonment at every interaction with authorities from street cops to national army officials or anyone in between.

My standing was tenuous at best. I didn't know the name of the apartments, didn't know the security code for the front entrance to get back in, and all I knew about whom I was staying with was the name "Exis." So when they asked me where I was staying and to take them there, I could hear the dirt being shoveled onto my coffin.

Relax, I told myself. *All they're going to find when they get into the apartment is a living room table covered with fingerprint cards, passports, and various official documents from the DIEX office. What could go wrong?*

I'm not sure what I was thinking but I led my new friends to the apartment building. Just as the MPs and I reached the main entrance security door two of the Jose's women were leaving the building. They spotted me, and one of the call girls did an immediate and instant 180 spin and went back to the apartment on the only working elevator in the building, which gave her additional time to warn Exis while the MPs and I waited for the elevator to return.

Anita, who was the unofficial manager and madam of the house, answered the door when I rang the doorbell and, to my amazement and relief, was ready to receive her guests in a tidy living room. I'm sure she saw my eyes gravitate to the table, which was now completely cleared. I had to stop myself from rushing over and hugging her.

"Is this man staying here with you?" one of the MPs asked Exis.

"Yes," she said. "His name is Charles, and he's studying at the Los Andes University in Merida."

I had a newspaper and showed them the classified section where I had underlined various cars that I had my eye on and told them that's why I was in Caracas. As they glanced around the apartment they saw a normal family setting—a TV blaring, two kids screaming for candy, and so forth.

Exis quieted the children with small white plastic glasses of lukewarm soda pop, so we could at least communicate without shouting. She even gave some to the MPs, which I thought was a nice touch. Their hopes of making a bust and exposing an international terrorist ring bent on mass destruction of government property and personnel were dashed. They thanked Exis for her hospitality and left.

I made my way into the bathroom and dropped to my knees, thanking God that I had made it out. All I had to do was wait and see how badly my ass would be chewed for having been so stupid as to leave the apartment. I knew it; Exis knew it; the women knew it; everybody knew it.

A few days later, I learned that my passports were ready. Although I knew the names I had selected were of Italian origin, I didn't think to look at them or to memorize them after I picked up the documents at the DIEX office. As I left the office, two plainclothes cops stopped me, but I couldn't tell if this was by design or at random.

I didn't know what to do. I had a fanny pack full of documents, and inside my pants I was wearing a money belt containing my stolen British passport, my Venezuelan *cedula,* and six thousand dollars American in cash. I also had a copy of the classified section of the local paper, with the Jeep Cherokees of interest highlighted in yellow.

"What's your name?" one of them asked.

Gosh, I wish they hadn't asked me that. How the hell would I know what my name is? I had two Venezuelan passports with my picture on them, but I didn't know the names, and a car title, on me.

The cops put me in cuffs and placed me between them for a motorcycle ride to the Interpol's local office. That office was quite a spot, and under any other circumstances I probably would have appreciated it more. The front doors were ten feet high and four feet wide, like medieval dungeon doors. Within one of the doors was a traditionally sized door, with a buzzer. One of the cops buzzed it, and then opened the smaller door—the medieval ones stayed put.

The door opened into a long, dimly lit hallway that we crossed to the other end, which had a door to the reception area. My cops spoke to some official for a moment and were told to bring me into another room, which appeared to be some kind of control room, like the CIA would have in a movie.

As a matter of fact, all I could think of was that I *was* in some kind of a movie. And just as in the movies, they had a world map on the wall with lights on every city and every country in the world that had an Interpol office. I remember noting the seeming lack of presence in Africa, where they had no lights, which made Africa look like the promised land of the moment. Sudan had no lights in it; it would be great to be in Sudan at that moment, I thought.

"What's your name?" one of the officers asked, which meant that the interrogation was officially under way.

I had no choice but to give them, as fact, the name, date of birth, and number from the stolen British passport. The local cops showed the Interpol officers that I had various passports and several car titles.

"What were you doing at DIEX?" he asked.

I told them I was conducting business for Jose, a licensed *gesteria*, and that the PTJ was running the numbers of one particular Cherokee I had my eye on to see if it was a stolen vehicle.

"We don't believe you," he said.

I showed them my classified ads with the highlighted selections of Jeep Cherokees I was using to find a car, which had locations and phone numbers, and I showed them a receipt from the PTJ for a particular Cherokee they were researching for me.

"We still don't believe you," he said. "Who are you?"

I gave them my British passport, which they promptly ran through the Interpol database, by name and not by number, because it didn't come up as a stolen passport. Don't forget, the real owner of the passport was wanted for murder back in Great Britain. The fact that it came up clean had to mean that the investigator who said the man was wanted for murder had been wrong. Everything was fine.

Such being the case, the Interpol office determined that this was a local matter, since all of the documents I was carrying, aside from the British passport that appeared to be legitimately mine, were Venezuelan. I was turned back over to the custody of the Venezuelan plainclothes cops, who drove me back to the local police station.

That day, massive protests were taking place in front of the U.S. Embassy, so the holding cell at the jail was full—well, not quite, because they managed to squeeze me in. I had been stripped of all documents I was carrying as well as my Swiss Army knife and the six thousand bucks in my money belt. The receipt I asked for never materialized.

There were several pieces of cardboard to sleep on in the holding cell, and when it was time to eat they brought out a mound of rice on top of a section of the newspaper. Everyone who could stomach eating like that would take a page of the newspaper from the bottom of the stack and use it as a plate for their serving. We all got plastic bags of Kool-Aid that we drank from straws poked through the top of the bag. After we emptied our bags, we held onto them, because they would serve as our toilets for that night.

After my forty-eight-hour stay, I was transferred, again on motorcycle by local cops, to the military base in Caracas, the base I had been near earlier. One of the officers there was nice enough to let me use his cell phone and even helped me dial the number to Mike and Peter's internet gambling club. It was not listed. Luckily, Mike was at work, and whoever answered directed my call to him.

I explained what had happened and asked him to get in touch with Jose and tell him to get to me as soon as possible. I also asked him to front Jose ten grand American, and that I would pay him back as soon as I got out. If for some reason I didn't get released, I assured him that my partner Nick would pay him. He told me not to worry about it, that he would handle it.

I really sweated that night. Mike had seemed very nonchalant on the phone. I didn't know him that well. What had made me think he was going to give Jose so much cash? I would have done it for him, but that usually does not matter.

In the meantime, I had been fingerprinted. I estimated that I had seventy-two hours, or less, before they figured out who I really was. It was obvious that they were doing their homework.

They took me to the roof, where the blazing sun beat down on a metal chair they had reserved for me. Having come from dark confinement, I was blinded by that light, my sphincter was being fried, and my handcuffs felt as though they were cutting into my wrists. They kept me sitting out there for about an hour before the colonel appeared. He was a tall, handsome man with a thick mustache. His uniform fit him well. Though he was about to ruin my life, I kind of liked him. "You aren't the man on the passport," he said.

"Yes, I am, sir," I said.

He shook his head. "You are wanted on drug charges, and you stay in gay hotels. Do you deny this?"

"I most definitely do *not* stay in gay hotels!" I said.

He let out a slight laugh. "What about the rest?"

"Yes, yes, I deny that, too!"

Sweat was pouring from my forehead and my hot gringo backside, my heart was pounding, and my mind was racing. I knew that I was on my way back to the States when they were through, but I kept denying everything.

Once they were certain that they had reached a dead end with the interrogation, they palm-printed me before they returned me to the cell. It was the first time I had ever had that happen, and I was beginning to realize that I was in a serious situation. They let me sleep on it, or should I say stare at the ceiling of my cell, and the next day, during an afternoon contemplation of my future, they called my name. I moved to the front of the cell, assuming they were going to move me again. Then, from down the hallway, I heard my name being called once more in the most beautiful voice I had ever heard—it was Jose. The hacks took me to a room where he and his wife greeted me. Their familiarity with the jails was revealed by the fact that they'd brought me a bag with some chicken in it.

Jose was soon negotiating my release with the colonel, who needed to make sure that I wasn't wanted by the British police or by Interpol before he settled on a skimpy bribe, because if I was indeed wanted, the bribe would have to be much larger. The colonel handed his lieutenant a form to take to the British Embassy and instructed him to get it filled out there with a seal and signature to confirm I was clean.

The lieutenant left the office with my *cedula,* which was going to come up clean when the lieutenant had it run through the database. If he had taken the British passport instead, its number would have revealed that it had been stolen, and the doors would have closed shut on me for many years.

All I had to do now, I kept telling myself, was make it out of the building—and I was extremely close to doing exactly that. When the lieutenant reached the embassy, the envoy ran the name and not the number, which came up clean because the *cedula* was not stolen. He returned to the colonel's office with the British Embassy forms that cleared my name, indicating that I had no warrants and was a citizen in good standing.

This shed an entirely different light on my situation. The colonel told Jose that he needed a vacation for him and his wife that, coincidentally, would up costing exactly six thousand dollars American, which I never saw again, as well as two round-trip tickets to Merida.

I found out about all of that later. All I knew at the time was that Jose had arrived and was now telling me that it was all over, that I could leave with him. Thanks to one of his contacts, I was able to get the record of my arrest pulled and destroyed. It was as if it had never happened.

After that fiasco I was scared stiff, scared straight, and terrified of even staying in Venezuela. Jose kept telling me that I could relax, that it was over, but he didn't know I was a fugitive to begin with, and if he had, he might not have answered my distress call in the first place.

My immediate business obligation was to receive new clients who were bound for the luxury townhouses, which Nick couldn't do because he was, at long last, in Australia with his family after many months in Venezuela. The resort had the potential to turn into a lucrative enterprise, and I loved running the business, but that scrape with the authorities had stripped me of all my enthusiasm. Luck like I'd just experienced never lasts, and I felt that every moment in Venezuela was tempting fate.

So I had to tell Nick that I needed to leave the business and the country as soon as was humanly possible, without even greeting the incoming guests—which would require him to immediately break off his long-awaited visit with his wife and children. And I'd have to pull it off without telling Nick that I was a fugitive, which would make it much harder for him to believe that one little scrape with the cops that'd worked out fine could scare me into another existence.

Nick was a great guy, very savvy, and had had his share of scrapes with the law and with *banditos*, and he insisted that what I'd been through was just part of doing business in South America, and he was right. I was not going to tell him that I had already used my get-out-of-jail-free card and simply could not stay where confrontations with authorities were so commonplace.

Over the phone, I apologized for breaking up his visit and for causing his premature trip halfway around the planet to come to a screeching halt, having only my half-truth to rely on as an excuse—I was scared, I was humiliated, and I could not take it. If he had known my situation, he would definitely have understood. As it was, he again accused me of having no balls.

I had been right about the Paradise Vacations being a potential cash cow, but I couldn't stick around. He told me that he was usually a good judge of character, that he had been deceived, that he thought he had a partner who was physically and mentally tough, but that I wasn't strong enough to make it in Latin America.

The excitement of a growing business, international clientele, fun and sun, and vacationing in paradise 365 days per year just wasn't enough for me when it came with risks attached that threatened my future. I told Nick that the business was a hundred percent his.

My plan was to get out of Venezuela, continue to travel, and find a place on this Earth that I could call my home.

The problem was that I could not decide where to go. I had bought a book about Africa, which I was seriously contemplating making a move to. Eventually I decided that I would spend a week in Merida, a city that I had heard good things about and where Exis had told the police I attended college.

10

EMOTIONAL DECISIONS

MERIDA, AT THE FOOT of the snow-capped Andes, which had a likeness to the Grand Tetons of Wyoming, was wonderfully picturesque. It sat at the base of Pico Bolivar, the highest peak in Venezuela, at over sixteen thousand feet. Merida was on the other side of the valley, across the river. Yes, it was a beautiful spot, but one thing I had learned from being on the run was that there were many, many beautiful spots in Latin America not nestled in the country where I had just been arrested and interrogated on a hot tin roof. But that fact did not deter me. *Gringo stupido.*

My second day there, I stopped by the Ocho de Mayo gym for a workout. There, I met a wonderful guy, Coach Kucho, who had been coaching the women's volleyball team in Merida for many years and was a legend in the field. His teams had won various national championships, and he'd been designated as an international referee. Coach Kucho was a great guy, a gem, who was highly respected throughout the athletic community.

The gym was right next to the stadium where the Venezuelan National Women's Volleyball team practiced. Coach Kucho was kind enough to invite me to watch their practice. I did so in awe as those tremendous specimens engaged in sprinting and plyometrics, among other exercises, in preparation for their volleyball practice, which would typically last for three hours after warm-ups. Those women were all business. I had presumed that volleyball was more a hobby than a serious sport. I soon learned that they'd been living in volleyball camps with their trainers and their families, that the sport was basically their lives. And there is no doubt that volleyball is a real sport.

It turned out that I knew one of the women on the team. A few months earlier I had met Donna on the beach in El Yaque. At the time, she had even offered to teach me how to windsurf. . . until her boyfriend strolled up and pulled her away. Still she seemed quite happy to see me, albeit a little confused. During one of their breaks, she introduced me to several of her teammates. Most of them were less than half my age.

I shook hands with four or five, and I tried my best not to come off as a perv. But one of them was so stunning that I practically stammered when I spoke to her. I forget her name now, but believe me, she was one of the hottest women I ever laid eyes on. Pity she had a boyfriend.

Another woman caught my eye, too. Her name was Mary Luz. She was a little taller than me—about five feet eleven. She had black hair and almost black eyes, and an athletic frame that certainly said that she could hold her own. I should have known better.

After the break, the team went out onto the field for a scrimmage. I couldn't take my eyes Mary Luz, in fact thought for sure that I was seeing double of her. It turned out that I was. Her identical twin, Mary Elena, also played on the team. I remember thinking that I should get the hell out of there—don't say goodbye to Coach Kucho, don't wave to Donna, and certainly not to Mary Luz. I thought that the best thing to do was to walk out of that stadium, grab a taxi to the airport, and take the next flight out of Venezuela.

As you can probably figure out by now, I didn't take my own advice.

A week later I was driving to Vigia to meet Mary Luz's family. Vigia was a few hours away by car, down in a hot and humid valley that supported banana plantations and agricultural production. Mary Luz's house had a tin roof, like Edwin's in Turbo, but with fewer holes in it, cinderblock walls, and, much to my surprise, running water and electricity. Despite the guardless fan (typical in Latin American homes), the house was like an oven inside.

Mary Luz's mother, Raquel, was in her early forties. She must have been a stunning woman, but years of poverty and heartbreak had taken their toll, and her face was marked with deep lines. She walked with a slight hunch more typical of a woman double her age. She greeted me warmly and led me across the cracked concrete floor to a metal card table and four rusty folding metal chairs. She even shifted the fan to face me, their guest of honor.

Raquel was a bundle of nerves and no sooner had she sat down than she jumped up; on a whim, or so it seemed, she decided that she would cook a chicken, but like most people in her predicament, you don't buy it until you're going to eat it. So, being the businesswoman that she was and as the sole provider for the family, she called over her next-door neighbor, a short, robust man who kept his hands in his pockets the entire time. For about ten minutes, through a barbed wire fence, they engaged in a spirited negotiation. Apparently they came to an agreement. Raquel ran in the house and grabbed a bottle of bootleg Chanel No. 5 cologne. The neighbor called to his son and returned his house.

Raquel led us to the "patio" (the sidewalk) in front of her house, where she reclined on her *sillon,*[77] which was made of black iron rod and entirely encased in white hollow plastic cord about an eighth of an inch thick. This covering apparently helped make it extremely comfortable, because it would stretch under the weight of its occupant. For the first time since I arrived, Raquel actually looked somewhat relaxed.

"Un momento," she said as she took a deep breath.

A few moments later, the neighbor's son returned with the squawking chicken in one hand and his handlebars in the other, and maneuvered his rickety bike with its bald tires and bent rim to the "patio," where he tossed the chicken to the ground at Raquel's sandal-clad feet. Upon landing, the chicken must have realized that the end was near, because it ceased all communication with us.

But the chicken, which had been delivered like the morning paper and merely been knocked unconscious, after a minute or two resumed screeching and flapping its wings, but its fate was inevitable. Raquel chased the chicken and caught it much faster than Rocky had when he was training for his rematch with Apollo Creed, wrung its neck, quickly and deftly cleaned it, quartered it, and placed it in a large pot.

The cooking would take some time, so Mary Luz and I offered to buy some sodas. We ended up walking around the neighborhood, giving her the opportunity to share some of her family's history with me.

Her father had abandoned her family when she was only five years old, leaving her mother as sole provider for herself and the children. Mary Luz and Mary Elena had to care for Pili, their younger sister by three years, while Raquel scavenged for glass bottles to sell to recyclers as a means of support.

Growing up, their main staple was large, green, freshly stolen *platanos*.[78] When the girls wanted to watch TV, they would walk down the sidewalks of the barrio and see the programs through the barred open windows of their neighbors' shanty homes. Raquel survived by selling fake colognes and perfumes door to door. Eventually, things got better. She recruited some women from the neighborhood, whom she trained to sell beneath her, in a multilevel sort of sales group.

She went on to tell me that her mother had graduated at the top of her high school class in Barranquilla, Colombia, at the age of seventeen.

Since college was out of the question for a woman in her social position at the time, she had crossed the border into Venezuela with an older female friend, who acted as her chaperone. They had been searching for better lives and employment opportunities, as the economic outlook in Colombia was bleak at best. Raquel's family was prodigiously traditional and religious, and she hadn't been allowed to have a boyfriend or leave the humble home without being accompanied by a member of the family—standard procedure for almost all Latin American women of that era.

If they lost their virginity before they were married, they were considered whores and immediately expelled from the family. If they became pregnant, there was literally going to be a "shotgun wedding" if their father and/or brothers could find the culprit. Social norms required that a family maintain its good name and standing in the community, so no single, pregnant woman was ever considered respectable.

When Raquel arrived in Venezuela with her chaperone, they had come upon a small pueblo near El Vigea where, as young women and as foreigners, they had been very vulnerable to exploitation by the local men. In small rural communities everyone knows everyone else, but they had been new blood in town. There, in Vigia, Raquel had met Jorge, a handsome and a well-to-do *finca* owner about thirty years older than she. He'd managed to impress her with tall tales, meals, and promises, eventually putting her up at one of the local hotels.

Once Raquel was in the hotel and Jorge was picking up the tab, he had become very possessive and insisted that she stay in her room and not leave unless he was present, turning her hotel into her personal prison. She'd become pregnant, and this had worsened her situation, for she couldn't return to Colombia and visit such a disgrace on her family. About a month into her pregnancy, her chaperone had gone back home, leaving Raquel alone, pregnant, and outcast, with only Jorge to confide in or even speak to.

Raquel hadn't dared contact her family but believed that her former chaperone had; but nobody had contacted her or come to her rescue, and it was more than ten years before she had again made contact with any of them.

On her own, pregnant with twins she didn't know she had, she had been unable to figure out why her abdomen was expanding so drastically.

After the birth of the identical twin girls, Raquel had agreed to name them after Jorge's favorite two cows, Mary Luz and Mary Elena. Jorge moved her and the girls into a shack of a home in a rural village where they had no running water, sewer, or electricity. After yet another baby, whom they named after another of Jorge's favorite cows, Ester, Raquel had begun to suspect Jorge wasn't truthful to her and soon discovered why she and her daughters were being kept in such conditions—Jorge was already married and had a family.

Raquel had also discovered that Jorge's children were actually older than her, and that she, in fact, was the age of a couple of his grandchildren. She had been crushed, and Jorge wouldn't even acknowledge her as his mistress or the fact that he had a second family, forbidding Raquel and the girls from even using his last name.

Raquel had become pregnant once more and given birth to a fourth, daughter whom they named Pili. That had been when Jorge disappeared from Raquel's life and returned to his first wife and family. It'd also turned out that Jorge ran a thriving business and even owned a *finca*. He'd not only left Raquel, he'd left her as an outcast in a foreign land with four young daughters to care for. In a profoundly desperate situation and an incredibly daunting task, Raquel had done whatever was necessary to keep her family alive and whole.

More than once, she'd visited a fortuneteller to ask what was going to happen to her and her daughters. She had been told that she would, in time, have a good future. The catch was that this would only transpire after many years, after her twin girls were married.

When Raquel's twins were ten years old, it had become apparent that, while they may have looked identical, their personalities could not have been more different. Mary Elena was mechanically inclined. She had built a bicycle from junk parts Raquel brought home, which she found while scavenging for recyclable items like bottles and cans to sell. After finishing the bike, Mary Elena had taken it out for a spin, which caught the attention of a gang of local boys who surrounded her and robbed her of her bike. She had been devastated.

Mary Elena had channeled all of her frustration and anger into her sports, with the goal of tracking down the boys who stole her bike and making them pay for it. When she wasn't playing volleyball, she could be seen running and doing push-ups.

From a very early age, May Elena would play on the all-male sports teams and was a superior athlete to the boys by a large margin. She became a sports star, not only of her village, but also in the surrounding area, where tales of her annihilating even the older boys became legend. Whenever one of the boys felt he was getting emasculated by a girl and try to bully her, he'd learn his lesson the hard way, often on his back, trying to deflect the blows that Mary Elena was throwing at him.

Mary Luz, on the other hand, wanted more to play with dolls and did so at her friend's house, because she had no dolls of her own. She wasn't at all the tomboy Mary Elena was, and instead had dreams of being a beauty queen someday and traveling the world.

One day, when Mary Elena was playing volleyball, a coach from the regional division had happened to be scouting the older kids in town. He could not believe that she was only ten. He'd immediately asked to meet with her mother. They had met at the house. Raquel told me that the coach had sat in the very chair I had been sitting in, and that he'd stayed for over two hours, obviously wanting, not only to get to know Mary Elena, but to ingratiate himself with Raquel, since it would be Raquel and only Raquel who would be making any decisions.

At the meeting, the coach had told Raquel that he wanted to take Mary Elena with him, enroll her in a first-class private school, and train her to be a world-class volleyball player. At first Raquel had not even considered it. She'd cursed at the coach and even hinted that she thought it an indecent proposal. The coach had remained undeterred, coming back every day for a week, and finally convinced Raquel that he was a decent man who would in no way disrespect her daughter.

As noted earlier, Raquel was a smart cookie, and had she been born in the United States, she would probably have been a CEO of a company. She'd certainly used her smarts when she negotiated with the coach. As part of Mary Elena's scholarship she would live with the coach's family while attending school. However, the coach would also have to take Mary Luz, who was older by a few minutes, give her a full scholarship as well, and treat her identically to how her volleyball-playing sister was treated. She explained that, while she may not have been as gifted as her sister, Mary Luz could play the sport well and would certainly excel in her studies and keep her sister company.

The coach had made a few calls and the next day come to the house with a bottle of scotch and a bottle of Gatorade. At the same card table where I sat that day, they had toasted the girls futures.

The village's education system could not compare to the teaching at the private school, so the coach had brought in the tutors necessary to bring them up to speed so they could resume their education in the new surroundings. They'd steadily progressed, studying hard in class, improving their grades, and practicing volleyball every day.

Several long years of this routine had eventually paid huge dividends. Mary Elena would become the star of the Venezuelan Olympic volleyball team, while Mary Luz would be selected to play on the Venezuelan National Team. Both would graduate from college, and Mary Elena would be one of only two women in the graduating class of mechanical engineers. She would return to the university and complete her master's in mechanical engineering. Later, she became a professor at the university and went on to start a very successful company, Todo Frio, which installed commercial air conditioning in large office buildings, government buildings, and schools.

Mary Luz had also graduated from college with a degree in languages, and became a beauty queen and my wife. But that's for later.

IN THE SUMMER OF 2003, I finally settled for an apartment called Residence Alberto, near the Pan American Highway, which went through Merida. I attended a meeting with the owner of the building and a couple of other prospective buyers. At the time it was a seller's market, and virtually all premium housing was sold before it was built. If you didn't buy before building, you ended up waiting in line with everybody else who was looking to buy.

In Venezuela, there was no financing of homes—you paid cash. This was the case regardless of how humble or elegant the home might be, and almost everybody owned their home outright, owing no monthly payments to a lender or property tax, and was required only to pay a sales tax upon the transfer of ownership.

This assured that, upon the loss of a job or in the case of any other financial crisis, people did not experience the stress that living on credit creates, as you see in the States. Nearly all of what people owned in Venezuela was paid in full.

I continued to pick up Mary Luz every night from practice, and soon she was practically living with me. You would think that it would be odd for a beautiful, well-educated star athlete to be dating an American ten years older than she (really twenty: she believed my passport), but almost all the women who majored in the Humanities dated foreigners. It made sense. If they were going to study three or four different languages, they wanted to try them out by traveling the globe.

Her friends started calling me "*Tio*," which means "uncle," I assumed because I was taking them all out to dinner every night and they were being kind. I *was* old, but not quite old enough to be called "*Papi*." But as soon as Mary Luz and I became romantic, she changed my name to "Tito," which is what I went by until I arrived in Miami many years later. The good folks who put me up in Miami had no interest in any of my monikers. But more about that later. For the time being, I was just another foreign guy with a few bucks who was living it up with hot female athletes.

My situation was a bit different. I had already pushed my luck traveling around Latin America. Now I had found a country that I loved, and I was ready to settle down, so to speak, with a woman whom I was definitely falling in love with. I certainly didn't trust her enough to tell her who I really was. To her I was a laid-back real estate developer who was probably living off of his trust fund, pretending that he was looking for business opportunities when all he really wanted to do was bang hot women.

I was dying to introduce Mary Luz to my friends, but that was impossible. She had met Peter and Mike, and while I really liked them and considered them friends, they were *new* friends. Mike thought she was "a nice kid." Peter liked her too but couldn't understand why I wanted to get tied down. And he didn't even know about my situation.

I soon got word that Paul Holt and his wife, Heather, were going to take an extended vacation in Venezuela, and they asked if I would accompany them on a wildlife tour. It happened that Mary Luz had a break coming up, so we planned it around that. I tried to get Paul to join me wind-surfing before we went on the tour, but he wanted nothing to do with it. In fact, he made fun of the fact that I had lost quite a bit of size since I got into the sport. It was a lot easier to get in the air at a 180 pounds than it would have been at 242, the weight that I had ballooned up to when we were powerlifting in prison.

To hell with Paul. I loved the sport. It gave me the same rush that I'd gotten when I raced horses as a kid, and so what if I didn't walk around like Arnold Schwarzenegger anymore. Heather was a pretty good athlete, but she was more content playing beach volleyball than wind-surfing. And Heather was not stupid. She always made sure that she was on Mary Luz's team anytime there was a game. Heather did not like to lose.

They seemed like two peas in a pod. They were obsessed about health and fitness, spending countless hours in the gym, always watching what they ate. I found it rather amusing that Heather was always quick to show off how much she supposedly knew about fitness—she had taken a physical training course in New York. Mary Luz was a former college volleyball star training to compete in wind-surfing competitions. But she just smiled when Heather went on a diatribe about a supplement that she had read about, or a new exercise that she had learned. It was obvious that Mary Luz liked her, and the two women often called each other sister.

We accompanied them on the wildlife tour with Tom, a guide from Arassari Trek to Los Llanos, hoping to spot examples of its abundant wildlife. We were looking for anacondas, ocelots, giant anteaters, armadillos, alligators, and wildlife in general. What we ended up seeing were alligators, several big ones, which eliminated all notions of taking a swim.

We also had a blast catching piranhas, fish with orange bellies and nasty teeth—a delicious dinner. As we ate we heard a host of howler monkeys calling from nearby, and Tom, our guide, said if we wanted pictures we would have to get closer to them. So we climbed about ten feet up the steep riverbank to the plateau where all of the trees stood, where we would find the monkeys.

I reached the top of the bank and looked into the branches of the trees, trying to spot the monkeys. I stood there beside Heather. I was really trying to make her feel welcome. I really liked the young woman, who seemed like the perfect match for my best friend. "Having a good time?" I asked.

"Fabulous," she said. "And I absolutely love Mary Luz. I feel like she's my long-lost Venezuelan sister."

"She thinks the world of you, too," I said.

At that moment Heather stepped on the tail of an alligator that was sleeping at the top of the bank. It wasn't a particularly large alligator, but it wasn't small either, and its violent recoil to free itself from under Heather's foot shocked all of us, but especially her. She screamed at a pitch that sent wildlife of all types and sizes running, swimming, and flying in every direction as if their very lives depended on it.

The alligator, with the footprint on its tail, was more scared than antagonized, so it passed on taking a bite of Heather's foot in favor of jumping into the river in its usual spot, which was blocked by our canoe. Luckily, nobody was in the canoe or they would have had more than just a funny story to tell because the alligator landed right in the canoe that Tom said was unsinkable, though it wasted no time scrambling back out of it and into the river.

Heather was badly shaken. Paul and I couldn't help but laugh, which sent her into a mild rage. I remember being surprised at this reaction. It was not as though she'd been injured. But getting rattled by an alligator might do that to even the kindest of folks. I could tell Paul was embarrassed by her outburst. I did my best to stifle my laughter. I tried to put her outburst out of my mind, and I even apologized. *Gringo stupido.*

Meanwhile, Mary Luz had put her arm around Heather and comforted her. They both shot Paul and me dirty looks.

That morning, Paul and I went for a short walk without our women.

"So what do you think about Mary Luz?" I asked.

"She seems great. But you want me to be honest?"

"Of course," I said.

"What the hell are you thinking?" he asked in a loud whisper. "You're a *fugitive*. You got the *feds* looking for you. Interpol is up your ass, and whoever the hell else, and you're thinking of making nice and settling down to play *house?*"

"I'm in love with her," I said.

Paul paused for a moment and looked at me like I was insane.

"Love is not an option available to someone in your position."

I shrugged.

"Please don't tell me that she knows who you really are," he said.

"No, I didn't tell her."

"Thank God, because the last thing you want to do is start telling a woman what's really up," he said. "I even keep things from Heather, and she's my soulmate." I remember cringing when he said "soulmate." Keep reading, and you will soon realize how ironic this statement was.

"You're the only one that knows my situation," I said.

He chewed on the inside of his cheek. "That's the first thing that I heard you say that makes any sense. My advice to you is to get out of Venezuela and stay under the radar."

"But I like Venezuela," I said.

"You sound like a fool," he said. "What's the difference if it's here or some other third-world country? They're all the same."

We heard the women calling for us and made our way back to camp without another word.

Paul was wrong. I had fallen in love with Mary Luz and her country. I even contemplated moving back to El Yaque. I know it sounds insane, but there was something about that beach that was drawing me back. I wanted to build a life there with Mary Luz. I was going to ride the wave of euphoria for as long as I could.

A FEW MONTHS LATER, I took Mary Luz for vacation in Cancun. She was really jazzed about it, which would be her first trip there and to the Mayan Riviera. The trip was of great value to me also, but a fugitive never really takes a vacation. Every airport was a hazard I had to carefully navigate, every document had to pass the scrutiny of government agents, and every question from the government had to have a logical answer; that's no vacation.

For me it was a business trip—I had business to discuss with Mary Luz. I wanted to tell her the truth and get her to move with me to El

Yaque, where we could build a life together in paradise.

I told Mary Luz in advance that it would be better for me to use a friend's passport because of my tax problems at home, and that many countries require visitor passports to be good for least six months before they expire, and mine was down to only three. I had bought a second stolen passport in Colombia that had a longer validation date.

My life was a constant lie, and it was getting to me. I needed to tell the truth to at least one person. But to succeed as a fugitive, you have to live many lives simultaneously, which most people just can't do. It's like Russian roulette, but each set of falsehoods, each fake life's circumstance, every false name, is tantamount to adding a bullet to the gun, and you're lucky if the only empty cylinder lines up with the hammer. But what do you do when all of the chambers are loaded? It was becoming easier for me to head at any time into a single screw-up that would send me to prison.

Mary Luz and I had been living together for over two and a half years by then, and I swore to myself that this trip would be different—it would make or break our relationship. It was time to tell her everything. But I intended to make it through Customs and enjoy our vacation first.

When I told her about using the friend's passport, she'd said it didn't matter, that she always called me Tito anyway. It may not have mattered to her, but the lies kept cutting away at my heart.

As we ambled toward Customs and Immigration after disembarking, the usual questions began to flood my mind, the biggest one being whether my passport had been flagged as stolen. There were more than a dozen people in line at the checkpoint, children playing and a young couple in love, parents and other travelers. While Mary Luz looked at those children with familial desires, I saw them as an enviable element in a life I couldn't attain. I also wondered how nice it would be to have so few cares or problems.

She smiled at the kissing young couple and waved at the children, her grip on my hand affectionately tightening. She was so innocent, and I was lying to her for a living and felt ashamed for not being able to provide those most basic objects of her desire.

Finally, it was our turn at the gate. The female immigration agent asked Mary Luz for her passport, and then entered the pertinent information into a computer, glancing briefly at her. She stamped the passport with a green-inked entry stamp and handed it back.

When I gave the agent my stolen passport, she performed the same routine. I had prepared my story in the event I encountered close scrutiny, or even the standard questions. More often than not, they would try to trip up a fugitive with questions ordinary travelers can answer without thinking but that pose a problem for somebody hiding from the authorities.

I had discovered that traveling with somebody is better than traveling alone, and that traveling with a group was even better than that, making a person less likely to be singled out. The agent began flipping through my passport, looking for a blank page, while my heart pounded through my ribs. Then she wished us a good day, stamped my passport, and handed it back to me as she pointed toward the exit.

"Let's get the hell out of here," I whispered in Mary Luz's ear.

Now that my heart was beginning to start back up I could finally focus on enjoying the trip.

The tropical breezes blew through the taxi, lifting Mary Luz's hair and wafting her perfume to me. The sea air was wonderful, just as it was in Margarita, but Mary Luz was sampling it as a new sensation unavailable to anyone living inland as she had. Our eyes met, and she smiled and kissed my cheek.

How and why a woman that incredibly beautiful could fall for me is something I will never understand. I immediately laid this thought on the canvas of lies I had painted, forcing me to turn away and look out the taxi window, wondering how I was going to break the news to her about the man she had fallen for. This begged the question: was I really the man she'd fallen for? How could I possibly be, when that man would never do such a thing to her?

We stayed in Cancun for a few days, then moved to the Isla de Mujeres, which is near the coast, only a five-minute boat ride from the mainland. While the island lacked the tourist sector's concrete-and-glass five-star hotels, it also lacked the slobbering hordes of drunken Americans who vomit used cocktails over their hotel balconies to a salsa beat, or so I'd heard.

Our second morning on the island, we were lying down in our hotel room, relaxing when she tapped me on the back to get me to turn over and face her, asking, "Tito, when are we finally going to get married?" It was a question I had dodged many times before, along with questions that led in that direction, but I felt that this time I had to open up and reveal the truth.

I didn't have to cough up blood or convulse in epileptic seizures for her to know that something was wrong. My mouth dried up I saw flashes of light, and my heart started beating out of control. She had been my rock for two years, the one thing I could depend on no matter what, and now I stood to lose her in a moment of truth.

"What's wrong?" she asked, breaking the silence that filled the room.

"There is something I need to tell you, honey." My strength vanished, and doubt flashed through my mind. What if she turned me in? I dug deep within myself for the courage to proceed, and took a deep breath. "Mary Luz," I said, "you know I love you more than life itself. And that's the only reason why I am going to tell you what I am going to tell you. My real name in not Charles. But like you said, you always call me Tito, so it doesn't matter."

"Why did you tell me that your name was Charles?" she asked after a long pause. I could see that her body was tensing up, as if she were expecting to get punched in the stomach.

"I. . .I'm a fugitive. A fugitive on the run from the federal government," I added. "The United States federal government."

She lay still and was silent, eyes closed, and tears began to stream from the corners of her eyes. She said nothing despite my pleading for her to tell me what she was thinking or feeling.

"If we got married now, we would have to submit documents to the local register, then they'd be published in their official paper. Foreign embassies would pick up the vital statistics and that could possibly lead to my arrest," I said. "I would do thirty years in prison. . . Not that it matters, but I did not *do* the crime that they have charged me with." She still said nothing. "I'm still the man you love. I am literally risking my life by telling you these things. But if I didn't, I know that I couldn't go on living this lie. I want to be with you for the rest of my life. There's no way I can do that if I go back to the States."

She remained silent. I hung my head as I rose and left the room to give her some space.

THERE'S NO WAY TO SAY what might have been if she had left me, but fate had a plan, not only to bring us together, but to make us a real team. Looking back, I see that this juncture was a milestone in our relationship. Mary Luz became my hope and my rock, the most certain thing in my life as a fugitive.

I begged Mary Luz to take a chance with me—to move to El Yaque, where we would build a life on the beach. I described to her the wonders of wind surfing, and how she would be a natural for the sport. I explained how I had built a successful business there, and that I was confident that I could do it again, twice as successfully because this time I would have her as my partner.

She listened, but, in the end, she chose Germany.

This was at a point in Mary Luz's studies where she was completing a certain body of work that included instruction in the German language. She won a partial scholarship to study in Germany, but she needed my support during her studies, as well as plane tickets. I probably should have told her that she should stay put and that if she was serious about building a life with me, now was not the time to travel to Europe. But I was still feeling guilty about the bomb I had dropped on her.

And if Mary Luz was going to go study German in Germany, it made sense to me that I should go study *Cubano* in Cuba.

11

BROKEN-HEARTED IN CUBA

ON THE FINAL APPROACH for a landing in Havana, I could see lush green farmland, pastures, and trees, but noticed immediately the absence of traffic on the streets. It resembled what you'd have seen flying into an American Midwest city that was stuck in 1950.

Once inside the airport, I took an escalator down to the first floor to retrieve my bags and could immediately tell that the authorities there were none too friendly. All bags were thoroughly tossed for contraband, which could, I guess, have been pornography CDs or electronic devices.

"Why do you have that radio and that cassette player?" a hard-looking guard asked. This was before the I-pod and the like. If you said that the devices were for personal use, you'd get waved through, but if you had an excessive number of high-tech goodies with you, they would be confiscated, so you could not sell them to the locals. Apparently, the last thing that the Cuban government wanted was for its citizens to get their hands on American goodies.

"I want to listen to music," I said.

"What kind of music?"

"Salsa, of course."

"Where are you staying?" he asked.

I told him I hadn't made formal reservations to stay anyplace in particular, so they directed me to a counter in the airport where I could book a room at a hotel, which gave me an answer to their question. Several agencies had counters to help in such an instance but weren't paid on a commission basis, which I could tell from how uninspired and slow they were in finding me a room, taking my cash, and issuing me a voucher to use once I reached my hotel. My reservation was for the Melia Cobia on the Malecon in downtown Havana, one of the city's top hotels. After displaying my voucher to the authorities, I was waved through to wait in line for a government-approved taxi. You can't knock the hustle.

A short, jolly man approached me. He was driving, not a taxi, but a faded blue Lada automobile, like many that Cubans had acquired from Russia during the Cold War. His wife, who wore a revealing sundress and dark red lipstick, had accompanied him. They were out to make a buck by transporting passengers despite the fact they lacked a license to do so. I saw this as an opportunity for more than the typical cab ride and took him up on his offer to be my driver.

His name was Ernesto, and he led me to a parking lot full of tour buses, where he loaded my luggage into his trunk and me into his back seat. He asked me if he could stop at his place to put more gas in the car.

Once there, he entered the house, and his cousin came out with a quart jar of gas and put it in the tank. It was black market gas that Ernesto purchased at a greatly reduced rate compared to the one at gas stations. Before leaving his house he introduced me to a couple of young neighbor ladies. I also got his phone number and said I would call him when I needed future transportation.

In no time, we were at the Melia Cobia, facing the ocean. The five-star hotel was likely Cuba's finest, with a large open lobby, ceilings three stories high, and escalators to the second floor. It was very nicely kept and had a swimming pool, a health club on parts of both the third and fourth floors, and its own disco and comedy club.

After checking in and unpacking, I crossed the street to take a stroll in the heat and humidity on the Malecon, where I noticed some locals fishing from the seawall and lots of single women. I had not walked thirty feet before one of them asked if I'd like to take her back to the hotel for a few laps. A short distance later, another asked me the same thing.

The Cubans called these women *Jenetes*, and the Malecon was literally loaded with them. I headed back to the hotel and checked my email on the hotel computer. There was just one from Mary Luz, to whom I had not spoken since her first night in Berlin almost a week before. It read:

> *Hi Tito,*
>
> *How are you? I am working hard at the University. I love Berlin. I feel like I lived here in another life. Too bad you can't come here because of your. . . situation. Hope things are good in Cuba and your keeping the house nice.*
>
> *Write back.*
>
> *Xoxo*
> *Mary Luz*

I read it over a couple times. I could not believe how much her English had improved in the two years we had been together. I also couldn't believe that she didn't mention that she missed me. And had that been a *dig* about my situation? I believe it had.

I took a deep breath. *She's been in Berlin for a week and only sent one email with not even a hint of missing me? Not even a thank-you for funding half of her semester?* And what was with this xoxo crap? Had she become so German that she couldn't sign off her letter with Love?

I hit *Reply* and wrote:

> *Dear Mary Luz,*
>
> *I'm glad that things are working out so well in Berlin. What do you think you did in another life in Berlin? I hope the funds that I provided are holding up. I guess you're busy with your studies (only one email and all). My business situation is preventing me from visiting, but you never know, maybe some time it will loosen up, and I'll be able to surprise you. I miss you every minute.*
>
> *LOVE,*
> *Tu Novio,*[79] *Tito*

As soon as I hit reply I dreaded having sent it. How could I have written such a passive-aggressive letter? And how could I be so immature? Mary Luz, twenty years my junior, was handling our long-distance relationship quite well, not to mention the fact that she was dealing with the fact that her boyfriend was a fugitive who had been lying to her for the past two years. And I was getting upset because her emails weren't mushy enough. The power of the pussy. They say that a beautiful woman's pubic hair is strong enough to pull a locomotive.

I walked outside and sat around the pool, feeling sorry for myself. I knew I should get back to Venezuela, but I just couldn't bring myself to go there and face an empty house.

On my fourth day there I dragged myself to *Finca Vigia,* Ernest Hemingway's house, which was located in the suburb of San Francisco de Paula, about ten miles out of Havana. I figured I might as well see what all the fuss was about, since Hemingway's mug was plastered everywhere I looked.

I remember reading *The Old Man and the Sea* in high school but I didn't know much about the man they called Papa. From what I could gather from our tour guide, Hemingway bought the property in 1940 and used it as his home away from home until his suicide in 1961. He seemed to love Cuba; at least that's what the Cubans said. One thing is for sure—Papa was drunk a good deal of the time. And the way things were going, I was tempted to break yet another rule and drown myself in alcohol. But I knew that would be tantamount to calling the feds and telling them where I was hiding. No, I had to stick it out sober, no matter what pain I was going through.

About a week into my Cuban excursion I received a second email from Mary Luz:

> *Hi Tito,*
>
> *I hope your doing well. School is great. I'm learning a lot. I blew out my knee, so I won't be playing for the team. I think it may be a blessing. It leaves more time for Berlin.*
>
> *Too bad you can't come. Hope your having fun in Cuba.*
>
> *LOOOOOOOOOOVE,*
> *Mary Luz*

Something stank, my suspicions were killing me, and I did something that I am only a very little proud of. I sat up the entire night at the hotel computer, trying to hack into her email account. It took me six hours of trying hundreds of passwords. Then I got it: VOLEIBOLCHICA.[80]

I discovered that she had some correspondence with a guy from Belgium, and over the next few days I could see the establishment of a relationship that exceeded the casual. She denied it when I confronted her, but she had no clue that I was reading her emails to and from the guy. I called her, which I shouldn't have done: I was pretty sure the hotel phones were tapped. Perhaps they might hear something that the Cuban government could find useful to trade to the Americans? But it didn't matter—she never came to her dorm phone. I didn't want to confront her by email, because then she would realize I had gotten into her email accounts, and she'd shut me down. Luckily, whoever picked up the phone in the hallway of her dorm building said that she was not there.

As irresponsible as the phone call had been, it was nothing compared to my next series of moves. I had been breaking rule after rule on the *Don't Do* list. So why stop then?

I walked out into the middle of the main drag, which I had been avoiding because of its density of *Jenetes*. Two could play this game, Volleyball Girl. Within ten minutes I had found the woman of my dreams: tall, dark, and fit. She had a carefree smile and. . . wait! She also looked a lot like you-know-who.

I arranged a deal, took her by the hand, and walked back to my hotel. Waldo, the doorman, who up until that moment had always greeted me with a warm smile and stories about Cuban baseball, met me at the door, arms crossed.

"*Como esta*."

He shook his head and said a few things to my date—something to the effect that she should have known better than to show up there. It turned out that local women were not allowed to enter any hotel in Cuba, under any circumstances. Even bribes wouldn't work. I know because I tried.

I called my old buddy Ernesto, the cabbie, and asked him to pick me up without his wife. He told me where I could find houses with government licenses to rent rooms to foreigners, signified by a green triangle with an "E" in it, either hanging on the outside of the house or in a window. The "E" stood for *Extranjero*, which is Spanish for "foreigner."

I asked him where the rooms closest to my hotel were located, and he led me to an apartment building on the highway side of the Malecon only half a block from my hotel. On the first floor of the boring, gray Soviet-style cement fifteen-story building, we went to a door with the requisite green triangle and knocked.

An attractive woman in her late fifties answered. I told her I was staying at the Melia down the street, but that they wouldn't let me entertain any Cuban women in my room.

"*No problema,*" she said. You gotta love Cubans.

She explained that she and her husband would move out of their bedroom and sleep on the couch so I could entertain. The heat was unbearable, but the apartment had air conditioning and a refrigerator full of Crystal beer, which they sold to neighbors and guests for one dollar a can. When they asked me if I could buy them a couple of beers, I said, "*No problema,*" and though I didn't drink, I bought a round for them and their neighbors with a ten-dollar bill.

They told me a little about how things were in Cuba and said they rented a room for fifteen dollars a day and paid a hundred a month for the government license to do so. Depending on where you were located, this fee might be less or more than what they were paying. The city was a high-traffic area, so the license cost more than the one they sold to landlords in the countryside.

The average Cuban was making twelve to fourteen dollars per month. With this in mind, it's obvious that to pay the hundred, they'd have to keep the room occupied. Doctors made fourteen a month, too. They carried black bags to identify themselves as doctors, and if you saw one standing on the street you were supposed to give them a ride if they needed one.

A truck with a large trailer, which they called the *Camello,*[81] was a free municipal mode of transportation for getting around the city for those who weren't hitchhiking. Car owners, such as Ernesto, were a rarity. I saw old bicycles, some of which had a one-horsepower two-cycle engine mounted over the rear tire that turned a belt to drive the back wheel.

After spending some quality time with the landlords and the neighbors, I tried, as delicately as possible, to explain that I would only be using the room when I was with a woman, and that the rest of the time I would be staying at my hotel. *No problema.*

I paid her a hundred bucks American and told her to keep the room ready for me for a week. I wasn't sure when I would show up, but I wanted to know that, whenever I popped in, it would be ready for me. She assured me that it would.

I went back out on the prowl—that is, after I trolled Mary Luz's emails. She had even begun telling our friends back in Venezuela about the Belgian guy. I wrote her a very casual email asking how she was. She responded almost immediately—fine, and so forth.

I stormed out of the hotel even more determined to hook up with someone. I maintain that it's very unfair to call these women prostitutes or hookers. The degree of poverty and confinement under which they lived often forced them to take money for sex. I really believe that, if they had been born in Los Angeles or New York, they would very likely have worked all week at a legit job but still hung out with guys that they met at bars, and, if they liked the guy, might have had sex with him. I got it—the shortage of money made them attach a fee to what they otherwise might do for free. Am I trying to justify prostitution? Probably. But that does not mean that I do not believe what I am saying.

As I strolled down the street, I encountered a thirty-year-old man dressed in a T-shirt, jeans, and tennis shoes with holes in them. He was accompanied by a young, light-skinned girl in shorts and a pink blouse.

"*Buenas noches,*" he said.

"*Buenas noches,*" I replied.

"Are you from Miami?" he asked.

From this minuscule exchange he could tell that I was an American.

How? I too was dressed in an old T-shirt, jeans, and sneakers. The only difference was that my sneakers did not have holes in them; but they were pretty beat-up, nonetheless.

He went on to tell me that the girl, his cousin, was from the outer provinces, had never been to Havana before, and had just divorced her husband, who was a cop. I didn't understand why he felt compelled to tell me this.

His cousin was quite attractive. I suspected that the guy wanted money, so I was quick to tell him that I was broke and was just trying to get back to my room. He said he didn't want any money. He said that he just wanted his cousin to experience having sex with an American. What a sweetheart.

They walked and talked with me over the three blocks back to the apartment. The outer door was like a barred jail door and the second door was wooden, but both had hefty locks. When I had opened both doors he told me that his cousin could come inside with me, which she did immediately. I told him again that I was broke but was assured that the experience would be good for his cousin.

I figured that they must have been desperate for cash. I told him to wait outside, because I didn't want to set myself up to get rolled. When I closed the steel-bar door, he looked at me and asked for a dollar. Can you believe a guy pimping out anybody, much less his own cousin, for just a dollar? I paid it.

Her name was Lina. I introduced her to the landlady, who joined us as we sat in the living room, talking and sipping coffee. After a while Lina, and I retired to my upstairs second-floor room, where we spent the night. I would like to report that we made passionate love. But that would be a lie.

The next morning I bought her breakfast at the house, and she went smiling on her way. The breakfast cost more than our date. No, I wasn't that heartless. I gave her some money and made her promise that she would not tell her cousin. She nodded, but I did not believe her.

My date left me in an even deeper state of depression. I couldn't lose Mary Luz. I had lost everything else in my life—my wife and daughter, my family, my property, my country—and I wasn't about to lose her.

I called Ernesto and told him that I needed a ride to the airport. I would buy a ticket to Germany when I got there and then I would surprise Mary Luz and win her back from that punk from Belgium.

But I wasn't done yet with irresponsible moves.

Later that day, Ernesto and his wife picked me up and helped me put my luggage in his car. We weren't two hundred yards from the hotel when I spotted a very pretty, long-legged blonde, in a miniskirt and high heels, walking down the street.

I yelled, "Stop the car!"

Ernesto hit the brakes and pulled over to the curb. This woman was special. Picture Cameron Diaz (who is half-Cuban, by the way) with curves. I asked Ernesto's wife to talk to her and arrange a date.

A few minutes later the woman, Katia, came to the car to thank us for the offer but said she couldn't join us because it was her turn to be in charge of operations at the bio-tech lab where she worked. She went on to say that they manufactured vaccines but now did a lot of sitting around because of the U.S. embargo against Cuba that had cut off the flow of the needed materials.

I could tell that Katia liked me because she stood by the car telling me her life story—some of which I actually understood. She said her father was the mayor of a small town outside Havana and was a full colonel in the Cuban army. She suspected he'd be none too happy about her seeing a foreigner, especially since she had recently been dating a Cuban army officer. I explained that I was on the way to the airport—that I had business in Berlin. But in a highly romantic gesture, I promised that I would postpone my trip if she would meet me for a drink after she got off work.

Katia laughed but said that was impossible. But she said that she was off the following day, and that she would meet me for dinner at the restaurant next to the hotel. I told her that Berlin could wait and I asked her for her number. She promised that she would be there at six. She said goodbye to Ernesto and his wife, kissed me on both cheeks, and walked off. She smelled fantastic.

I told Ernesto to bring me back to the hotel. He and his wife could not believe it. I checked back in. That night I tossed and turned. For the first time since I hit Havana, I was thinking about someone other than Mary Luz. Who knows—if Katia and I hit it off, maybe I would say good riddance to Mary Luz and wish her and the Belgian a nice life.

Yeah, right.

Katia showed up a minute past six, wearing a white sundress, sandals, and no bra. We ate, and she had a couple of glasses of wine. When I asked her to come back to my rented room, I thought she might be offended. Instead she went on a little rant about how ridiculous the rule that forbade locals to enter the hotels was.

We got to my room about nine. A couple of the neighbors, whom I had bought the beers for—two middle-aged women—were sitting outside at a makeshift table.

"Buenos noches," I said.

I was expecting a warm greeting. Instead, all I got was a snub. They were more interested in looking Katia up and down. They didn't seem pleased. She shot them an evil look and kissed me on the lips. I led her into the apartment.

I would like to report that we made love like porn stars. Instead I broke down and told her the whole story of what was happening with Mary Luz, the love of my life. Katia proved quite understanding and eventually fell asleep, her head on my chest.

The next morning I woke up and looked out the window to see four Cuban cop cars, with their lights on, surrounding the house. Not good, I thought. There certainly was no escape, especially in broad daylight. I tried to convince myself that they might not even be there for me. There were the two people from the room upstairs, the landlady, Katia, and me in the house.

The cops came in and told the landlady to show them her books. Every time someone rents a room, there has to be a record containing the name on their passport and their country of origin, amount charged for rent, and so forth. She had a license to rent only one room but had a full house and was defrauding the government by pocketing the money.

"What room are you staying in?" the officer in charge asked me as he examined the lady's books.

"The room in the back," I said.

"You have no license to rent out that room," he said to the landlady. "You will have legal complications or may be fined for this."

The officer turned to me and asked, "When was the last time you were in to Cuba?"

The truth was that I'd been there a few times before, but I had used my British passport. "Never," I said. "You must be mistaken."

"No, I am not mistaken. I remember you."

He began searching room to room until he found Katia. When Katia called me Tito, I quickly explained that it was my nickname. On this trip I was using an American passport, so the cops thought she was lying.

They led her into one of the bedrooms and interrogated her while I was sort of arrested and taken downtown in a police car caravan, along with my luggage. I wasn't handcuffed, and the police were congenial. All of the ones in the caravan were uniformed and clean-cut. Those in my car seemed intrigued that they were actually sitting with an American. One of them even asked me if I was a Yankees fan.

In the cop shop, they sat me down on one of three metal chairs, accompanied by one officer and my luggage, which sat on the floor beside me. Images and notions of dark, cold, smelly prison cells were running roughshod over my fugitive instinct to remain calm. The tourist zones didn't have power outages but the domestic housing areas and prisons did. Would they drive bamboo shoots under my fingernails or just smash my big toes with a mallet? As a victim of American anti-Cuban propaganda, I had no pleasant thoughts. I knew that I was in serious trouble.

I had been seated in semi-darkness for about twenty minutes when two plain-clothed detectives appeared and took me into a back room, where they asked me why I had come to Cuba using different passports with different names. They said they had run my American passport through their database and found only my current entry.

"I'm an American, and I was afraid from the news and propaganda that I wouldn't be treated well in Cuba," I said. "My roommate is a travel agent, and he let me use his British passport to visit Cuba."

"What's the name and number on the British passport you were using?" they asked.

Being interrogated can make it difficult to accurately recall such information, but I had used that passport for some time and had all of the information in it etched on my brain, and I disclosed it to them. They ran the information through their database at the airport and it checked out.

"Do you have the British passport with you?" They wanted to check the picture.

"No," I said.

But they had all the relevant dates and numbers from immigration forms I'd filled out to get the visa under which I had entered Cuba in the first place. When these matched, they wanted a copy of the passport, because, as they told me, they felt that the agents at the airport should be more careful when checking the pictures on the documents. The more they talked about that British passport, the more I was certain that I was done.

"I'm a fugitive, and I bought the damn thing in Colombia." Is hon-

esty really the best policy? Relax if you're innocent, but if you're guilty, then lie your ass off.

"I had brain surgery recently, and I can't quite remember the details," I told them.

I showed them an old six-inch scar from a hair transplant surgery that had never healed properly. This seemed to slow their roll, because they started to look at me very strangely. If I'd had a copy of the British passport with me, or the original, they'd have known immediately that it was my photo. Apparently, though, they hadn't run the number, or they'd have been alerted that it had been stolen years before. That's really what saved me.

Their focus shifted to the lapse in security involving my repeated presence in Cuba using different passports. That tourists could pass through Immigration and Customs on borrowed passports spoke very poorly of their security measures. I tried my best to explain that I was apolitical, and that, from what I had witnessed, the folks in Cuba seemed to be pretty damn happy, so the government must have doing something right.

One thing I found amusing was that, of all the countries I entered illegally, the country that went the farthest out of its way to investigate, examine, and verify a passport's authenticity was Cuba. They also seemed extremely professional. This glitch in their system drove them into a frenzy to tighten up their procedures. They asked me how similar I was physically to my roommate, the travel agent, from whom I had borrowed the British passport. They really needed a copy of the passport so they could check the photo.

I figured that, if I vaguely described my appearance and the other guy's as similar, I would see the end of this little encounter. I was right. I could not believe my luck when they told me I was free to go.

After long and steady contemplation I have concluded that the fact Americans were not allowed to travel to Cuba was probably the sticking point. I had figured that, in such an instance, I would at least be kept in a holding cell for a few days. I will bet you that I could not have sold that story about why I'd entered and left a country, under different identities with different passports, in any other country in the world.

The angle that probably served me best was the tale of being afraid of entering Cuba as an American for fear of being mistreated, as one would be led to believe when watching American news. But my cojones honestly weren't as big in recent weeks as they had been. Fear of life in a Cuban prison as a purported spy will do that.

I desperately wanted to go to Berlin and confront Mary Luz, but even I was not that stupid. Traveling to Europe with a stolen British passport a year after 9/11 would be suicide. I should have gone back to El Yaque and rebuilt my life. But I decided, instead, that I needed a change—a change of appearance, that is.

12

THE CHASE IS ON

THE FIRST THING I REMEMBER after regaining consciousness is that my eyes were swollen shut. "I can't see! I can't see! I'm *blind!"* I shouted. Everything was black, and when I touched my face and neck, I felt nothing; everything above my collarbones was numb. All I could think about was how insane I had to have been to allow this sort of thing to happen, and over something as trivial as a facelift. Granted, I hadn't had it done out of vanity, but to increase my chances of staying out of prison. If I was going to travel to Germany, I had to do everything I could to try to avoid getting caught.

What felt like a week was actually only two days in bed in a Mexico City hospital, waiting for my sight to return and listening to the nurses' jokes in Spanish about me. I couldn't understand what they were saying, but what else was there to joke about—not to mention that the word *gringo* kept popping up. My surgeon, however, spoke excellent English and, after a careful and gentle examination of his work, assured me that everything was normal, including the dramatic swelling in my face and eyes. On the third day, I was still wrapped up in gauze but began to see slivers of light.

The second thing that went through my mind was my money. I had left nine thousand dollars American in my shorts, and I had to admit that I had been pleasantly surprised that it was there when I checked. I gladly paid the hospital bill and graciously tipped the nurses who had been so kind to me during my stay. In my experience, the negative impression many Americans have, and perpetuate, about the Mexican health care system and its professionals is deeply flawed.

Although my face was still pretty numb and my neck entirely black and blue, I returned to Maria Rosa and Manny's home to recuperate after five days in the hospital. While I indeed looked like a car-crash victim, I was confident that I'd be pleased with the results.

When my recovery was nearly complete, I had been planning to go back to El Yaque. I could not explain the lure of that beach, but I really believed that I could make something great there. Maria Rosa suggested that I stay in Mexico until I was completely healed, but I was afraid that, if I waited any longer, it would be too late. I had documents, a new hairline, and a new face. All I had to do was go to Germany and get my girl back.

REMEMBER WHEN I SAID that the only way I was going to back to the United States would be in a box? About seven years into my run, I went back, in a Boeing 747. About forty-five minutes into my flight, I was reading a guidebook on Germany when an announcement came on to the effect that we had to make a landing in Miami because we had mechanical issues.

Huh? I asked the stewardess to repeat the announcement. She did so with a smile—that is, after she tried her best not to cringe at the bumps and bruises on my face. I probably should have listened to Maria Rosa. What was I thinking, traveling to Berlin, to win back my girl, looking like Freddy Krueger? What was the worst thing that could happen? She breaks up with me on the spot and goes off with Johan the Belgian. Actually, the worst thing that could happen was that our plane would land in Miami, and the agents, who happened to be the most vigilant in the history of United States travel since 9/11, would figure out that my passport was stolen, and I would get thrown in prison until I'm seventy-eight.

Life is full of choices, and the way I saw it, I had two—either I could hijack the plane and get them to drop me off in Mexico, or I could land in Miami. I seriously considered both options but luckily kept my head.

Although I had the urge to visit the rest room, I thought a return trip would pique the curiosity of the flight crew, and the last thing I needed was to give them a reason to single me out to the swarms of government functionaries who were performing military exercises and anti-terrorism drills at each and every turnstile, drinking fountain, candy machine, gift shop, urinal, toilet, metal detector, restaurant, and cocktail lounge throughout the airport.

I tried to relax. I fought like hell to clear my mind of the worst-case scenarios racing through it. My only chance would come in the form of being permitted to remain on the plane while they attended to whatever mechanical difficulty they needed to fix. (Not that I believed that bullshit anyway.)

I had no such luck. After the plane came to a stop, we were told to disembark and to proceed to Immigration.

I tried to keep my composure and blend in with the crowd, none of whom had to urinate as badly as I did. I wasn't running in place or anything, not yet anyway, and I knew that anyone who took off to use the rest room would raise suspicion. I was in the last group of twenty-five passengers to go through the checkpoint, and when I handed the agent my passport he thumbed through it, glancing up to confirm my picture's authenticity. He stared at my face.

"I was in a car accident," I said. "I went through the windshield."

He nodded. The guy obviously wasn't one for small talk. He found a good place to put the United States' entry stamp. When he slammed it against the passport, I let out the heaviest sigh imaginable.

I was not, however, able to celebrate for long. I still had to clear Customs. I wondered why we had to go through both Customs and Immigration just to go to Germany, and whether the flight had been flagged for some reason. Was I walking into a security net the American authorities had cast? Had somebody blown the whistle on a terrorism plot or drug-smuggling operation? I knew that there was no way my documents could withstand that level of scrutiny.

I also remembered that I had the shaving cream can with the false bottom in my bags, and that it had always passed at checkpoints of every kind, even under X-rays. The way the hundred-dollar bills were rolled up made it appear to be full of shaving cream, but if the agent handled the can and simply tried, even unwittingly, to twist the bottom, he would easily discover the secret compartment with the cache of cash.

I retrieved my bags from the luggage carousel and joined the line at the Customs counter to have them "revised." As I stood there trying to blend in, an Asian man with long dark hair, wearing a black leather jacket, approached me. As he reached me he unzipped his jacket to reveal his U.S. Customs badge on a chain around his neck.

"Follow me," he said.

I must have been flagged by Immigration, and I concluded that, if there was a problem, this was where and when they would address it. They must have been waiting for me to get my bags before singling me out. The guy, and another Customs official, escorted me into a back room, where I was interrogated about where in Mexico I had been, and why I was going to Germany.

I told them about my car accident in Mexico City. I had been a passenger in a professor friend's car. He'd inadvertently swerved, avoiding a drunk who had darted out into the street, and we had gone off the side of the road. The professor was fine; I'd wound up on the hood of the car, with shattered cheekbones and so forth. (Yes, I had thought it out before I left Mexico.)

I was ordered to strip, which is never fun. (It is amazing how small your dick gets in these situations.) As an international fugitive, I had never done drugs, sold drugs, or transported them, and I definitely had none in my possession. Despite that, I could not afford one little slip-up, or I would belong to the United States of America.

They asked me if I knew the reason why I had been pulled from the line. I said, "My face was scaring the children on the flight."

That actually got a laugh from the two of them. The Asian agent told me that the stamps from two drug-source countries in my passport had triggered heightened scrutiny. That could be very useful information to a fugitive. He said that Colombian cocaine and Mexican heroin had been making their way to Europe, so they looked close, found that I had been to a number of South American countries, and determined that I needed to be "revised."

I nodded. "That makes sense," I said.

After the strip search, I was told I was free to go. My bag was then X-rayed and my shaving cream can went undetected. I was free to go—*almost.* Everyone who survives to that point proceeds to a button, which, when pushed, either results in a green light or a red light. If you cause a red light, your bags are searched by hand; if it turns green, you are free to go.

I didn't even make it to the button before I was waved over to a table to open my bags and stand by while my undergarments were held up and laughed at—that's what it felt like, anyhow. Again, my shaving cream can sailed right through.

Then a female agent asked, "Sir, why are there so many stamps in your passport?"

I told her that I was a travel agent and was on a familiarization trip to build my competence.

"Thanks, and have a nice day," said the woman, who happened to look a great deal like my favorite aunt. I had the strongest need to hug her, but I stopped myself and moved along.

"Hey!" the Asian agent called out to me. "What's the name of the travel agency you worked for?"

"International Travel," I said.

I know it's a pretty lame name for a travel agency, but I knew I needed one I could remember even as I was about to piss my pants. I had been ready for that last ploy. I had business cards, a website, and credit cards, which I showed him. He nodded and finally he waved me through.

Let's go back to my *Do Not* List for a moment and take a look at Rule #7: *Do not make emotional decisions.*

Once again, I had ignored it. I'd reasoned that the only way to address the matter of the Belgian was to travel to Germany and see Mary Luz in person. I believed that, if I didn't, I would lose her.

For a moment I was able to forget the image of the castle and lightning strikes that gave birth to the German monster Frankenstein, and my head cleared enough to allow reasonable notions to speak to me—*wake up!* I was on a transatlantic flight to Europe with a stolen British passport, an act so stupid that even standing outside a Venezuelan military base, taking notes, paled in comparison.

Great fugitives are not born; they are made. I had passed the point of no return hours before and only now was contemplating my status under the law. I was so embarrassed. The only thing I could have done that might have been worse would have been to fly directly to England.

Until I made it through the immigration checkpoint at my destination, I was stuck in traffic. Not in the sense of commuting, but in the sense of being on foot in the middle of the freeway with cars and trucks speeding by at seventy to eighty miles an hour. I could get squashed at any time and be whisked off to a foreign jail until America was ready to receive me and imprison me for my remaining years.

Airline food never tasted so good. Was it my last meal as a free man? Eat up, *gringo stupido,* I told myself.

As the plane touched down and began to taxi toward the landing gate, I really wanted to use the rest room, but it was the wrong time to do that, because that's what smugglers do. *I'm no smuggler!* I thought loudly enough for anyone in the vicinity to hear. Or so I imagined. I may have been a bail jumper who looked as though his face had been bashed in, but I was not a smuggler. As if it made a difference.

During the flight I had purchased some Polo cologne for myself, and a little gift for Mary Luz, which the stewardess delivered to my seat. I was reminded of my first visit to Mary Luz's home, when I met her mother, who traded fake cologne for our meal, and who had subsisted by selling the same in a makeshift multilevel company. Now, I was on an international flight buying cologne to smell good for her daughter, a student in a foreign university. I tried to keep these pleasant thoughts in my mind.

After disembarking and passing through the jet way, I approached German Immigration and Customs. I knew from experience that, when they scanned my passport and entered the data into the database of known terrorists, smugglers, and the like, I would be arrested if my passport had been reported as stolen.

How the hell do you blend in when you look like a car-crash survivor? I had to stay calm, go with the flow, no matter how badly I wanted to hang back to delay the inevitable: the government agents, the computer database, the cameras scanning the crowd for suspicious behavior, anything out of the ordinary. The key was act and look cool, even as my insides were boiling.

After what felt like eternity, I was finally face to face with the tall blond German bastard who seemed to have walked off the set of *The Damne*[82] and who could shatter my existence by merely doing his job.

"Passport, please," he said.

I could do that. I handed him my stolen British booklet; he merely glanced at the picture and went straight to the stamps. I hoped that he had not noticed the ones from Colombia because they might cause another "red flag" event.

"Why are you in Germany?" he asked.

"I'm here to check out the language program at the University of Regensburg," I said.

"Are you here to study?" he asked.

"Possibly," I said.

"Aren't you a little old to go to college?"

"It's never too late to learn," I replied. "I've always been interested in the German language and its culture."

What came next was either a smile or a smirk. I hoped it was the former. "What happened to your face?" he asked.

"Car accident," I said. "I went through the windshield."

"I'm sorry to hear that," he said.

He told me that I did not need a student visa, which is what Mary Luz had obtained, since I was just touring the university, but if I decided to attend classes, I would have to apply for one. Had he determined otherwise, I stood the chance of having to undergo a closer scrutiny of my stolen British passport. The fine young man who, moments earlier, I had referred to as a German bastard, admitted me as a tourist and stamped my passport with an entry stamp next to my Mexican departure stamp from Mexico City. He had not scanned my passport but rather entered my name, or passport information, into the database, which might have averted alarms. He did not hold me up while he waited for a bribe. He merely handed me back my stolen British passport and wished me a good day.

"Yes, sir," I said, almost skipping forward.

My nervous system was a wreck, but I was breathing a sigh of relief. I think that passage of my life would qualify as a near-death experience.

I finally made it to the rest room. When I stood in front of the mirror, I looked at myself. Who was I? I was pushing fifty, and I had risked my freedom by traveling halfway around the world trying to win back the heart of a woman twenty years my junior who was in love with another man. I considered myself a good person, but the truth was that I had lived most of my life either breaking the law or fully entrenched in the gray area. Had I taken so ridiculous a chance in coming to Germany because I was unconsciously trying to get caught?

I splashed water on my face and did my best to clear my head. The more I looked at myself, the more I could not believe that I'd come there looking like I did. *Maria Rosa and Manny call themselves friends?* I grumbled. *Why didn't they shoot me in the calf or something instead of allowing me to travel to Germany looking like this? Probably because they knew that I still would have made the trip.*

From Frankfurt, I took a short flight to Munich, and then I caught a train to Regensburg, in Bavaria, where the university was located. Mary Luz had no clue I was coming to see her.

We had been together for over almost three years, so I was understandably heartbroken. She had only known the Belgian for perhaps three weeks when she was already speaking of love for him, possibly even marriage. As far as I could discern from her emails, she had only seen him in person during that one competition when her team was in Belgium.

All of this was too much for me to absorb or comprehend except for my conclusion that I should not have waited to marry her, and that she'd probably viewed my hesitation as an indication that I didn't think seriously about her, about us, about a commitment. I factored this in with what I knew about her family. Her father had not married her mother, though he fathered four children with her. I also knew that Mary Luz had always craved stability. She probably thought that she had found it with this older, hardworking, wealthy man who treated her like a princess—until that same man told her that he was a fugitive who had been lying to her the entire time they were together.

When she came back to her room she found me sitting on the floor in the hallway outside her room. To say that she was not delighted to see me would be an understatement.

"Why are you here, Tito," she asked, "or whatever your name is today?"

"Why do you think?" I said. " I came to —"

Before I could finish my sentence she grabbed me by the hand and led me inside her room. It soon became obvious that she wished to keep me a secret. In Venezuela, she had been proud to introduce me to her family and to her friends. It wasn't unusual to see a girl with a boyfriend twenty or so years older than she was. In Germany, however, this was an anomaly, perhaps even borderline taboo. She did not introduce me to one person while I was there, as if she did not want people to see that she had an older boyfriend.

"What happened to your face?" she asked.

I was about to give her the car-crash story, to at least gain some sympathy but I caught myself. *No mas* lies when it came to Mary Luz, I had promised myself. I told her that I'd gotten a facelift because I had had some problems in Cuba and thought that it would be prudent to look younger to match the age on the passport. She did not ask how old I really was. I wish she had, because it would have at least meant that she cared.

Then there was the matter of the Belgian. It must have been a hard choice: did she want Johan, the dashing young motorcyclist from Belgium, or the middle-aged international fugitive with the fucked-up face?

I stayed with Mary Luz in her dorm room for a few days and saw how I was nobody the students wanted to socialize with, which was the opposite of the reception I'd gotten from students in Colombia and Venezuela, where I was welcomed. I tried to keep it light with Mary Luz, but she just moped around, saying that she couldn't play tourist with me because she had too much studying to do. I noticed that she didn't do much studying, though. She did a lot of sleeping, in a tight ball, ignoring my affections.

Finally, early one morning, after lying in bed feeling lonelier than I have ever felt in my life, I reached my boiling point. I could not take it anymore. "Honey," I said, "I don't know what's going on with you, but I feel like you don't want me here."

She stirred but didn't say anything.

"I know you're awake," I said. "Stop pretending."

"I want to go to Belgium," she said.

"Why don't you just call your new boyfriend and ask him for money for a ticket?" I said.

". . . Why are you so cruel?" she countered.

At this point I had to take a number of deep breaths and try to maintain my balance. I've never hit a woman in my life, been raised better than that, but I have to admit I would probably have thrown a fit if it hadn't been for the fact that Security, and then the police, would be banging at the door. And that is something that I obviously could not risk. I had risked enough.

"You know what, honey? I'll give you the money for the trip to Belgium. No hard feelings."

She rolled over slowly. "Really?"

"Yes," I said. "I just want you to be happy."

She hugged me and kissed me a few times. Lightly, on the cheek.

The next day, she left for Belgium to see her new boyfriend. I got a hotel room with the intention of visiting some museums, but all I did was lie around the room for a couple of days, dreading the thought of having to deal with flying again. I must have checked my email every hour from the hotel's business center. *Nada.*

On my third day, I did get an interesting email from my old pal Julio. He had just landed in Spain. He was staying at his friend's *finca* right outside Seville. He knew that I was in Germany, so he invited my girlfriend (the one he had been hearing so much about for the past few years) and me to join him for a few days. I wrote back that I would see him the next day without my girlfriend. She was busy getting banged in Belgium.

JULIO AND HIS GIRLFRIEND were staying in his friend's *finca*, which looked like a seventeenth-century castle, though it had actually been built in 1844. The friend was not there, but he had left Julio a staff of several cooks, housekeepers, and butlers, along with an armed security staff and a driver.

We ate delicious food and relaxed in the mineral pool. I don't ever remember seeing Julio so focused. He had brought along a girlfriend from Madrid who didn't talk much.

He quickly figured out that I was having problems with Mary Luz. Instead of pretending nothing was wrong, I broke down and told him how heartbroken I was. I thought for sure that he was going to bust my balls and tell me that there were plenty of fish in the sea or some such lame cliché. Instead, he was quite understanding and actually a soft shoulder to lean on.

After I calmed down, he informed me that he was leaving for Sicily two days later and that his girlfriend was going back to Madrid. He invited me to come to Sicily with him.

"I've got some business there. Big business," he said. "If this deal goes through with the Sicilians, it'll be a game changer. I need a good pilot."

"Thanks, Julio, but you know that I'm retired," I said.

"I know but it doesn't hurt to ask."

I smiled.

"Why don't you come anyway?" he asked. "We'll hang out and see if Sicilian cooking can compare to Colombian. Which I doubt."

"Sicily? That's near Africa, right?"

"Yes," he said, a bit bewildered.

"I was thinking of going to Africa anyway," I said.

He started laughing. *"Africa?"*

"I heard it's nice there," I said. "Not much Interpol."

He laughed again and got up. "I fly on out on Wednesday morning," Julio said. "Let me know if I should get you a ticket."

"I sure will."

Julio's friend had the most sophisticated computer system that I had ever seen. But I guess that's not saying much, considering that I spent most of the technology revolution in Latin America. That night I hopped on it and checked my email. I was actually surprised to see an email from Mary Luz. I pulled it up as fast as I could.

> *Dear Tito,*
>
> *How are you? I miss you. I'm back at University. Things didn't work out with Johan. He is a nice guy, but he's not you. I take my final exams next week, and then I plan to go back to Venezuela. I don't know where you are, but I'll be hear waiting for you. If you left, I hope we can get back to normal life when I come home.*
>
> *I love you the most.*
> *Mary Luz*

The next morning I walked out to the pool, where Julio was getting some sun. His girlfriend was asleep on a float on the opposite end.

"So, *amigo,*" he said. "You looking forward to seeing Sicily?"

"Mary Luz emailed me," I said, avoiding eye contact with him.

"And you're going to go back to Germany?"

I nodded. "I love her," I said.

"I understand," he said. "In theory."

"I'm sorry."

"You have nothing to be sorry about," he said. "If you ever need a job, or a friend, you know where to find me."

He got up and we hugged. That was the last time that I ever saw the best friend I ever made while on the lam.

BEFORE I WENT TO THE HOTEL, I stopped at a jewelry store and purchased a one-and-a-half-carat diamond engagement ring. It was half the size of the diamond pinkie ring I had sported when I was twenty-four and living large in Vegas. But now I was a different person. Though my funds were dwindling, I knew that somehow I would find a way to earn a living. And as tempting as Julio's offer was, there was no way that I was going to do anything illegal.

I had not called Mary Luz. When I got to her dorm room, she wasn't there, so I waited out in the hallway for about forty-five minutes, just as I had a week earlier. I was sure that my presence got her fellow students gossiping. When she arrived she did a double-take. I stood up, and she flew into my arms.

We made our way into her room, and she threw me onto the bed and started undressing. I motioned for her to wait a moment. The expression on her face was priceless—it was if she thought I was going to rebuff her. But her pained expression turned into bliss when I reached into my pocket, got on one knee, and presented her with the ring.

"Will you marry me?" I said.

"There's nothing more that I want, my love," she said. "But I don't want to get you in any trouble."

She was right. Getting married—well, really the act of *applying* to get married—was probably as risky as trying to board a plane from Mexico to Germany with a stolen passport.

"Don't you worry," I said. "I have it all figured out."

If I *was* going to try, there was only one person I trusted to get done without negative consequences.

13

A DESTINATION WEDDING

IN 1985, WHEN I MET Warren "Blackie" Anderson, I was in Boron. Blackie was the Asian connection for the infamous Coronado Company, featured numerous times on CBS's *60 Minutes*. In fact, he was interviewed in prison several times by national news organizations.

Blackie was a born rebel, health nut, and vegetarian. The hacks[83] were clearly jealous of his fame and the influence that he had over other prisoners. They would mess with him in trivial ways like pouring meat gravy onto his mashed potatoes, or commit more serious acts such as shipping him out and shuffling him to fourteen different facilities during his eight-year stay as a guest of the United States government. The BOP[84] refers to this as "diesel therapy."

No matter how often they moved him, Blackie continued to show that he could influence his fellow prisoners, and the BOP would strike back. For example, after initiating a food strike in Tucson's Federal Correctional Institution, Blackie was shipped to the Federal Medical Facility in Springfield, Missouri, where he was placed in a solitary confinement cell for the insane. Many years later, mob boss John Gotti died at the same facility.

I spent a few years in the same unit as Blackie but at opposite ends. He once asked me to bunk with him, but since he was always being harassed and searched by the cops, and forced to submit to UAs,[85] I declined. It was better to be his friend from afar than actually live with him.

We spent hundreds of hours walking and talking, lifting weights, and hanging out together. He did most of the talking while I listened to hundreds of adventure tales about travel and mischief in so many countries that I couldn't keep count. Listening to them, I became infatuated with travel and vowed to do the same, to see the world if I ever had the opportunity. I thought that I would be doing it under different circumstances.

Blackie also told me his story. He had graduated from a California high school in the 1960s as a hippie kid and started selling pot around the state, eventually moving two hundred pounds of it each week. When he was eighteen, he got busted by the state.

After Blackie's release on bail, he was warned by his attorney that he was going to Folsom State Prison to serve his time, and about how the inmates would be fighting over who was going to make the sweet eighteen-year-old vegetarian surfer his wife. By the time I met him, Blackie had done his fair share of weightlifting, and despite his lean and narrow build he could squat over four hundred pounds in the bucket, which made him world-class for his age and weight. But none of that would have mattered at Folsom.

Blackie weighed the possibilities and his opportunities, and decided against a romantic entanglement in a cellblock, choosing a life on the run instead. After posting bail and paying his attorney, though, he was broke, which meant that he couldn't possibly afford what it would take to leave the States. He talked his connections into fronting him a couple hundred pounds of pot, which he sold very quickly, paid back his debt, and repeated the process a couple more times.

Thereafter, he had two things: enough money to live on for a while, and good credit with his marijuana suppliers. As a vegetarian and overall mellow fellow, he decided to go to India and become enlightened. Before he left, he read the Eden Press pamphlet *The Paper Trip*, which offered detailed instructions for acquiring a dead person's identity.

In the early 1970s, a U.S. passport application was not as thorough as it is today; not even a Social Security number was required. Blackie used a name from an obituary column to obtain a birth certificate, and used that to obtain a state health ID card, which he then used to get a California driver's license. With the license and birth certificate he got a passport under the dead man's name, bought a flight to New Delhi, and left.

Blackie hung out with other foreigners in the southern state of Goa, where he convinced a guru to tutor him on enlightenment. He recounted one experience to me in tremendous detail—the time that he spent more than a solid year sitting below a particular tree each day, focused and meditating intensely on trying to see the wind. (I have to admit it wasn't the most action-packed part of his story, but when you're doing time, you take what you can get.)

After close to two years of direct tutelage under the guru, Blackie became enlightened to the fact that he had exhausted his bankroll on trying to see the wind, and that he needed to raise some capital. This was during the Vietnam War, and there were plenty of American draft dodgers living around the world in places where the United States could not find them, one of which was Kathmandu, the capital of the Hindu Kingdom of Nepal, in an area affectionately dubbed Freak Street.

Upon arrival in Nepal, Blackie had learned from other foreigners that he could buy inexpensive and fantastically potent Nepalese blonde hashish almost anywhere; it was legal. This naturally led to his involvement in a scheme to smuggle hash to the American market.

He had come up with an ingenious plan. He hired a furniture carpenter to build a dog cage with a hidden compartment in the bottom. While the cage was being built, he bought a Lhasa Opso dog. He then stuffed the hidden compartment with Nepalese blonde hashish, sealed it tightly, and drove the dog to New Delhi by land because Nepal was already red-flagged as a drug-smuggling hub. The dog would take Pan Am's China Clipper flight to San Francisco, which went out twice a week.

The small, long-haired dogs had originally been bred as guardian sentinels for the Buddhist monasteries in Tibet and, as an added bonus, could be sold in the States for five hundred bucks each. As an added precaution, Blackie fed the dog some laxatives the night before, which acted as a natural deterrent to overzealous inspectors.

Blackie notified his California connections that the dog was due to arrive, and they would pick up and clean both the cage and the dog, sell the dog, and bag and sell the hash as fast as they could. Blonde hash was brand-new to their customers and it became a smash almost overnight and would sell out as soon as his distributors hit the beaches. The sale of the dog typically netted enough to pay for the shipping and initial cost of the hash, so the trip was about pure profit.

Within two years, Blackie had the operation running so smoothly that he was able to relocate to Thailand, coming back to Nepal once a month to check on the business and collect his sizable cut. He first moved to Bangkok, then to the island of Kai Somoi. Then he visited the northern city of Chang Mai. Through some friends, and using his status as a native English speaker, he managed to meet some Thai citizens at or near the top of the power structure. After some time he began to date a Thai princess, whom he eventually married, which meant he would meet the people at the top, the people in charge, including Thai generals and above.

Blackie's pot and hash suppliers back home wanted him to send them some high-quality Thai pot to complement the blonde hash. To do this, he decided he would enlist the help of some local farmers, so he could control the quality of the product. By actually dictating the variety of marijuana to be grown, and by overseeing the plants from seed to weed, he could remain free of middlemen and pay his farmers far more than they would make off any other crop they might grow. He negotiated deals with village elders, supplied them with very high-quality seed, and paid the farmers well, and this led to the cultivation and production and, ultimately, increased export of better product.

Out of this operation Blackie is credited with having developed Thai sticks, which is a method of packaging the pot by tying the buds to short bamboo sticks from four to eight inches long, in diameters as big as an inch. The sticks were placed in nitrogen vacuum-sealed plastic bags that held ten kilos apiece and kept the product very fresh and tasty. Soon Thai sticks became the rage in California and eventually throughout the country.

At first Blackie was shipping the sticks to the California coast by sailboat, an exceedingly laborious and time-consuming avenue. Then he bought a large yacht and hired some old surfing buddies to man it. There was a pool on the deck to which they added water jets so they could practice surfing and fight boredom while under way.

Then they progressed to using shipping containers they would fill with sticks, sending them to America on commercial cargo ships. But things in the States heated up, and this forced Blackie to negotiate a deal with the Mexican Army through which his containers would go to Mexico, and the army would then deliver them into America for one-third of the action. Under this arrangement, Blackie was left with only a twelfth of the take—which was still around ten million dollars a container.

Sometime later, Blackie and his cohorts started shipping the sticks around Thailand on 707s from the Thai air force, which precluded problems with roadblocks and clandestine landing strips where busts potentially could occur. Then the American authorities decided to launch a major investigation into the Thai pot smuggling ring. When the United States government is really intent on capturing a major trafficker, they turn to Centac, the group above the CIA. When someone gets on Centac's radar, one of two things happens: he either gets prosecuted or assassinated. Centac was Blackie's undoing, and without its help I would probably never have met the marijuana smuggling legend, at least not in prison.

One factor set Blackie apart from the rest of the busted smugglers: he spent most of his time and money outside America, so his assets, which stretched around South America and Asia, remained out of reach despite his having been prosecuted.

Now I was about to visit my old friend for the first time on his offshore turf, outside prison and outside the United States.

I had emailed him about my marriage dilemma, and he'd promised he would help any way he could.

When I landed at the airport in Bali, the lines to pass through Immigration were extremely long and wide, requiring that everyone stand in line for hours. Blackie had instructed me to put a twenty-dollar American bill inside my passport, and to go through the diplomatic line and checkpoint to save time. As a result, Mary Luz and I were whisked through with a thank-you and were quickly on our way.

We caught a taxi to the road running adjacent to Double Six Road to meet Blackie and his wife, Nancy, an accomplished Indonesian model, and their new son Ace. Blackie owned and operated a small resort, restaurant, and gym that a French movie-set designer had developed. It was so spectacular, I had heard that Blackie had rented his entire compound to some rich Arab sheiks for their millennium party for a cool million dollars.

The compound was literally on the beach, and as soon as you left its confines you would be swarmed by hordes of local vendors to the point that you could not sit, lie, or even walk without having to verbally swat at them. I found this a great opportunity to practice my filthy

Spanish slang.

The vast majority of Blackie's clients were foreigners, some of whom were expatriates who lived in Bali. He told me of his discovery of Kuta Beach on the Island of Bali when he visited during a surfing tour of Asia in the 1960s. The several acres he had purchased came with nothing but tropical vegetation, but he'd soon built a house and tennis court and was living well. In subsequent years, the tourism industry had grown and grown, and some major hotel chains had purchased property on both sides of Blackie's acreage; this had served to drive up the value of his own property exponentially.

One of our first nights there, Blackie took Mary Luz and me out to eat at one of the beach-side restaurants. During dinner, we saw a crowd of thirty or forty people chasing a young man down the street and wondered if the crowd was taking the law into its own hands, because I had heard how thieves are treated in Indonesia. Blackie's father, who was also visiting, and I followed to see why the crowd had formed, as it seemed to have stopped on the sidewalk.

When we reached it, we noticed that a couple of men had tree limbs, which they were using to strike the back and body of a thin fifteen-year-old boy; we could hear his ribs cracking as the blows fell. The crowd surrounded him and showed no signs of letting up in the quest to kill this boy, who eventually fell down, at which point they began to kick him. In only several minutes, the beating was over and the boy was dead. A few minutes later, the police arrived in a Datsun pickup. No one from the crowd seemed to be in any sort of hurry to leave. The crowd, and the police, spoke for several minutes, and then, after the crowd dispersed, the police got out of their truck and lifted the boy into the back of it to take him to the morgue, DOA, I assumed. Not once did the police look as though the incident was out of the ordinary for them. It was the price you paid, in Indonesia, for stealing a one-dollar bottle of shampoo.

When Blackie's father and I returned to the restaurant and shared the details of what we had witnessed, Blackie explained that it was simply how thieves are dealt with in Indonesia. As a society or community evolves without exposure to other cultures or methods, certain ideas take hold and evolve into forms of conduct that may seem normal to those who don't know differently. Just as that small and isolated village in Colombia had its burros, or an urban city like Compton had its Crips and Bloods, Indonesia had its own code of justice.

I walked back to the restaurant a little shaken. When I asked Blackie about it, he said that it was the way it went in Indonesia. As I've said, I tried not to pass judgment on the cultures that I interacted with—I had done a good job of not acting like an American who assumed his way of doing things was the word of God. But that doesn't mean that there weren't times when I felt shitty about something that I witnessed.

Blackie and I went for a walk on the beach, just the two of us, and I explained my situation to him and how I was going to lose Mary Luz if I didn't marry her. He promised that he would look into it.

The next day, while working out, he explained that he could in fact get us married right at his estate. His wife would set it up, since she was a native, and she would make sure that none of the documents got into the wrong hands. He asked me if Sunday would work. I said sure, forgetting even to clear it with Mary Luz. Later that day, she stormed into our suite, peeved that I had set the wedding date and the itinerary without even asking her.

"I asked you already, in Germany, and you said yes," I said. "I thought that would be enough."

She did not stay angry, however. In fact, I had never seen her as happy as she was that week. The night before the wedding, she did get a little sad that her sister and mother could not be there, but I explained that we would have some kind of a ceremony back in Venezuela. This cheered her up.

The next morning, Nancy, Blackie's wife, took Mary Luz into their suite, and Blackie and I got ready in mine. A couple of days earlier,

Blackie had called a tailor who fitted Mary Luz and me; the wedding clothes were delivered that morning. I wore a dark brown *beskap*, which looked like a thick shirt. It had no folded collar, and the front part of it was asymmetric, with weird sideways-designed buttons. And get this—I wore a sarong. If my friends in South Dakota could have taken a gander at me, I can only imagine what they would have thought. But Blackie wore one, too—he actually owned one—and as I looked in the mirror I have to admit that I didn't look too bad.

He led me out onto the beach, where about fifty guests had gathered. I found that a bit odd, because the only people I had really gotten to know on the island were Blackie's wife and father. But apparently, when folks get married in Indonesia they invite just about everyone who ever met the couple. I wasn't complaining.

All the guests were dressed in traditional clothing too, and sat in chairs in front of a beautiful arch decorated with an array of brightly colored flowers. To the right of it someone had drawn a ten-by-ten-foot heart in the sand and decorated it too with hundreds of flowers. In the middle of the heart were our names—Mary Luz's and my British one. I got one of the workers to change it to *Tito* for the pictures. No use confusing our friends back in Venezuela.

We stood there in the intense heat and humidity, and Mary Luz kept us waiting. And waiting. I started thinking that maybe she had gotten cold feet. Maybe that Belgian motorcycle guy had emailed her and—I finally got a grip, and after what turned out to have been only eight minutes, my beautiful bride came walking past the guests.

She wore a dark purple *kebaya*, which was made of lace, and she too wore a sarong, but I had to admit that she looked a lot better than I did. Her thick hair was layered and spun into an extravagant ball. She had never looked more beautiful. Keeping with tradition, at least Blackie's tradition, neither one of us wore shoes.

An old Indonesian man read some words that we wrote to each other about loving each other until death or extradition and so forth.

Blackie and his wife served as best man and maid of honor.

After I kissed my bride and we were pronounced husband and wife, the guests all danced and consumed a feast of delicacies. It was an amazing night, and I will forever be grateful to Blackie and his wife. After the wedding, he let us use his most dramatic suite; I cannot even imagine how much it cost.

Finally, we were lying on the bed. I assumed that Mary Luz was content at last, but she surprised me once again. "Honey, how much longer are we going to stay in Bali?" she asked.

"A couple more days," I said. "I can't wait to get us situated in El Yaque. You're going to love it. And after we get going, we'll get your mother to move down there. If anyone deserves that life, it's her."

"Actually, I was wondering where we are going to go for our *honeymoon*," she said without a hint of irony.

I broke out laughing, which, of course, set her off. "Why do you mock me?" she demanded.

"Honey, people come from all over the world to honeymoon *here*," I said. "We have one of the best suites on the whole island. Doesn't this count?"

"I want to go to India," she said, holding back her tears.

"India? Why?"

"Why not? I always wanted to go, and we always go wherever you want to go, and—"

By then she was yelling, and I was afraid that we were going to get a noise complaint. I calmed her down and said that I thought it would be prudent to get back to Venezuela, that I didn't want to take any more risks, considering my circumstances.

"You didn't mind taking risks going to Cuba," she said from the bathroom.

Oh, so *that* was what this was about.

The next morning Blackie asked me if everything was okay—that there had been some talk of fighting coming from our room. I was embarrassed, but he quickly put me at ease. I told him that Mary Luz had an insane desire to go to India.

"That's not a bad idea," he said.

"*What?*" I said. I hadn't exactly told him about my situation—no sense making him an accessory—but he knew that I was trying to travel under the radar, hence my need for his help with my wedding.

"I said it's not a bad idea," he repeated.

"Let's just say that this probably isn't the best time for me to travel any more than I have to."

"I understand," he said. "All I'm saying is that it may look like travelers without an agenda if you were to spend some time in India."

He didn't need to say more. My passport was full of stamps that could raise suspicion.

14

A PASSAGE TO INDIA

WE LEFT FOR MUMBAI on an evening flight, and by the time we had cleared Customs and Immigration it was about 11:30 p.m. All I knew about India was what I had heard from various people in the backpacker information grapevine. The recurring theme among those tales was that you would either love it or hate it, that there was no middle ground.

The arrival terminal was clean and organized, but once we joined the general public we were mobbed by hustling hordes peddling and pitching wares and services of every nature, legitimate and illegitimate alike. Mary Luz and I made our way to a line to wait for a taxi. The line paralleled the curb, and were about thirty people on it. All of the drivers claimed to be running the least-expensive and efficient transportation, but some were unregulated, and we did our best to ignore them. Those hucksters actually tried to grab the luggage right out of our hands in an attempt to coerce us into hiring them.

I have never been a jealous guy. Seriously. Not that I would let anyone disrespect my woman, or any woman for that matter, but I never understood how some men would get angry if another guy glanced at his date, his girlfriend, even his wife. It was the price you had to pay if you dated an attractive woman. But I still could not believe what happened while we waited in line for a taxi. Almost every guy who walked by (except the tourists) looked Mary Luz up and down in such a perverted manner, it would have gotten each one of them kicked out of any reputable strip club. But once again my hands were tied. If I had planted my shin in the crotch of one of these pushy bastards, as I wanted to, I could be certain of having to turn over my ID, however briefly, to the authorities who had to summon the ambulance. And that would have been the beginning of the end.

Eventually, we reached the head of the line and loaded our bags into the trunk of a taxi. It was a Fiat, with the steering wheel on the right. There was no meter. He started to drive off before I even gave him our destination—not a good sign.

"How much is it going to cost to get us to the Sheraton?" I asked.

"About fifteen dollars in rupees," he said.

I knew that was a bit steep, but considering the time of night and how tired we were, I accepted the offer rather than bother with negotiation. As we pulled away from the arrival terminal, I presumed we were headed for the Sheraton Hotel, the five-star establishment where we had reservations.

I could not have been more wrong.

The road was dimly lit and nearly void of traffic. As we sat there waiting to turn onto the roadway, I was startled by a tapping on my window. I instinctively pushed the door lock down with my left elbow.

"Please not to worry. He's my brother in-law and needs a ride home," said the driver. "Is it okay if he rides with us?"

"Fine," I said, as if we had a choice.

We had been driving for about ten minutes, and Mary Luz had already fallen asleep on my chest, when the driver said, "We cannot go to the Sheraton—terrorists have taken over the entire hotel!"

What? We had just been inside an international airport, and we had not heard a word about anything out of the ordinary—especially a terrorist attack. It would have had to happen in the last five minutes, but there was no way to know, since the radio had been removed from the taxi. So there I was, on my honeymoon with my beautiful bride, out on a deserted street in the dead of night with two men wearing matching turbans. I had no cell phone, but I had no reason to panic, our benevolent and kindhearted taxi driver assured me. He was going to come to the rescue.

"My cousin has a hotel, good like the Sheraton but at low cost," said the driver. "No terrorists ever go there."

Even in my state of exhaustion, I was beginning to grasp what was happening. "If you don't have a radio, how do you know the Sheraton's being held by terrorists?" I asked.

He said, "I heard from my company dispatcher to stay away from the Sheraton zone, because the police have barricaded the streets."

I asked him to contact the dispatcher for an update so we could hear the report firsthand. He ignored me. When I repeated that we wanted an update, he told me that he'd ask someone on the street what the latest developments were.

By then, we had awakened Mary Luz. I tried to comfort her and get her to go back to sleep, but she was wide awake. I filled her in.

"So what are we going to do now?" she asked.

"Your husband wants to waste time asking people what is happening at the Sheraton," said the driver, "so I am accommodating him." What a sweetheart.

I demanded that he call his dispatcher to verify the claims about the Sheraton. He again ignored me. Then I told him to take us to a tourist office, so *we* could call the Sheraton for ourselves.

"All the tourist offices are closed," he said.

At that point I was fuming, and Mary Luz massaged my shoulder to try to calm me down.

"Then take us to a public phone so we can call the Sheraton!" I said.

"There are no public phones available," he said.

"But we paid for the hotel in *advance*," Mary Luz said sweetly. "And it's our *honeymoon*."

"Very good," the driver said. "The hotel that I am going to bring you to is very romantic."

"He's running a scam," I said.

"I am *not* running a scam," he insisted. "I am keeping you out of danger. As you know, many people dislike America, and since many Americans stay at the Sheraton, that is why it is under attack."

The driver then backed the taxi up while turning the car to face in the direction from which we had just come. As he stepped on the gas he began a conversation with his brother-in-law. If this had happened during daylight hours, I would have forced him to pull over, taken his keys, unloaded our luggage myself, and then waited for another taxi. But to try that in the dark on a deserted street would only have served to invite robbery as we tried to find another ride. The driver himself might very well have been the one to summon the thieves. In Latin America this is called a "takeout kidnapping," but it usually entails being taken from ATM to ATM to withdraw funds from your account. In Mumbai, apparently, it was to make you patronize the hotel that paid commissions to the taxi drivers.

Mary Luz got me to calm down. I told her that the hotel had better be a showstopper. We were tired, sweaty, physically and mentally exhausted, and infuriated—all things a shower and good night's sleep could fix.

After another forty-five minutes we finally reached the hotel—not that we would ever have guessed the square cement building actually took in guests. Nonetheless, we were grateful to be there. We got out of the cab at the hotel entrance while the driver went to ring the buzzer beside the steel security door to wake the manager. I had feared he might quickly hop into the car and drive away with our luggage as his commission, so I had taken his keys to ensure an amicable conclusion to our interaction.

While the driver was summoning the manager—who, when awakened, had been sleeping on a filthy mattress behind the steel security door—I moved our luggage next to the building. The cab ride had lasted somewhere in the neighborhood of two hours, and it was now nearing three in the morning. We had no idea where in Mumbai we were—or whether we were still *in* Mumbai.

I looked at Mary Luz. I wanted to say that it was all her fault, that we could have been back in Margarita, lying in a cabana, watching the sun set into the ocean. I wanted to tell her that she had acted like a spoiled brat demanding that we go on honeymoon, *another* honeymoon—to this godforsaken country of all places. I wanted to tell her that she was lucky that I'd even came back to Germany for her after the stunt she had pulled with the Belgian. I wanted to say a lot of things, but I didn't. I just pulled her close to me and told her that I loved her.

As the steel door opened, the driver began to tell the hotel manager to jack up the price on us for our having been so belligerent, and he demanded a larger-than-usual commission for having burned so much gas to get us to this fleabag squatter camp. None of it was in a language I could understand, mind you, but I would bet that I was not too far off.

I tried to remind myself that things could have been worse—we could have been in the hands of terrorists, in fact. So I stood there and tried to relax and enjoy standing with my new wife and our luggage in the off-blue concrete hotel hallway. I actually smiled, that was, until the driver shouted, "You owe me thirty dollars!"

Mary Luz was ready to go to war, but I gave him the money and sent him on his way.

I turned to the manager. "Please show us to our room," I said.

"I have only one room available to you, but it has two beds," the manager said. "The rest room and bath are down the hallway, and you share it with the other guests. All rooms with private baths are taken."

Of course they are. I knew from my backpacking days that rooms in a hotel like that should have been priced at about five bucks a night.

"If you pay with American currency. For you and your lovely wife . . . sixty dollars," he said with a big smile.

"We'll take it," I said. I thought, with any luck, the terrorists would show up and put me out of my misery.

It was 3:20 a.m. when the manager finally handed us our key and walked us down the hall. When we entered the room, a crazy thought popped into my head: could it be possible that the hotel owners in the Tijuana ghettos actually owned this hotel, too, and kept this baby running just in case someone came up with a Worst Hotel in the World contest, and this spot would assure that actual hotels would not win? Even after all Mary Luz and I had been through that night, the room was so appalling that we actually contemplated calling another taxi.

There were no windows but, as promised, there were two beds—thin, unmatched mattresses, one of which was on the bare floor; the other rested on a crumbling concrete slab.

"Does that thing work?" I asked as I pointed at the decrepit and rusty ceiling fan.

"When its motor has warmed up it should work," said the manager, turning it on.

Why the damn motor was not already warm was beyond me, considering that we were sweating out of every pore on our bodies. The only amenity besides the fan was a flickering twenty-watt light bulb hanging from the ceiling.

Each mattress had a single dingy white transparent sheet folded at its foot. The mattress on the concrete base even had a single, off-colored flat pillow, which turned out to be almost as hard as the concrete base. Normally we would have pushed together the twin mattresses but the concrete slab made that impossible.

"Do you think that we could get another pillow and some towels?" Mary Luz said.

"I have no key to the lock on the room with the linens. I will get a pillow for you at 7:30 a.m., when the person in charge of that comes to the hotel," he said. He held out his hand. "In India, it is customary to tip those of us who work within the service industry."

"I'll be happy to tip you at 7:30 a.m.," I said. "That's when my banker is coming to give me some funds."

"Very good," he said with a smile, and left.

Mary Luz and I did our best to fit onto one of the beds.

When dawn arrived, the fan still had not warmed up. As hot and sweaty as Mary Luz and I were, we decided to avoid the communal shower and get the hell out of there. She managed to talk the manager into letting her use the phone to call the Sheraton. (She did not tell him that she was calling there, or I'm sure the phone would suddenly have stopped working.)

There had been, of course, no terrorist action the previous day. We told the manager that we were checking out. We called the Sheraton and, forty-five minutes later, a car picked us up and we were transported there without incident.

From the time our plane touched down to our arrival at the Sheraton, eight hours had gone by, about the same number as the flight from Bali to Mumbai. We checked in, having to pay for the previous night since we had reserved it, but that was fine, since we preferred not to wait another seven hours to check in at 4:00 p.m. We got to our well-appointed room, which felt like the Four Seasons compared to the dump we had come from. Mary Luz and I made up, made love, and fell asleep until the next morning.

AFTER BREAKFAST, THE CONCIERGE recommended that we walk about ten minutes to the highway. He said that there we would find buses bound for different destinations. He offered to call us a taxi, but after our experience we were trying our best to avoid them. I had, anyhow, always preferred public transportation when traveling, mostly because it gave me the chance to mix with the locals.

At the bus stop, a boy of about twelve was standing in front of three buses, barking out the names of cities we did not recognize. The truth was that we could not understand him. But this did not have a substantial impact on us, because we had no plans or particular destination in mind.

We boarded the bus that was leaving first. We hastily claimed two of the thirty or so broken seats and watched the bus fill up. Not long after the bus got under way, an attendant came down the aisle collecting everyone's fare, which was determined by one's destination.

When it was my turn to pay I asked, "Where does this route end?"

A ride to the final stop would cost me fifteen rupees (about one dollar American); we would have to board another bus to continue on.

The exterior of the bus was painted in vivid colors, mostly red and yellow, like an American carnival bus, in contrast to the interior, which had hand-painted advertisements. The bus had no air conditioning, so we traveled with the windows down, picking up and dropping off passengers as we went.

In many places traffic was a potpourri of India's commercial and private daily life, and this was never more obvious than during the days we spent in Mumbai, India's most-populated city. I am not sure how many people called Mumbai home when we were there, but at the time of this writing it is about twenty million, about two and a half times the size of the five boroughs of New York City.

We witnessed people pushing each other in homemade wheelbarrows, camels pulling wooden carts, folks wearing their Sunday best and riding scooters and motorcycles, wildly overloaded buses and trucks, and elephants and cows all on that two-hour bus ride. It was not pleasant; commercial vehicles had an obvious disregard for air quality and commonly belched plumes of black diesel exhaust into the air.

Speeding trucks of every size transported goods and commodities of all kinds, honking continuously at oncoming traffic in an apparent game of chicken. The trucks were driven like racecars and would dart out into oncoming traffic to pass the car ahead of them or intimidate the oncoming cars in the other lanes, all the while their drivers liberally used their horns, brakes, and leaden feet. Many of the cars would compensate for the recklessness of the truck drivers by letting them cut in front of them to avoid collisions with oncoming traffic when the trucks passed.

The margin of error for all involved in this approach to commuting was minuscule, and I would have guessed that a tremendous number of motorists would not have survived their encounters with careless aggressors. But one of our fellow passengers told Mary Luz and me that the residents of Mumbai have adapted to this style of driving, and that most make it to where they are going in one piece, although accidents do occur.

The fellow went on to say that the fatally injured victims of the mayhem might lie beside the road, or on the road, until such time as they are scraped up with a square shovel and discarded by the agency charged with keeping the highways passable. Meanwhile, all who pass do so more slowly than they would otherwise.

One of the most curious features of Mumbai life we witnessed was what we later called the "median hotels." With only inches to spare, quite often no more than a foot, dozens of people would sleep between lanes of speeding traffic in an obvious tempting of fate. This sort of disregard for their own lives reflected faith in a spirit that survives the death of the body. They truly believed they are putting at risk a meaningless vessel the soul can take or leave on its eternal journey, during which it has had and will have many human incarnations. Death, in this scheme, would occur so quickly that they would feel nothing, as in Russian roulette.

After about an hour and a half on the bus, Mary Luz noticed steam coming from under the warped hood and feared that the radiator might leave us stranded beside the road before we reached the final stop.

The driver pulled over to top off the radiator and let the engine cool down. A couple of minutes later, I noticed four men board the bus. I asked the attendant how much longer we had yet to travel; he said the final destination was still two hours away. This exchange was cumbersome because of the language barrier.

The bus resumed its service. An hour later, the four men who had boarded during the radiator stop stood up, pulled out daggers, and began shouting menacing orders at all of us. We were being robbed. Two of them posted up in the front of the bus, and two stood in the back.

Two of them then started down the aisle with canvas bags. The first to lose their belongings were the driver and the attendant. Then the driver was ordered to continue to drive as if nothing was happening. When my turn came to put my valuables into the canvas bag, I gave him only my cash. He ignored my fanny pack, because that was where my stolen passport and my thousand-dollar ink markers lay.

At the beginning of the trip the attendant had stacked my backpack, which held the rest of my markers, on the roof and covered it with the other luggage, so I felt good about my chances of keeping it intact. The driver was ordered to stop the bus, and the thieves sped away in a waiting pickup truck with just my money, leaving the luggage on the roof entirely unmolested. In light of the fact that the thieves used a yellow *Tata* pickup truck for their escape, I found it curious that they did not use it to carry luggage they could have easily stolen from us, too.

Our fellow passengers started muttering and quickly cursing as soon as the robbers drove off. Was this the fault of the driver? they asked. Should he have told the four men that they couldn't board the bus? Was the driver the mastermind behind the robbery? Had he punctured the radiator to cause the stop in so remote a location as to facilitate the boarding of the four knife-wielding men?

Was the driver the same man who had driven the taxi from the airport when we first arrived in India? I myself wondered. I guess I was just trying to fit in.

I wasn't that angry. I had lost about two hundred dollars American, and Mary Luz about fifty. I was grateful that we were not hurt, and that the four markers and our luggage did not get snatched. The rest of the passengers, however, were as steamed as the radiator. Several of them demanded to speak to the police. They were hell-bent on accusing the driver of complicity in the robbery.

When we reached our next destination, the police were waiting to question us. We could not understand much of what was being said, but they seemed to take what the passengers were saying very seriously. My first objective, however, was to talk the driver into getting my luggage from the roof of the bus, and us getting the hell out of the area. The attendant did, in fact, toss me my backpack, so we could. But he was not quick enough.

Just as we were walking away, a police officer signaled that he wanted to talk to Mary Luz and me, the foreigners. I braced myself for the worst but, actually, was quite surprised. They turned out to be extremely cordial and gave us a ride to our hotel, about thirty minutes away, while they interrogated us in broken English. We did our best to give them our version of the details of the robbery. We both said that we didn't think the driver or the attendant had been in on it. We also asked them what would be the best way to get funds wired from our family—that our money had been stolen.

They finally left us alone at the hotel at around 5:00 p.m. We showered and changed into fresh clothes so we could find a restaurant, fill our stomachs, and forget the day's festivities.

OUR PRIMARY MODE OF TRANSPORTATION as we explored India was the trains, which are very punctual despite the enormous volume of riders. The people of India have to wait in lines that stretch for dozens of meters from the ticket counters, while international tourists and travelers are afforded their own counter, where the lines are typically much shorter.

We tried to get a first-class sleeper but had to settle for a second-class one because the other was sold out.

"How bad can second-class be?" Mary Luz wondered.

I just smiled as we strolled down the length of the train to our section. The floor of our cabin was three feet by six, with three bunks stacked on either side. My bunk was the one on the bottom right, and Mary Luz's the one above it. We were the last cabin occupants to arrive and quickly set about making ourselves somewhat comfortable. I turned to shed my backpack, which placed my butt in the face of one bunkie[86] and struck another bunkie with my pack as I swung it from my shoulder to the floor. It was not my fault—the place was like a phone booth with mattresses. In the process, I had managed to strike or offend each of the cabin's other four occupants. Mary Luz sat on her cot and looked on in horror.

I don't know Hindu from Spanish slang, but I do know sentiments of disgust when I hear them in any language, and those people's venom was definitely directed at us. We tried our best to ignore them, which wasn't easy considering every time I looked away they leered at my new bride. Again, had I not been in my situation, things probably would have gone down a little differently.

"Honey," I said, "I have to use the rest room."

"You do?" she said, horrified at the thought of being left alone with the four of them.

"I'll be right back," I said, loudly and resoundingly.

"I'll come with you," she said.

"You have to watch our stuff."

"But I have to go, too."

"I'll be quick. Then you can go," I said.

I kissed her on the forehead and slipped from the cabin into the crowded aisle to the rest room. When I opened the door to it, I was brutalized by the stench of last week's failed attempts on the part of others to hit the hole in the floor with their sewage. Even the sink was filled with horrors, and dozens of flies were enjoying every moment of it.

I stood in the place with the least shit underfoot and closed the door long enough to pee in the sink, only to see that what went in there leaked out through a crack in the pipe underneath. The lack of privacy alone kept me from peeing instead into the wind between the train cars.

When I returned to the cabin, I shook my head at Mary Luz, who asked, "What's wrong?"

"You can't go in that bathroom," I said.

"Screw it," she said. "I've got to go, and I mean *now!*"

Who was I to argue? She returned thirty seconds later. "It's closed," she said. "There was a piece of paper in the door with words I didn't understand, so I knocked on the door, but nobody answered. Then I opened it up, and a glob of liquid shit come oozing out from beneath the door, almost touching my feet. *Asqueroso!*"[87]

"I'm sorry, honey," I said.

"I don't know what I'm going to do," she said. "The door to the next compartment is locked, and I really have to go."

I took out a plastic water bottle and cut the top off it. In a hurry she sat on her middle bunk and placed the water bottle under her skirt while straddling it.

I lay down on my bunk and covered my face with a towel to bring the number of men leering at her doing her business down to only four. Soon they started to point and laugh at Mary Luz, like a pack of a pack of sophomore classmates at a hazing, knee-slapping and making hand gestures only true curs and vulgarians can muster. I threatened a few of them, but it didn't matter. They could not be embarrassed.

It was shameful but unanimous among the Indians in the growing audience that now included those passers-by in the aisle. In all, more than fifteen lecherous jackals, misogynistic hyenas, motherless children of pornographers one and all, leered and jeered at Mary Luz in her time of desperation. They got what they were unwittingly begging for. Her fortitude, which had been trained in the poorest of barrios and honed on the volleyball court, won out.

"Move into your bunk," she said when she finished.

"Why?" I asked.

I looked in her eyes and saw blood on the moon. "Just move *now!*" she told me, as she reached under her skirt for the container of urine.

"Yes, ma'am."

The mocking got louder, with a couple of our bunkies now standing in the cabin. At the perfect moment, my new bride lifted her plastic toilet and pelted the pervs with the warm, fresh contents of her bladder. She hit the one who had exhibited the most egregious behavior right in his face. They all ran off to find a rest room.

I never loved my wife more than at that moment. The rest of the train trip, no one dared mess with us.

AFTER A COUPLE OF HOT, humid days in New Delhi, we took another train to Vasanari, India's sacred holy city. This time we were able to ride first-class. After we checked into our hotel, we took a boat along the slow-flowing and filthy Ganges, past several ghats,[88] series of steps that lead down to the water. There, rather appropriately given the condition of the river, is where the bodies of the dead are placed to rest at the top of rectangular wooden stacks of boards. Eventually, the bodies are set ablaze; the flames need several hours to consume the corpses of the departed.

Thousands of people, in any given week, make a holy pilgrimage to this site to bathe and pray for the dead, who are cremated in a closed-off area. After cremation, but often before cremation is complete, the doors to this area are opened and the ashes of the departed swept into the river, along with any remaining unconsumed body parts. These human remains join the raw sewage, which provides a robust and intriguing aquatic adventure for the many children who also use the river as their swimming pool.

Two things came to mind. First, the river reminded me of what the River Styx must look like. One of the books that I read in grad school (Geiger Federal Prison) was Dante's *Inferno*. Dante travels through the fifth circle of hell on a boat (probably much like the one we were traveling on) across a toxic black river. The souls of the wrathful and the sullen lie in the river. I looked down at the Ganges, almost expecting one of those bastards to jump up and try to get on our boat.

I also wondered why they didn't have a similar gimmick in Medellín. Wouldn't it have worked well when I lived there? Think about it: they investigated hardly any murders anyway, and they were running out of crypts. It would have been a win-win for them.

When we left our boat, Mary Luz asked if we could find an Internet café. I must have shot her a dirty look, because she explained that she wanted to check on how her mother and sisters were. I knew that, in order for our marriage to work, I had to begin to trust her, and I let my resentment about the Belgian go.

On New Year's Day 2002, we rented a white Ambassador and instructed our turban-sporting Punjabi driver to drive to Agra, so we could see the Taj Mahal and spend a couple of days exploring the city. About the legendary palace, I will say only this: if the Taj Mahal is one of the Seven Wonders of the World, I would not want to see the eighth.

As you may have deduced, I am not a big fan of Indian men, especially in their disrespect of women, particularly foreign women, particularly my wife. For the entire ten days we were in the country, Mary Luz had to endure catcalls, lascivious looks, snickering, inappropriate laughs, and what I assume to be insensitive and disgusting remarks. I did my best to ward off these men without attracting the attention of the police. I had been hoping that she would admit defeat and ask me to cut short our honeymoon and get our real honeymoon started in El Yaque. But my bride was as stubborn as they come. She just grinned and bore the hostility that came her way—until our visit to the Taj Mahal.

The assailant was of average size for Indian males, about five foot six and 145 pounds. He was about thirty years old and soft around the middle. He had jet-black hair and did not wear a turban. Mary Luz and I had just concluded our visit. We were facing up on a stairway in line to enter another attraction, the Red Fort. I was standing behind her, and this guy was beside her. His wife and two kids stood in front of him. Mary Luz, for some reason, had been issued an Indian citizen ticket, which was a different color from the one I had received, which was meant for foreigners. She was holding the ticket in her hand, so the guy may have believed she was native. I could see him staring openly at her ass, and I have to admit I was kind of hoping that he made the next move.

At five-foot-eleven and 125 pounds, she possessed a distinctly athletic build. She could easily have spiked the guy's head into the ground. She may have been a beauty queen, but she'd also played on the Venezuelan National Volleyball Team, one level below its Olympic team. More to the point, she had grown up under conditions that prepared her for much tougher situations than this one. Let's put it this way—I hadn't gotten to touch Mary Luz's ass until she was good and ready, so I doubted very much that she was going to permit this guy to. After a few seconds of panting and drooling—mind you, while he was standing right behind his wife and kids—he grabbed a handful of Mary Luz's behind. Perhaps he didn't sense that I was actually with her, or didn't care. I was about to do something but I caught a glimpse of Mary Luz's face and actually backed up a step. She immediately launched into a tirade. If the man had thought she was Indian, the English that she spewed must have come as a shock. He immediately began backing up the stairs in retreat behind his family.

Having exhausted her vocabulary of English profanity and epithets, Mary Luz switched to the Spanish slang I have so much trouble with, punctuating it unintentionally with spit droplets that made the man blink and wince. Spanish profanity is a masterpiece of linguistics, and so was the slap to the face she managed to land, following it with a flurry of glancing blows to the assailant's chest.

The man's wife may have appeared complacent, standing there with her mouth agape, frozen in amazement, but I was hoping that she was taking mental notes on how to handle her husband from then on.

After a moment, I suggested we forgo the tour of the Red Fort. Mary Luz agreed, but not without giving her attacker a long, menacing stare. He remained behind his wife, looking down at the stairs, his two children clinging to his legs.

Then it was my turn. "Watch this," I said softly to Mary Luz as we turned to leave. I was fairly certain that the assailant had sensed that I might punch him, because he tensed up and covered his cheeks with his hands. Instead, I'd reached out and grabbed a big handful of his fat little ass as hard as I could manage, twisting it to one side. I had hoped that I could leave him with a black-and-blue-mark reminder of the day that a woman had kicked his bigoted ass. As we marched off, I looked back—he was still cowering behind his wife and kids.

When we got outside, Mary Luz turned to me and said, "Tito, can we please go home?"

"Why?" I said. "You're not having a good time?" She playfully hammer-punched me a few times in the chest.

We were on a plane out of India the next day.

15

GO FLY A KITE

IN THE SUMMER OF 2002, the Professional Kite Rider's Association (PKRA) sanctioned El Yaque's first competition, a weeklong event that drew the world's best. Many consider it the event that put El Yaque on the extreme sports map. Superstars Martin Vari and Mark Shinn, and many others, participated. But I would argue that there was no one more responsible for the rise of popularity in the sport in Latin America than my pal Deisy Arvelo.

Venezuela's top model was extremely athletic and in the vanguard of the kite-boarding and wind-surfing scene. Between photo shoots, she would train for extreme sports in El Yaque. Although she first got into wind surfing, she soon switched to kite surfing after seeing how exciting it was.

Deisy's kite-surfing training occurred before its emergence as a popular extreme sport. With her discipline and constant practice, she became the best female kite surfer in Venezuela. Her celebrity as a top model helped to promote the sport. When she wasn't on the water, she was on the beach, sunbathing in one of the more than a hundred bikinis provided by sponsors. We're talking color-coded and labeled plastic file boxes full of bikinis. She was working with the top bathing suit designers and wore only the latest fashions in the best color schemes. Everybody knew that her trips to the training center at the beach were trips to try on and model another yard of dental floss, if you know what I mean, so everyone watched her like a hawk, or a wolf. All you ever had to do to find her was to ask the nearest stranger where she was. She was very outgoing and friendly, and willing to pose with fans for pictures or to sign autographs, even for the occasional drunk. As the owner of a beautiful body and a charming personality, she could likely have succeeded in Venezuelan politics. I was already an avid wind surfer, but once I started hanging out with her and training with some of the sport's best, I never looked back.

Kite-boarding combines elements of snowboarding, wake boarding, sky diving, gymnastics, parasailing, and wind surfing into an incredibly exciting and exhilarating activity to enjoy as a participant or as a spectator. And from what I could see, El Yaque was about to become one of the epicenters of the sport. I knew that I was too old to try to make a profession out of it, but I wanted to be part of it.

Mary Luz, Deisy, and I were having dinner at an open-air Italian bistro in Porlamar[89]. The sun had set, and we were still at our outdoor table when a group of demonstrators, followed by the police, stopped right in front of us. The bistro was located on a street corner at a busy intersection, which made it a very attractive opportunity for the demonstrators to cause disruption. Soon they blocked the street and began throwing rocks as they rolled out old tires to set ablaze.

In response, the police started to fire tear gas canisters into the crowd, and advanced in our direction. The wait staff shouted at us to take cover inside the kitchen to escape the gas. We followed them inside, closed the doors, and sealed off the doorway with towels.

The wait staff remained unbelievably composed. They handed us rags doused with vinegar to breathe through, which I would not have thought to do. The towels under the door did not create a perfect barrier against the gas, but the vinegar acted to lessen the irritation it would otherwise have caused.

In April of that year, opposition leaders had attempted to carry out a coup d'état on President Hugo Chávez, who had been elected in 2000. In fact, Chavez had been ousted from office for forty-seven hours before being restored by a combination of military loyalists and an uprising of the poor.

Born Hugo Rafael Chávez Frías on July 28, 1954, in Sabaneta, Venezuela, Hugo Chávez was the son of schoolteachers. He attended the Venezuelan Academy of Military Sciences, where he graduated in 1975 with a degree in military arts and science. He went on to serve as an officer in an army paratrooper unit. In 1992, he, along with other disaffected members of the military, attempted to overthrow President Carlos Andres Perez. The coup failed, and Chávez spent two years in prison before being pardoned. He ran for president in 1998, campaigning against government corruption and promising economic reforms.

After taking office in 1999, he set out to change the Venezuelan constitution, amending the powers of the congress and judicial system. Under the new constitution, the name of the country was changed to The Bolivarian Republic of Venezuela.

Toward the end of 2002, large pro-Chávez and anti-Chávez marches were taking place, often simultaneously. On December 6, a Portuguese taxi driver killed three and injured twenty-eight at Plaza Altamira. The opposition blamed Chávez. A few days later, the opposition declared the strike to be of indefinite duration, and said that only Chávez's resignation could end it. As shortages of gasoline and later basic foods took hold, the government responded by developing an informal emergency import network with the support of other governments in the region.

Chávez was facing challenges both at home and abroad. He got a reputation for being outspoken and dogmatic throughout his presidency, refusing to hold back any of his opinions or criticisms. He outraged oil executives, church officials, and other world leaders, and was particularly hostile toward the United States government, which, he believed, had been responsible for the failed coup against him. Chávez also objected to the war in Iraq, voicing his belief that the United States had abused its powers by initiating the military effort.

Relations between the United States and Venezuela had been strained from the very beginning of his presidency. After taking office, Chávez had given oil to Cuba and resisted the United States' plans to end narcotics trafficking in nearby Colombia. He also helped guerrilla forces in neighboring countries, and he threatened to stop supplying oil to the United States if there was another attempt to remove him from power. He was no fan of the United States of America, and I was an American, as much I pretended that I was not.

You may think that the last place that an American would want to find himself ringing in the year 2003 was Venezuela. That is, unless that special someone was a fugitive. After some real soul-searching (and a lot of kite-surfing), I had come to the following conclusion: I could not think of many other regimes that would be less likely to hand me over to George Bush and company than Hugo Chavez and his government. Not only that, I loved Venezuela. Traveling around South America and the world, I had been trying to find a place where I could build a new life, settle down with a woman I loved, start a family, and earn an honest living. It had taken me almost nine years, but I'd finally found what I was looking for. And to be honest, air travel in a post-9/11 world was getting to be too risky.

Then there was the money issue. I needed to make a living if I was going to build a life and start a family with Mary Luz. I took the advice of Baron Rothschild, who, when Napoleon was sweeping through Europe, said, "The time to buy is when there's blood in the streets." That sounded like sound advice to me.

As I started to look for potential investments, many folks, like my old buddy Paul Holt, thought I was insane—and Paul wasn't one to run away from risk. "You have to get the hell out of Venezuela," he said. "Chavez is crazy. He'll never let you build a business there. He's a socialist, and he despises Americans."

I barked back, "I'm staying here with Chavez!"

He shook his head in amazement, saying that I would be sorry.

I have to admit that I wasn't upset over what was taking place. As I've said, the more Chavez beefed with the United States, the better it was for me, and I *was* following Baron Rothschild's advice.

A high degree of fear that the government might confiscate all of their holdings or properties ran through the hearts of Venezuelan businessmen and investors, so most people were not buying. Their notion that getting ten cents on the dollar was better than getting nothing was one of which I quickly grew fond. The selling was fueled by riots in a growing revolution and unrest that some people thought might escalate into civil war. Many countries advised their citizens to leave Venezuela and sent national and commercial airliners in to transport remaining countrymen. I had a stolen British passport and wasn't going anywhere.

Here was the way I looked at it: the devaluation of the Bolivar meant that I could buy, for example, three million dollars' worth of deeds for only a million. At the time, no one in his right mind was actually buying property. Folks were selling everything that they had, figuring that it would be better to get something for it than sit and wait for the government to take it. I was not so sure.

There happened to be a piece of land right near the beach on my beloved El Yaque, and I start asking around about it and rather quickly found out who owned it. It took me a few days, but I managed to arrange a meeting with the owner, who had trouble believing that anyone was interested in buying his property. As a result, I was able to acquire that prime piece of oceanfront heaven for about two thousand bucks American.

I realize that this may sound like a ridiculous deal, but Venezuela, at that time, was completely shut down. Foreign investors were frantically pulling money out of the country in suitcases because they believed that Chavez was going to nationalize all the industries. I figured it would be the perfect time to build condominiums that would capitalize on El Yaque's position in extreme sports, and I would sell to Europeans, who I had learned did not grasp (or care about) the political situation in Venezuela. *Gringo stupido?* Not so fast.

I was confident that that I would be at a huge advantage because there were virtually no jobs in the architecture, engineering, or construction fields. I estimated that I would be able to employ the best workers in each of the aforementioned fields and pay them between ten and twenty percent of what I would have had to in normal times. I was wrong—I ended up paying most of them about five percent, and they were grateful to have the work.

Another factor that gave me confidence to move forward with my plan was the fact that my wife was building a pretty good business of her own. Mary Luz's well-honed volleyball skills allowed her to easily hold her own against the guys who played at the beach, which made her very popular; being drop-dead gorgeous didn't hurt, either. She was able to parlay all this attention into a profitable business. She opened a Spanish school, where she had no trouble getting students. In fact, she taught up to ten Spanish classes a day during the week, each of which was fifty to sixty minutes in length. She had such a steady stream of enthusiastic new students that she eventually had to start a waiting list.

One of her clients was Steve Potter, an Englishman in his early thirties who had done very well in real estate in Great Britain. He mentioned that he wanted to buy an apartment in El Yaque and prepaid three hundred and fifty thousand American for one that would be double the size of the other units in the building I was going to erect. And

I had not even broken ground.

I found an engineer, Alejandro Medina, who had already built a couple of high-rise apartment buildings and had experience in constructing multilevel concrete structures. Even though he was a top engineer, he was out of work. When I made him an offer, he almost jumped across the table to shake my hand and accept it. Many weeks later, he admitted that he had thought I was *loco*.

Alejandro ended up becoming the most important person that I hired. As soon as he came aboard, he paid a visit to all of the local vendors and construction supply outlets. He hired a contractor with a crew that worked with steel, and other experts experienced in building with reinforced concrete to pour the foundation and main structure. We built the whole project, five stories, with only one cement mixer that held just ten bags of cement at a time. We would mix the concrete and deliver it to the dump location in a one-cubic-meter cart, and once we were finished with the first floor, we used a winch to hoist the cart, loaded with concrete, to the upper floor where it was needed.

He stressed the importance of keeping the workers happy. We hired a woman to cook our meals, three per day, right at the construction site. As we completed the first floor, the workers moved right into the building. As we finished other floors, they moved their campsite, if you will, up. This saved them housing and transportation costs as well as travel time.

I gave the supervisory job to Mary Luz's mother. She had moved to El Yaque a few months after construction began, and as I had suspected, she quickly became a shrewd manager. She would find and acquire materials, driving forty-five minutes one way to the local city to do the purchasing. She was also in charge of payroll, which was handled on a cash basis. Had we paid the workers by check, we would have had to give them a half day off to go to the bank in the city and stand in line waiting to cash them, and we could not afford such a work stoppage.

When we started, I was living in an apartment block on a dirt road slightly uphill from the site, which I had rented. We hired a night watchman for the site, but a couple of times I went to check on him at 3:00 a.m. and discovered he was gone. When I confronted him, he insisted that he had been there.

I went home and complained to Mary Luz. She came up with a solution. "Put a television in there," she said. "I bet he's dying of boredom."

"Really?" I said.

"Don't you remember my mom telling you about how we used to watch TV through our neighbor's windows?" she said. "People love TV. It makes your life go by fast, which is important if your life isn't going that good."

She was right. I bought him a television, and he never left the premises again when he was supposed to be there. In fact, he often came into work early. Eventually, he asked if he could bring his wife and kids to the job site to watch TV. How could I say no?

We began work on the rooftop swimming pool, which was going to be the center of social activity, like the rooftop pool at Blackie's in Bali.

The edge of the pool would be at the front of the building; for anyone sitting in the pool, it would seem as though the water was flowing over the edge right into the ocean. That rooftop pool had the best ocean view of any of the hotels on the Island of Margarita. And by "ocean" I mean the cavalcade of passers-by who became part of the seascape of everyday life in our paradise. From the shore directly beneath this vantage point, you first had bathing beauties, tan and trim bodies soaking up the sun and fun; secondly, you saw the water-sports enthusiasts who would use the beach as a home base from which they launched their forays onto the sea, speeding along on their windsurfing boards or flying under their kites. You would see the sea birds too that called El Yaque their home and, beyond all that, passenger liners cruise past with the Island de Coche as their backdrop, ten miles in the distance. Luxury travel magazines and travel websites can offer photos, but to actually experience it on a daily basis is reserved for the few who dare to truly enjoy life.

After the El Yaque Club was up and running, I promised myself that I would get into the water every day and kite-surf. I don't know if it was because I had grown up in South Dakota and lived for so many years in Las Vegas, not to mention the ones that I spent in prison, but being in that warm water, and actually finding a sport that was as exciting as horse racing. . . I planned to do it for the rest of my life.

Most of the locals were really welcoming to us. We employed as many people as we could, and we even started setting up scholarships for talented young Venezuelans—getting them equipment and lessons, and sponsoring them in out-of-town competitions.

There were some folks who did not like a bunch of foreigners changing the dynamics of their towns. One guy in particular was less than pleased for a reason that really surprised me. I had managed to lose a kite board while out kiting, and I knew that many lost boards washed up on a beach called El Pilar that lay downwind and down-current from El Yaque that was a small fishing community where few tourists and foreigners ever ventured. El Yaque kite surfers always combed the beach there after losing their boards and spoke with the fishermen who lived there to see if they had picked up any. They also knew that they would probably have to pay a hundred bucks in order to get their five-hundred-dollar board back. Time was of the essence, because there was an unwritten rule that if the owner of the board didn't show up that day, the finder would sell it to somebody else.

I had been forewarned that the Spanish spoken in El Pilar was laced with fishermen's terms and would be impossible for me to understand, so I brought Mary Luz's mother, Raquel, with me. As we drove up to the village (better described as a camp) at about 7:00 a.m. in my white Chevy Blazer, which contrasted vividly with the rusted-out and dilapidated fishermen's cars that they used strictly for going to and from the gas station for boat fuel, we came upon a group of small shacks or huts directly beside the ocean, each with a roof of palm leaves. There were pilings perhaps six inches in diameter driven into the ground, and to these were nailed or tacked a few warped boards, along with oil-stained cardboard walls. All of the huts had dirt floors and makeshift beds, very basic and quite dirty. There were some mattresses, but most of the fishermen seemed to prefer the traditional hammock, next to which they stacked empty beer bottles and cases until trash day, whenever that might have been. I also wondered when laundry day was, because I saw dozens of young children running around in diapers or completely naked.

They had a few small outboard motors too, and some handmade fishing boats, beside the hut nearest the ocean. I strongly suspected that nobody in that camp could read or write, but they clearly had a grasp of how to repair boats and motors, not to mention being able to solve other mechanical and electronic challenges. Imagine if they had had the opportunity to attend school—I bet that Americans would have gotten more worried about Latinos competing with them. Look at how shook-up many Americans get when Latinos come to America to clean their houses and cut their lawns.

We quickly found a woman who appeared to be in charge of the camp. She was about sixty, short, thick, and toothless. She was weathered from sun, wind, and salt spray, and had a couple of deep wrinkles in her forehead that could have doubled as rod holders in a fix. The camp's resident dogs barked wildly at Raquel and me as we approached the woman. I was a little worried that they might attack, but once the woman kicked the leader in the ribs, the rest of them backed off and minded their own business.

Raquel initiated the conversation by asking her if any kite-boards had washed ashore. One of the men brought out a couple of boards, not custom-made, that came from one of the kiting schools in El Yaque.

It soon became clear that my board was not in the camp.

I struck up a conversation with a man who looked as though he was the mayor of the town. I doubt that he was, but he was definitely the alpha male. He, too, had pronounced wrinkles in his forehead but not as severe as the señora's. He stood five-five and weighed at least two hundred pounds. He had a very thick and muscular frame, over which were draped a pair of oil-stained board shorts that spanned the distance between his knobby knees and his navel. His round, protruding brown gut, and the rest of him, offered a prime example of the perils of spending life beneath the glaring tropical sun.

Raquel had to translate most of what he said, and at first I thought that she too was having trouble understanding him. His first comment to me was that the gringos had severely altered and crushed his lifestyle. He explained how he had been fishing all of his life, some forty-four years, but that since the arrival of the gringos, and especially kite-boarders, things had changed. And the change was definitely not for the better.

Raquel turned to leave, but I asked her to ask him to continue. By then my Spanish was pretty good—I had been in Latin America for a decade—but I was still struggling with this man's dialect. He reminded me that, when he was a young man, El Yaque had been a fishing town, but then the gringos had started doing crazy things in the water. He opened his eyes wide and explained that they had not been content to sleep on the beach or even in huts. They'd had the audacity to build houses and hotels, with running water and electricity. And they did not even relax. They spent their days trying to ride on wave boards for which they had paid hundreds of dollars. The stupid bastards kept losing them, and then they would have to come to his village and pay again. At this he laughed deeply and shook his head in amazement.

Then he got into the reason why he was upset. For all of his adult life, he had been able to get by working just one day every six weeks. On that one day, the entire village would work together to string nets with their boats and fish until their boats were full, and the entire village would share in the catch. Afterward, there would be a celebration of the catch that would last for several days. Dancing to the radio under the stars, drinking beer and *aguadiente*, and baby-making in hammocks were the activities of choice.

Only when the village's credit line for the essentials—booze, cooking fuel, gas, and food—got maxed out, and when they faced having to sell their hammocks for beer, would the village again hit the ocean for a day of fishing and do it all again, usually once every six weeks. Whatever fish was left over, they used in barter for other goods. This had gone on for many years, he explained, until people like me started to show up.

It began with the kids in the village who saw foreigners wearing sneakers with little pictures of a basketball player on them. Eventually the kids learned about Michael Jordan himself, and they even wanted clothes with the Jumpman on them—not T-shirts featuring local beer companies that they got by the dozens for a few fish. Being caring parents, the village's adults began to work harder, fishing once every four weeks, so they could actually lay their hands on hard currency that they needed to buy the Jordan gear and other cool athletic clothes.

Soon the wives and the girlfriends got in on the act. They saw, and began to demand, CD players and radios with cassette players in them, so the fishermen had to get to work every three weeks. Eventually, this poor bastard had been forced out of bed once every two weeks to go fishing, just to support his family.

"Lo que sigue?" [90] he cried. It was all because of the gringos.

Though he was winded by the time he finished this rant, he was kind enough to invite us to sit down for a breakfast of an *arepa* with rice, coconut, and fish. I sensed that they went an extra mile to make the meal a nice one to honor us, their guests.

I share this story because I still find it hard to comprehend. Consider the fisherman's time and place for a moment. Health care was free, and the country was socialist. Here was a pocket of adults having children on a beach, totally isolated from the developed areas and ways of their fellow Venezuelans, choosing to stay out of society until such time as they required fuel, food, or manufactured goods. They lived without luxuries, amenities, modern plumbing, or electricity, yet they were fully aware of civilization, which lay only a few miles away from the village.

They lacked any notion of capitalism or entrepreneurship and they were likely illiterate. Their personal motivation extended only so far as to labor one day in forty-two. They were completely satisfied with living in six-week cycles where one day's catch got them by. Their existence mimicked that of the shore-dwelling natives of outlying tropical islands in the South Pacific. The use of outboard engines was, perhaps, the only difference.

Then along came a slight exposure to modern society, and it was enough to disrupt the fabric of daily life. This forced them to up their workload by three hundred percent. On the one hand, you had the adults who were willing to sacrifice in order to please their children, who came to desire stylish clothes and sneakers, and then to please the women, who came to desire technologically advanced entertainment accessories.

The fisherman, and, according to him, all the other fishermen in the town, were livid. They had had everything that they needed for a happy life—huts, warmth, fresh fish and other seafood, hammocks to sleep in, and mattresses to screw on, and they had even found women of the same mind-set.

Catch fish. Drink beer. Make babies. Repeat. Life was pretty damn good until the gringos came.

The man did not complain that the additional fishing depleted the fishery, or that the villagers' health or well-being had been negatively impacted. There was no unique and ancient culture in danger of being erased from the face of the Earth. There was no unique tribal language or dialogue that stood to be lost due to an influx of outsiders, no threat of pollution or disruption from outside activities or commercial enterprise as might happen if, say, a huge mining operation suddenly sprang up or nearby forests were being harvested indiscriminately. The only clash seemed to be between the desire for more on the part of the women and children, and the desire to work less on the part of the men who would rather fornicate than fish.

A part of me envied the simplicity of this village's perception of life and of the outside world. Its fragility, however, could not be overlooked. Aside from health and education, poverty threatened nothing. In a socialist country like Venezuela, free health care made education optional, even silly. The only mistake the fishermen had made was that they'd failed to keep the blinders on the women and kids.

That guy was an exception. Most of the folks who lived in and around El Yaque welcomed us with open arms. In stark contrast to these villagers, who were happy to fish one day in forty-two and to coast the rest of the time, the fishermen in El Yaque were quite pleased to work more and to contract with the kiting and windsurfing schools and equipment rental shops that catered to the growing tourist trade. Fishing soon became a boring occupation to some, and they made the switch to working, as rescue boats for crash victims or aides to wind/kite-surfing instructors, or to providing water taxis for visitors to Margarita.

The idea of harnessing the wind as fuel for locomotion quickly became a passion among the island's youth, many of whom became world-champion wind surfers. I even witnessed some youngsters making such use of a newly paved parking lot on the island, where they rode a disregarded, elongated board to which had attached wheels and a patched-up sail—I guess you would call it a wind skateboard. The El Yaque locals jumped right in to exploit the new tourism industry to enhance their lives and the opportunities of their children, just miles from the village where screwing and drinking beer were the top priorities.

Mary Luz and I had discussed having children, and I was quite excited about the prospect of raising ours there. I am not about to say that the United States is a bad place to raise children, but it seems to me that American parents have become way too protective. Though they believe that they're doing the right thing by protecting kids from possible harm, they are also robbing them of the opportunity to make decisions on their own. They schedule play dates, hire coaches to set up and run their games, and generally prevent them from being creative when it comes to dealing with problems. Most parents would not allow their children to play *futbol* on the street, using garbage cans as goalposts, to explore their neighborhoods, and certainly not to take discarded trash and turn it into a wind skateboard.

Raquel and I said our goodbyes to the fisherman and his wife. Back at my truck I noticed many of the adults were lounging around, and the children playing effortlessly. Raquel hurried me along. "Come on, we have to get back to the club and get ready for lunch."

BY THE BEGINNING OF 2007, the El Yaque Club was running on all cylinders. But I wasn't spending all my days riding a kite—I worked diligently building the El Yaque Club, and I spent much of my time meeting and greeting people, who began to come, not only from Europe, but also from other parts of Latin America. Eventually I was introduced to Captain Arthuro, of the National Guard, who oversaw the airport and our part of the island; and he, in turn, introduced me to Comisario[91] Duran, who was one of the top members of the Venezuelan secret police. Soon they invited me to play in their weekly poker games.

I know what you're thinking—*gringo stupido* is at it again. As an international fugitive, my initial response was of course to run as far away from these guys as humanly possible. But I also realized that they might have become suspicious, or at least offended, if I refused their offer. The truth is that I had become a law-abiding guest of Venezuela (except that I was a fugitive).

During our card games, *Comisario* Duran regaled us with stories of how he was investigating major crimes, helping in the bust of a smuggling ring, negotiating with guerrillas for the release of a kidnapping victim, even helping to catch an international fugitive. I do not have some snappy analogy for this. There I was, an international fugitive myself, listening to a commander of some sort of national law enforcement spill details of how he had captured an international fugitive.

At one such poker game, which was held at the *comisario's* apartment, I met a handsome young man in his early twenties named Carlitos. He didn't play much poker but was an impressive guy, part of a family that had a chain of stores that sold imported gourmet items like chocolates, cheeses, top-brand liquor, cookies, and other goods. In addition, he had a coffee concession at the airport. I hit it off well with him; he was a big fan of the El Yaque Club, and soon he asked me if he could put one of his specialty stores in it.

The locals did not know or much care about the club, because it was mostly an international destination, not really the kind of place where islanders gathered. But Carlitos knew the caliber of clientele that we attracted. He was quite eager to open a store at my location and wanted nothing but a first-class operation, so he and I decided to create a gourmet type 7-Eleven, with an Internet cafe, deli, liquor store with ice, and international phone services. We also decided to build a bar and restaurant next to the store.

Naturally, Carlitos's contacts were young people, and once he told them about the club we got great word-of-mouth mileage from them inside the country. When the club was finished, we secured all of the parking with a large electric gate in our lot, not visible from the road. Each of our regular clients received an electric remote control, which he or she could use to open the gate, and there was a back entry directly into the hotel from the parking lot.

Mary Luz came up with the name we chose for the new gourmet store, the Wind Guru Cafe. Soon we became the social heart of El

Yaque for the young and hip. The mornings were especially popular before the sun became too intense.

One day, Carlitos told me that two Americans were waiting to see me. At first my heart stopped; and then I thought it might be Heather and Paul Holt. I headed to the restaurant, quite tentatively I might add, where I saw two men wolfing down enormous amounts of food. Then it struck me—they were Peter Jacoby and Mike Nichols, who owned the Internet gambling site and had helped me avoid getting into an altercation at that café in Margarita where those guys had tried to con me into paying tabs and the police had been called.

Mike and Peter had established one of the first internet gambling websites, with offices in Costa Rica, which was the capital of internet gambling, and they took turns managing it on a monthly basis. They had grown tired of the weather in San Jose, so they had relocated their business to Margarita. They were the only two American friends that I made the entire time that I was on the run. Of course, I never confided in them about my situation. The only people who knew about it were Julio and his family (and they didn't know that I had relocated to Venezuela), Paul Holt, and Mary Luz. I had vowed that they would be the only ones that I would ever tell. And Mary Luz and Paul had sworn never to tell a soul.

I spent the next couple of days hanging out with those two. I have to admit I did get flashes of homesickness, but they quickly passed. I was living a life beyond my wildest dreams—until a few days later, when I thought for sure that I was going to die.

I had stored some kites below an upside-down Zodiac raft under a large, thatched-palm roof. When I removed them, I noticed a healthy population of mosquitoes and a pool of stagnant water in a part of the boat, in which the mosquitoes were breeding.

A few days later, I felt very achy and became weak and nauseous.

I had just been to the Isle of Coche and eaten some seafood cocktails I'd bought from locals, who were selling them on the beach. They were so good I had returned with the friend who had recommended them, and ate some more. Not long after that, I was walking down the beach and was stricken with immediate diarrhea, the runs, which were so urgent that I had to walk into the ocean and do my business. After being forced to perform this degrading act a couple more times, I decided I had better get back to El Yaque.

When I got home, Mary Luz was in the middle of one of her tutoring sessions. She looked up at me in horror, as if she had seen a ghost. She cut her lesson short and quickly enlisted her mother to take me to a clinic in downtown Porlamar.

The clinic's staff said I should be in the hospital because I was dehydrated and had both hepatitis A and dengue fever.

My second night there, I got some more bad news—I had AIDS. That's what they told me, anyway, in front of Mary Luz's mother, who I thought was going to stick a needle in my heart. Soon she was on the phone with Mary Luz, yelling and screaming. A couple of hours later, Mary Luz arrived in tears and began to scream at me. I could barely move, and I remember thinking it was all a dream.

And it was—sort of. It turned out that my test was a false positive. I cannot explain how relieved we were. While I still thought that I was going to die, I felt some comfort in knowing that it was not going to be from AIDS.

I told Raquel that I very much preferred to stay at home and pay a nurse to attend to me. In Latin America, everything is possible and everything is impossible. As it happened, Raquel's friend, Nurse Josefina, was the one in charge of the government clinic in the zone where El Yaque was situated. I was very fortunate when Josefina herself agreed to provide my care.

Hammock hooks in a home's concrete walls were fairly common in Latin America, and I had some in my living room. We hooked up a hammock and used the extra hook to support the bag with the saline solution that dripped through an IV tube into my arm. Normal SPOG or SPOT readings relative to liver functions are about 250; at 6,000, your liver will shut down. My readings were nearly that high, so I was told that rehydrating was imperative in addition to the IV drip. I was told to drink as much water and beet juice as I could.

My urine was the color of Coca-Cola, and my stool as white as snow. I was constantly swinging from very cold to very hot and sweaty, and would take a cold shower or apply ice and cold wet towels to cool off. This went on for more than a week. Overall, I was laid up for nearly a month. It was the only time in my life I felt I might die.

By February 2007, I was living a life that I could only have dreamed of. I had a successful business in which I entertained and hobnobbed with powerful local government officials, wealthy business people, and the international elite. I had become immersed in a sport that I loved, and I lived in a place that was known as one of its best venues. I was madly in love with my wife, and though we still didn't have children, we certainly tried almost every night. I was a respected member of the community who, seemingly, got along with almost everyone I had come in contact with.

After a huge amount of kite-surfing training, I won the Venezuela National Masters Kite Surfing title. I competed with my friend Lilian Tintori, who won the Venezuelan National Woman's title the same year. She introduced me to Leopoldo Lopez, whom she married a few years later. At the time of this writing, Lopez is a political prisoner serving fourteen years in a Venezuela prison. Upon his release, he may just become the next president of Venezuela.

Life was good. I was still looking over my shoulder ever so often, but I truly felt that I could not be in a better place politically. Hugo Chavez and his "Socialism of the 21st Century" were securely in power. In the 2007 election, he won sixty-three percent of the vote. Chavez had also aligned himself with Fidel Castro and thus further alienated himself from the United States. A year earlier, he had delivered a speech at the United Nations General Assembly in New York damning President George W. Bush, actually calling him "the devil." I figured that there was no way that I was going to get extradited, even if I did get found. At worst, I would have to bribe some official. And anyway, who was going to tell on me? My wife? My best friend? *Gringo stupido.*

16

THE PARTY'S OVER

IN NOVEMBER 2007, I received an email from Paul Holt to tell me that he was in heated, nasty, and bitter divorce proceedings with Heather. She had testified at a deposition in the case and had exposed me in full to the United States Marshals and the FBI. She'd told them that Paul and I were affiliated (*affiliated in what?* I wondered) and that I was living in El Yaque. I had always insisted upon not being photographed, but at a birthday party years earlier, on Margarita, she had managed to take a picture of me, which she had apparently given to the authorities.

Until that time, all the information they had on me was unreliable at best; after the deposition, they knew my whereabouts, my contacts, my appearance, my home and cell phone numbers, and who knows what else.

I was in shock, in total disbelief. Heather had been one of Mary Luz's best friends, and I considered her a good friend of my own. Ever since I started dating Mary Luz, we had spent many days and nights traveling and frolicking with them. They were our best friends. We trusted them, and they trusted us.

I arranged a safe call with Paul to see if it was really true, and he sent me a copy of the deposition to prove that the authorities knew my whereabouts and more or less everything that I was up to. I felt as though I was being punched repeatedly in the stomach as he talked.

I couldn't sleep for two nights. I spent every waking moment combing through my records and documents for any reference to Paul or Heather—receipts for the bills I had been paying for them, staff payroll, and so on. The last thing I wanted to see happen was Paul charged with aiding and abetting.

I had come to realize by then that the worst is often brought out in people when they go through a divorce. He was my best friend, so it was hard for me to not take his side, but I could not imagine what he could have done to drive her to do such a thing. But that was really beside the point. I lay in bed at night racking my brain to figure out if I had done anything that would have warranted the situation I was suddenly in, but I couldn't for the life of me come up with anything. I knew for a fact, and still do, that I had done nothing to harm Heather.

The scariest part was that they had always seemed a happy, loving, adventurous couple. Both were health nuts—he an amateur bodybuilder, she a private trainer. They often trained together in the gym for two hours at a time. Both of them were true hard bodies.

Paul was more than a good provider. He had invested in underpriced real estate, mostly commercial, that he renovated and sold, or sometimes leased. They'd home-schooled their two daughters, so that they could travel around the world, often taking extended vacations in Five-Star resorts.

Paul seemed as well to back his wife in her aspirations. When she decided to get special certification in personal training in New York, he'd paid for it. When she was feeling insecure about her breasts and wanted breast enlargement, he'd paid for the operation in Los Angeles. But when I spoke to Paul on the phone and asked him what had gone wrong, he summed it up quite succinctly: "Once she got her tits and her body, and a lot of clients, it wasn't long before she starting sucking dicks and fucking them."

One of those clients turned out to an attorney—yes, a divorce attorney, with whom she fell in love. Soon they were out for blood. He pumped her for all the information she had on Paul's assets and contacts, which was when my name came out. She left Paul and took their children (two daughters, six and three). Soon she was snorting coke and binge-drinking as if she were back in her notorious college days.

Even as Paul went through this, I still could not figure out why she had turned me in. But it didn't matter. I scoured my records for anything and everything relating to Paul and Heather, destroyed it, and left Venezuela. Paranoia is the fear of a nonexistent threat or enemy. I was not paranoid. I was scared, but not irrational.

I concluded that the smartest thing for me to believe was that I had two days, at the most, before the authorities came to my door or my bedside. When they failed to find me where Heather had said I lived, they would check the airport to watch security footage of me checking in at the ticket counter, which would give them a time and date signature. Once an image was identified, they'd know which flight I had boarded and which name I'd used. Then they'd check the passenger manifests to confirm. My time was running out. I wondered whether the authorities had already given my photograph to the counter help, with instructions to watch out for me.

Before leaving Margarita, I called Carlitos and asked him to get me two cell phones, one for me and one for Mary Luz, so I could talk to her on a clear line. I took the ferry to Puerto La Cruz and caught a bus to Caracas. The taxis at the bus terminal were always the same, which would make it easier for authorities to find the one I'd taken and where I had been dropped off. So I caught a cab to a hotel, where I stayed until the driver had left, then walked down the street and caught another taxi to the house of a friend of mine. I explained my situation vaguely and said I needed to keep moving, so he let me use the telephone to make flight reservations.

At the airport I bought, with a backup passport, a ticket to Costa Rica with a stop in Panama, so I could get off the plane there and proceed overland after going through Immigration. That passport had a name that Paul knew nothing about, which meant Heather didn't either. I figured that, even if they tailed me by discovering my flight, they would think I was in Costa Rica.

Knowing the authorities had my picture, my major concern was the security cameras at the airport and the ferry terminal. Because I suspected that they were waiting in Costa Rica, I disembarked in Panama City and set about getting some help accessing an international communication system.

Having put another country's border between the authorities and me served to greatly diminish my fear of detection. At that point, the authorities had nothing but cold leads to my whereabouts, and I had room to move and plan in obscurity.

When I bolted, I had been about ninety percent done with the construction of the El Yaque Club. I had accounts in escrow and clients living in their new apartments, and I had been planning on securing occupancy permits and filing the condominium by-laws, so I could give the apartment owners their titles. Luckily, Mary Luz had my power of attorney, and was planning to negotiate some deals while I was away.

I had sold roughly one-third of the building and used those proceeds to complete the project, which was now paid for free and clear. This left me two-thirds of the building and the commercial property (the Wind Guru Café and our restaurant, so far) as a net profit. I had just pulled off a multimillion-dollar profit. Not bad for *gringo stupido*. And believe me, that is exactly what most folks thought, considering the political climate in Venezuela at that time. Too bad I couldn't enjoy my success.

My project started a building boom of sorts in El Yaque, and while I was away I was planning my next moves. I remained productively occupied with my homework, schooling, and with working out at the nearby gym.

The change of scenery did serve to calm my nerves, so I set about contacting some people in the know to see if I could uncover information or resources that would help me avoid arrest. I checked with a contact in the Venezuelan Federal Police and asked him to run a search on me to find out what the government's computer had. He told me that there were no Americans wanted in Venezuela, but there were a couple of Colombians, and that he'd give me a heads-up if anything changed. Over the next two weeks I put out some other feelers.

Everyone said the same thing—there was no record of anything to do with an American fugitive.

Interpol did not have a red notice on me, and Venezuela was not in any mood to help the United States, which already, in fact, knew right where I had been living. If a warrant had been issued, I would have known about it before they could act on it, and since there was no extradition treaty between the United States and Venezuela, and given the hostility that Chavez openly exhibited toward Bush and the government, I was pretty confident that I would be safe back in El Yaque. I even thought about asking Venezuela for asylum, since I knew that the United States had refused to turn over Louis Posada,[92] who had won asylum and was living in Miami.

So can you see why I thought that Venezuela would not be likely to hand me over to the United States, when the United States would not hand over Posada? It was around the time George Bush proclaimed, "people who harbor terrorists are also terrorists."

I continued to fool myself into believing that I was justified in going back to El Yaque. The truth was that I missed my wife, my home, and my friends, and I was being told exactly what I wanted to hear, that I could not be in a safer place than Venezuela. I also thought that, because I had never done anything illegal while a fugitive, in Venezuela or elsewhere, the law would protect me from the United States, where I would not likely get a fair trial any more than Posada would.

Even as I write this, I cannot believe how stupid I sound.

IN APRIL, I SNUCK BACK to El Yaque, back to my idyllic life, back to my beautiful wife, back to kite-surfing and working with the local youth. The construction was progressing very well, and I managed to obtain all the necessary occupancy permits and titles for the apartment owners to complete the project.

I had a devoted wife and good friends. I owned a small resort and other holdings. I was living the dream. I missed my family back in the States, especially my mother, who was not getting any younger. I knew that I could not contact her or my brother or sisters, because, even after all those years, I was sure they were still being watched by the feds.

I went on to enjoy my life. I figured that, since the United States was fighting terrorism in two wars, it probably had better things to do than worry about the venom of some deranged woman who was trying to soak her ex-husband for money in a divorce.

Then, one day a few months after I returned, one of the apartment owners told me that he needed a place because he had rented out his apartment to a tenant. Since it was the high season, the club was full.

As he and I strolled through the lobby, I was thinking hard about where I might find him a room when I suddenly noticed a conspicuous anomaly in paradise. Seated at the tables in front of the Wind Guru Cafe were several large men in slacks and dress shirts, on a beach where everyone wore shorts and T-shirts. A minute later, I spotted several black Chevy Suburbans, new ones, with blacked-out windows, parked nearby.

At that moment I knew it was over.

As I passed one of the tables, two of the over-dressed guys got to their feet and tackled me. Almost immediately, several other members of their team jumped in; the entire team held me down and choked me. When I tried to shout to get Mary Luz's attention, I could not manage to utter a single sound; I thought they were going to choke me to death on the spot. I couldn't tell whether they were working for a drug cartel, a government, or somebody else. At that moment it really didn't matter.

I had several pistols pointed at me. Someone put a black nylon bag over my head, and then the goons quickly and deftly picked me up and dragged me to one of the Suburbans and tossed me into the back seat with three or four of them. Two of the others got into the front seat beside the driver. They drove as if they expected me to be rescued in a hail of bullets by a small army. I only wish I had been that thorough.

There was one road into and out of El Yaque and, at the edge of the village, a steel pole that the police could lower and use as a checkpoint. If you were a tourist or a local and not a *bandito*, they'd raise the pole and let you through. My caravan obviously had planned for the police checkpoint and simply drove around it, through the ditch, and up the other side.

They began to shout questions at me, asking, "Where are the planes, the boats, and the money?"

I had been kidnapped. I may have actually breathed a sigh of relief. "I don't know what you're talking about," I said. "The only money I have is in the bank, in the construction account, and since the banks are closed, I can't get at it right now, but I promise that I will get it tomorrow."

They continued to drive at breakneck speed.

"How much can you pay us?" one of them asked.

"I have about two hundred and fifty thousand," I said.

He laughed and said, "*Deja de mentir, puto.*"[93]

"I'm not lying," I said. "I just built the Beach Club. My money is tied up."

They continued to grind me until we entered the National Guard compound. They opened the gate with an electric remote they pointed at it, and we drove into a tunnel-like garage where the Suburbans fit bumper-to-bumper.

My handlers took me to a barrack-style army safe house. I began to demand to talk to the person in charge of the kidnapping. I was sitting on a steel chair in the middle of a room, and they kept interrogating me about planes and money, and all I replied with was more demands to see the person in charge.

They brought in a digital camera and snapped my picture, which they proudly displayed to me and to each other, like monkeys with a crescent wrench. When they again demanded to know where I had money I told them to get in touch with my partner, Carlitos, because I knew that he had contacts at the airport. I was somewhat confident that if Carlitos were permitted to talk to the head of this operation, he could likely negotiate a deal for my release.

I had been abducted at about 5:45 p.m. and had been interrogated until perhaps 4:00 a.m., when they finally relented, telling me that I could lie down on the steel bunk bed in the corner of the room. I was cuffed to the top bunk and they assigned two guards to watch my every move.

I spent the next few hours trying to find a comfortable position. There was too little room between the upper and lower bunk for me to sit upright. If I lay down on the lower bunk with my arm straight up in the air, the blood to my hand was cut off by the angle of the cuffs. I ended up standing in place with my free arm on top of the bunk and the cuffed arm in whatever position I could find that didn't cut off the blood flow.

At dawn the demands for money resumed, and I told them that, now that the banks were open, I could pay them what I had if they contacted Carlitos or my wife. But I was not permitted to speak to Carlitos, or Mary Luz, or to the kidnapper in charge.

I still did not know whom these guys were working for, but I knew that they had to be well-connected if they could just cruise into government facilities and make use of interrogation rooms. The routine went on all morning, and we accomplished absolutely nothing.

Finally, at about noon, I learned that I was to be escorted to a plane for a flight—destination unknown, at least to me. Before leaving the barracks, I was permitted to use the rest room. One of the guards had a small tube of toothpaste and instructed me to use my finger to brush my teeth when I used the toilet. From there I was placed in the same back seat with three new companions and their firearms, and was driven out the electric garage door to an airstrip where a National Guard plane was waiting for us. The plane was a turbo-prop with high wings.

The guards were armed like soldiers. I was seated near the back with guards all around me.

As the plane gained altitude and made a long banked turn, my side of the plane got a perfect view of the El Yaque Club rooftop pool and my guests.

Adios, my life.

The guards on the plane were dressed in camouflage, carried AR-15 and AK-47 rifles as well as knives, and told me they had been fighting Colombian guerrillas, the FARC. I was about to tell them about the time I was held by guerrillas but I thought better of it.

As we approached the International Airport in Caracas I could see the many terminals. Due to the high volume of air traffic, we had a very long wait for an open runway. I was again marched off the plane at a location away from the main terminal and placed in a brand-new Chevy Blazer, which waited among many outside. The team on the tarmac included a few plainclothes, short-haired military-looking types, all wearing aviator sunglasses. They handcuffed me and put me in the back seat. All I could see was a team of guards who surrounded me, and all I could smell was the new leather interior. I continued to ask to talk to the person in charge but I was, again, ignored.

I remembered how Julio had said that kidnappers always move slowly, which would make the people who have to come up with the ransom even more desperate and anxious. The bad news was that I had been telling the truth about my finances. I only had the quarter of a million in my account. If we'd had to pay three hundred thousand American in ransom for a college kid from Campo Valdez, I could only imagine what they would ask for me. And it was not as though I could call home for help.

Once again I was in the middle of a caravan, except that this time there were five vehicles instead of three. The bridge between the airport and Caracas was under repair, which had clogged traffic, but the drivers of the Blazers were not shy about forcing other cars off the road and pushing their way through to get where they wanted to go—bumper to bumper, as you would see in NASCAR races. It was clear that the caravan was not going to be stopping for anyone.

After a few minutes, we detoured onto a narrow road that took us through hillside ghettos for about an hour until we pulled up in front of a hilltop military installation. The security gates opened. We drove to a guarded and fenced-in compound where I was led into a large, white three-story building. Once inside, they took mug shots and fingerprints. I had no valuables. I was traveling light, with just shorts, a T-shirt, and a Casio watch with a plastic band (which they took).

After I was fingerprinted, they put me in a large cellblock with about twenty other men, all of whom I later found out had very high-profile cases. I met several who had been locked up in that cell for very long periods of time. Horrific scenarios started to play out in my mind. I had been reading about how the United States government had, in some cases, abused the Patriot Act and detained people for years.

Take my first bunkie, for instance. He was a Muslim kid in his early twenties who said he'd been arrested for setting off a bottle rocket in front of the American Embassy without knowing or suspecting that the United States now included such fireworks in the definition of bomb. As a result, he had been classified as a terrorist and had been unable even to get a lawyer. It had been six months since he was arrested.

This was the same prison that Louis Posadas had escaped from while dressed as a priest years earlier. Many inmates had known him, and most were very eager to talk about him to an American.

The prisoners said that they had pooled their resources and bought paint, cleaned up some cells, and built additional cells. They now had running water, a flushing toilet, and a light, all of which had been provided by their efforts and money. They also told me that they were usually taken outside for fresh air and a walk every two weeks, but that the remaining time was spent in the windowless cellblock.

The padlocked cell of six feet by seven typically gave us only three feet of floor space between the bunk and the wall. The toilet was at the end of the hall by the shower, a South American shower with an electric shower-head that we would turn on to heat the water that flowed through it. When we wanted hot water, we had to greatly decrease the flow so the heating element would work as intended. For those instances when running water was unavailable, there was a large blue plastic barrel, or garbage can, full of water with a bowl for a scoop, which we used to shower or fill up the toilet for a flush.

I was only allowed out of the cell to use the toilet. The other prisoners were friendly and shared their food with me, which was all rice-based, usually served with *plantanos*. All in all, the conditions weren't nearly as bad as they had been in the Caracas Municipal Jail, where I had been forced to use a baggie for a toilet.

My main complaint was that I was being denied access to communicate with my wife. When I got there, I'd immediately started asking the other prisoners how to get a phone call out. One guy said he had a cell phone but was unable to call out except at certain times because of a jamming device he said the jail used. He told me that he would do his best to get a message to my wife.

I also continued voicing my demands for a lawyer, a phone call, and for a face-to-face with the man in charge, and I always got the same answer: "How much money do you have? Where is your money?" This only served to convince me that I could buy my way out of the situation if I could just speak to the boss. I had to remain patient—as if I had a choice.

After three days, however, I became convinced that this was not a typical kidnapping like Hector's in Medellín. I deduced that these guys must have been working for a government—perhaps the Venezuelan, or even the American. I knew that I had not broken any Venezuelan laws. I had a Venezuelan wife, a clean business, and I was responsible for helping young people, the community, and the economy. The more I thought about it, the more I realized that I was a poster child for a responsible member of the community in good standing. What the fuck was going on?

Additionally, Mary Luz was working for the Chavistas and teaching local children for free for the president's political party. In light of all of that, I found it difficult to believe that the Venezuelan authorities were behind my kidnapping and subsequent treatment. I knew that, if I could get in front of a Venezuelan judge, I would not end up in the hands of the United States government. I desperately needed to talk to Mary Luz, to Carlitos, or a lawyer friend—somebody with some influence. On my own, I was utterly defenseless.

I ended up staying in that military installation for five days.

On the morning they told me I was being moved, they led me down a narrow corridor, past a refrigerator containing food, soda, and some booze owned by certain prisoners. I do not ever remember my mouth watering as ferociously as it had at that moment.

I was again fingerprinted on the way to a paved parking lot, where three 4x4s waited. These trucks were a stark contrast to the other vehicles in which I had been transported. They were battered and had to be at least twenty years old. The new guards that surrounded me were not like the undercover types from the day of my arrival but looked more to be military personnel. They had automatic weapons and knives, and wore camouflage fatigues.

The vehicle they put me in had cracked windows and faded paint. When we moved out of the compound, we traveled bumper-to-bumper, and actually scraped other cars and touched bumpers to get through the traffic jam at the bridge.

I still could not figure out what was going on. I was thinking that it was entirely within the realm of possibility that these Venezuelans had been promised residency in the United States and/or American security jobs in return for helping in my apprehension. Chavez was busy in the media, making a show against Bush, which could only have served to make it easier for these people to carry the operation off without a warrant. Nobody worked for free, and we all know that the United States could pay the most.

On our way, the pedestrians were rightfully stunned when our three trucks from the demolition derby drove up onto the curb before coming to a jerking stop. Most of them looked positively baffled at the spectacle before them. There I was—with filthy uncombed hair, a half-ass beard, dirty surf shorts, a grimy wind-surfing T-shirt, and bare feet, surrounded by my own security detail of fully armed soldiers and plainclothes police to guarantee my personal safety.

We reached the international airport, where I was whisked inside and taken to the basement by elevator. Standing in a hallway, sandwiched between two armed guards, I was unceremoniously told, "You're going to the United States."

I let it sink in for a moment but then I started to shake my head. They did not care when I told them that I had real estate and a Venezuelan wife, and that I wanted to speak with an attorney or to be taken in front of a judge. They left me with two other guards, Venezuelans, who asked if El Yaque was a good place to pick up girls. They also told me that they were paid only two hundred dollars a month, and that, if it was up to them, they would turn me loose. I believed them.

I was held for an hour in a small, cramped room. Then I was taken by eight men, two plainclothes and six soldiers in camouflage, who carried knives and AR-15s. It seemed excessive. They led me down a long, wide hallway with a bright tile floor. We then took a large commercial elevator, easily big enough for all of us, up three or four floors to a secluded area in the main terminal.

I was escorted through the terminal in the opposite direction that departing passengers walk. We went straight through Customs, Immigration, and all of the way to the check-in counter, which we passed. We proceeded to the jet way and onto a plane while I pondered the fact that, upon entering an aircraft with an American registration number, I was apparently on American soil. As a pilot, I knew how the law works in regard to aircrafts. The registration number of the American Airlines plane began with "N."

At the doorway of the jet, I was transferred into the custody of two agents in slacks and sport coats, both Latin-looking. One of them looked Mexican-American and spoke excellent English and Spanish, and told me he was with Homeland Security. I didn't even know what Homeland Security was. I had assumed I'd be handed over to the U.S. Marshals or to the FBI, but since 9/11, Homeland Security had become heavily involved with international fugitives as well.

I was seated in the middle seat on the left side of the plane, approximately five rows from the back, clearly the only one who knew nothing about what was happening. In the ten minutes it took to get into takeoff position, one of the agents bragged to me that, a few weeks earlier, "they had pulled the same shit" on a fugitive in Ecuador.

As we started to taxi along the runway, a stewardess made an announcement, and I learned that we would be traveling to Miami. Then we took off. I knew in my heart that I would never see my wife again.

I had sworn early on that the only way I would return to America was with pennies on my eyes or in handcuffs. I felt no thrill in realizing that I had been right. The three-hour flight was anticlimactic. After recalling the rest-room scene in the movie *Catch Me If You Can,* I asked to use the rest room. Leonardo DiCaprio was able to escape through the floor of the rest room on his plane, in the movie, but my captors stood in the doorway while I relieved myself, so I couldn't close it. The highlight was when I got to choose what I wanted for my meal—a chicken breast with mashed potatoes and gravy, mixed vegetables, and a brownie.

WE LANDED IN MIAMI a little ahead of schedule and taxied to the terminal. My agents waited until all of the passengers had disembarked before leading me out of the plane and into the jet way—one in front of me, and one behind.

Four U.S. Marshals were waiting to take me into custody, and the two from the plane vanished as soon as we reached the terminal. They didn't even bother to say goodbye. They had mentioned doing some shopping at the Lincoln Road Mall in South Beach before returning to whatever Latin American country they worked in. I guess that they were in a hurry. I was led through Customs and Immigration to a cell near the luggage carousel. I was placed on, and cuffed to, a steel bench, where I sat for thirty minutes before being taken to the marshals' service van.

What immediately stood out to me, having been gone for almost fifteen years, was how the people at the airport were so overweight, much heavier and bigger than I remembered and certainly much larger than the Latin Americans. I also observed how much newer and fancier the cars were, and I wondered if there was any correlation between the two.

It was a less than thirty-minute ride to the Federal Detention Center in Miami, which is basically a skyscraper prison. We came to a stop in a sublevel basement parking garage, rode an elevator to booking, and I was stripped down, bent over, and examined for keys, weapons, and things that might aid in my escape. I was outfitted with an orange jumpsuit to replace my shorts and T-shirt, and led through a maze of holding tanks, where I helped some of the non-English speakers fill out forms we were given. My mind was still racing, and I maintained my demand for a phone call but was told by senior staff, "Boy, you made that phone call fifteen years ago."

I spent that night in segregation and, the next morning, was moved to a two-floor cellblock in the general population that was cold and hygienic. I noticed that I was one of the few white inmates—mostly everyone was black or Latino.

I got celled up on the second tier. My bunkie was a white guy in his early twenties with full tattooing above his waist and down his arms. He claimed to have been in Coleman Federal Prison on terrorist charges for some time. I could not believe how many prisoners had told me that they were up on terrorist charges.

Since the toilet in our cell did not flush, we used our T-shirts to stifle the stench somewhat, which made for an extremely chilly night. As I shivered, my bunkie slept like a baby in the bottom bunk. He had been given Thorazine, the lucky bastard.

The next day, he got into an argument with a black inmate who later charged into our cell and gave him black eyes. In federal prison, anyone who gets in a fight, even the victim of an assault, goes to the SHU[94], which I have always thought was unfair. To prevent being issued an incident report and going to the hole, my bunkie ate in the cell for a couple of days to let his eyes heal.

There were four television sets for our viewing pleasure. And when I say viewing, I *mean* viewing, because if we wanted to actually hear what was happening on the television instead of just watching, we had to buy radios (twenty to forty dollars) from the prison commissary and tune into the FM channel designated for the station.

After a few days, I was transferred to the first floor, which I believe was connected to the U.S. Courthouse. For each court visit, we were shackled and handcuffed and led to a waiting cell, where we were placed on anchored steel benches until our court appearance or returned to the cellblock. We stayed on these cold steel benches, or sometimes on the concrete floor, from early morning until every single detainee was done with his appearance.

I was finally granted phone access—or so I thought. Nothing in prison came easy, though, and this was no exception. We received three hundred minutes on the phone each month. The last two digits on our Official Prison Number determined which day our balance was reset. For example, if the Official Prison Number ended with a 04, it would reset on the fourth day of the new month. There were thirty days in most months—thirty days, three hundred minutes at twenty-three cents a minute.

Of course, it was not that easy to get started. Each inmate also needed a PAC[95] number. This was supposed to be handled by the counselor for our cellblock. If an inmate was caught using another inmate's phone account, he would be thrown in the hole and have his phone use suspended. All calls were, of course, monitored and probably recorded, so the odds of getting caught were pretty high.

It took me a few days to obtain a PAC number from staff members who suffered from a tragic and highly contagious condition called "cop," a virus that impaired the authoritarian cortex in the brain. Once that region is compromised, individuals have reported that they lose almost all ability to act in a humane manner at their job. In the first decade of the twenty-first century, it reportedly reached epidemic proportions among prison personal.

After I had been inside for at least a couple of weeks, I was told that I would finally get my PAC number. They had been claiming that they'd run out of numbers, but they had finally arrived. I was ordered to go to my counselor between noon and 1:00 p.m. I arrived there at 12:10, only to be told by the lieutenant that I was late—that it was 1:10 p.m. When I pointed to the clock, which clearly read 12:10 p.m., he threw me out of the office and promised that, if I protested for one more second, I would get thirty days in the hole.

Two days later, I received my PAC number and was finally able to call my wife. As soon as she heard the message "This call is originating from a federal detention center" I heard her scream. She said between sobs, "They killed Carlitos! They killed Carlitos!"

I was stunned. Mary Luz was crying uncontrollably and had lost all composure, but she managed to tell me that, about a week after my kidnapping, Carlitos and his driver had been assassinated in a barrage of bullets and thereafter doused with gasoline and burned beyond recognition. It had been all over the news, and locals on the island had already plastered pro-Carlitos bumper stickers all over town. I speculated that Carlitos had some less-than-reputable associates who feared their own scrutiny by authorities because of his relationship with me, now that I was in the frying pan.

Calls from federal facilities were limited to fifteen minutes, so most of the conversation was devoted to Carlitos. As I trudged back to my cell, I was burdened with even more questions and more problems than I thought I had. I knew that Mary Luz would not be able to run the club without him, so I did not know how my wife would survive. My biggest burden was the guilt that I felt, especially knowing that it would be nearly impossible to pay my respects to his family.

I suspected that I would never get to speak to anyone in his family about Carlitos, and I was right. When I finally obtained an attorney, one of the first suggestions he made was that I was not, under any circumstances, to discuss my properties or finances. He guaranteed that everyone who had anything to do with me had his phones tapped and emails monitored. For all intents and purposes, I was in a communications blackout.

I never did learn who killed Carlitos and his driver.

When I had been in federal custody for about six months, the Venezuelan government came up with bogus money-laundering charges against Mary Luz and me. This caused the confiscation of everything we had. And when I say everything, I mean it—they even took my wife's wedding ring. She and her mother were thrown out of our house and left homeless. I heard that they finally found refuge at a family member's house, and that Mary Luz was forced to take the bus ninety minutes each way to and from Porlamar to teach Spanish in El Yaque.

Many of her students stopped their lessons after my arrest and Carlitos' murder. She barely got by.

I tried to fight back. My friend Alejandro Cossu was one of the top real estate attorneys in Venezuela. He was highly respected and extremely attentive and efficient in handling all matters I entrusted to him. His penthouse office was in the Gigante, the largest shopping mall on the island, which he had secured through agreements to handle the legal matters for the mall's owners.

LIKE EVERYONE ELSE IN VENEZUELA except Mary Luz, Alejandro had had no idea I was a fugitive and certainly had broken no laws while handling real estate transactions for me. But that didn't matter to the Venezuelan authorities who sealed the front door to his office with crime scene tape and positioned two armed guards by the doors, barring him from entering, for two full years. His files, his records, and his computers were off limits to him. The Venezuelan Supreme Court eventually ordered that everything taken from him be returned, but by then his practice was ruined.

I sent a lawyer from the United States to find a law firm in Venezuela that would dribble the ball for me. The fact that the case was against the government had made finding one difficult, but after Alejandro's debacle, it became impossible. My American lawyer, Bob Van Norman, kept looking, but the one attorney willing to involve himself was not at all aggressive in trying to keep our counter-lawsuit alive. In Venezuela, you are either pro-government, or you are anti-government; whoever is in power controls the courts. At the time of this writing, we are still fighting that battle. The Venezuelan government still has all my property. The last I heard, a high-ranking general was using the El Yaque Club as his private residence. The good news is that the general has been taking great care of it, and it is in fine condition.

I eventually agreed to a plea bargain and was sentenced to 120 months in federal prison. I have not seen Mary Luz since.

Acknowledgments from Dan "Tito" Davis

There are a lot of folks who helped me get to the point where I could write this book.

I would like particularly to thank the following seven individuals who I am forever grateful: Patrick L. Donahue, Stephanie Donahue, Shannon Donahue, Marlyn Erickson, Marcelleen Davis (my mom), and Tim and Deb Davis.

For providing inspiration, hospitality, comradeship, clarification of memories, and helpful advice, I am also obliged to Alisha Brown, Alan Laird, Johnny Brockelsby, Mark Stemler, Mike Vasey, Albert Flangas (RIP), Terry Hofer, Pat Hall, Bill Gikling, Bill Durst, Brent Beckley, Peter Conti, Catherin Lee, Brad Smith, Marty Gannon, Budd Zuckerman, Chris Whitnell, Marilyn Charville, Dave Perry, Craig Mundt, Delia Mundt, Mike Langbehn, Troy Erickson, Dan Island (RIP), Jack Knodell, John "Hurricane" Hirning, Jorge Shaber, Jackie Shaber, Mario Olivares (RIP), Hugo Calo, Manuel Camejo, Alejandro Rodriguez Cossu, Renato Elia, Sergio Stefan, Colleen Blakley, Keith Trader, Hugh and Cindy Cunningham, Mike and Ginger Vaughan, Curt Byrum, Tom Byrum, Mark Hughes, Neil Schuster, Joe Saint Veltri, Frank "The Legend" Sanders, Fabiola Tavio, Mike Feather, Luis Benedetti, Richardo Campello, Denise Rochebois Campello, Freddy and Denise Vargas, Mike Blomvall, Beat Steffan, Lillian Tintori, Leopaldo Lopez, Bernd Armbruster, Nick Judge, Elias Juan Elia Maaraoui, Paula Basmagi Elia, Wilferdo Maldonado, Murray Sampson, Nancy Hood, Stef Waig, Luis Rivero, Tim Sampolinski, Juan Carlos Del Rio, Michael Schulze, Alejadro Medina, Carmelo Dagher, Gary Angel, Rob Corner, Jack "Little Man" Floyd, T.J. Knutsen, Dan Gutting, Sloan Kiser, Deisy Arvelo, Ricardo Arjona, Porter Nuttall, David Stwarka, DeanO Henrichsen, Dustin Knode, Gilbert Athay, Hilda Paredes, Jamie Tullo, Jimmy Matuska, Robin Reoh, Mike Emme, Mike Bradeen, John Reinholt, Joni

Kopecky Oligmueller, Joris Haazen, Ogden and Zannie Driskill, Lincoln and Ashley Driskill, Katerie Driskill, Andrea Driskill Wood, Lindasue Smollen, Curt and Peggy Mundt, Alan and Angie Gross, Chuck and Barb Lien, Pete and Nancy Lien, Dan and Nancy Kelley, Dick and Rosie Seaman, Gary and Marlise Fisher, Jim and Anai Gruel, Boyce and Kathy Kennedy, Victor and Cindy Silbaugh, Marty and Julie O'Malley, Mark Doyle, Miguel Bruggeman, Miguelito Bruggeman, Keber Mota, Marla Merlano, Bob McCormick, Barry Sheinkopf, Zachary Coleman Curtis, Lera Gavin, Mike Feather, Michael Gargarnese, David Rockwell, Mike Herida, George Hamshire, Bill Gardiner AKA "Sharkey", Marty Baumgart, Pat Vidal, Rich Sagen, Paula Young, Jean Kopecky, Danny Wiseberg, Rex Haskins, Gary Johnson, Rodney Snyder, Rosti Sobek, Lisa A. Mahoney, Rudy Smites, Scott Rodgers, Scotty Hansen, Robert Van Norman, Roger Tellinghuisen, Mark Dreier, Paul Ortega, Ganny Parker, Fred Reilly, Donald Roth, Chris Mosses, Butch Ballow, Chad Carrico, Mahesh "India" Patel, Donald Myers, Ismail Beciri, Frederick Barbour, Barbetta Bork, Berat Shabani, Aaron "Ace" Smith, Angelo Sadler, Leslie "John" Hamilton, Steve Barrow, Scott Halverson, Carlos Gomez, Karl Irwin, Frankie Sosa, Jimmy Robinson, Neil Johnson, Paul Peterson, Steve Glerum, Nicole Fedo, Michael Randy, Robert Mills, Shawn Meyer, Charles Dunbar, Tyrel Kaltenbach, Shawn Bergstrand, Dave Myrland, Russell Frauendorfer, Josh Hedland, Chris Chapman, Steve Atherton, Steve Hollis, John "Stud Muffin" Andrix, Cilia Ines, Doug "Ughy" Minnich, Tim Sampolinski, Alain Galarneau, Gerald Porri, Warren "Blackie" Anderson, Michael Spruce, Tony Sanders, Frankie Guido, Chad May, Thomas "Beany" Burblies, Gabi Steindl, Dioni Guadagnino, Jort Herder, Big Air Lee, Yessica Alabaz, Elgys Schuffelers, Patrick J. Sharkey, Jim Karel, Irwin Spruce, Jeb Hughes, Tony Darwin, Chris and Yenifer Valentine, Victor Martin, Paul Niemann and Joe Loya. My apologies to those whose names I forgot to mention.

Endnotes

1. Officially called *Policia Federal*, the Federal police force of Mexico.
2. Prison sentence.
3. Federal prison sentences are given in months. It's tricky. They may give a poor bastard 96 months, which doesn't sound that bad; that is, until you get out your calculator and figure out that it is eight years, of which you have to do a guaranteed 85 percent.
4. Without trees or stone to build with, homesteaders had to rely on the only available building material—prairie sod.
5. The prospect time is when prospective members of a motorcycle club learn about the club, get to know their members, and get evaluated to see if the prospect will get accepted as a member. Prospects are the bottom of the food chain within the club but are often feared and respected by people outside the club.
6. A thousand pills.
7. Locals who did not attend college.
8. The UNLV Running Rebels' coach who was fired for violating NCAA rules.
9. Spanish for "white boy."
10. A name given to Hughes Airwest planes.
11. Interest.
12. About $180,000.00 in 2016.
13. About $3.5 million in 2016.
14. The Racketeer Influenced and Corrupt Organizations Act, commonly referred to as the RICO Act or simply RICO, is a United States federal law that provides for extended criminal penalties and a civil cause of action for acts performed as part of an ongoing criminal organization. The RICO Act focuses specifically on racketeering.
15. Note from co-author Peter Conti: There's no such thing as the mafia.
16. Correction officer.
17. Drug traffickers.
18. Solitary confinement.

19. Jose Gonzalo Rodriguez Gacha (May 14, 1947–December 15, 1989).
20. When someone is on parole they must get permission to move to another state.
21. Highly potent marijuana from female plants that are specially tended and kept seedless by preventing pollination in order to induce a high resin content; also: a female hemp plant grown to produce *sinsemilla.*
22. A one-year sentence that is usually served in a jail rather than in a prison.
23. Cactus, cut into long strips, the spines removed and sangria.
24. Town.
25. The Zapatista Army of Nation Liberation was a leftist political and militant group that had declared war "against the Mexican state," although the war has been primarily defensive.
26. Tavern.
27. A *chancla* means "flip-flop." Since Mexican prostitutes pride themselves on their shoes, a *chancluda* is a prostitute who wears flip-flops, the vilest and cheapest of the lot.
28. Guatemalan money.
29. The town of Deadwood, South Dakota, got its name from its trees. An immense beetle population attacks the trees in this area and leaves them standing but dead.
30. Mexican federal government (their version of the FBI).
31. Bitch.
32. Meetings.
33. What is your name?
34. Rural farm worker.
35. Bandit.
36. Derogatory term for "homosexual."
37. Silver or lead.
38. Soccer.
39. Hit men.
40. Weekend home.
41. Deep fried, cheesy dough balls.
42. An inexpensive Japanese-made motorcycle, usually a small Kawasaki or Honda.
43. Soap operas.
44. Drug traffickers.

45. Fucking.
46. I would like to make love to you.
47. Easter Week.
48. Almost twenty-five miles.
49. Enter.
50. "Cheating bastard of a husband."
51. "I'm going to kill you, you son of a bitch! You faggot!"
52. "The cheap bastard."
53. The Lost City.
54. Sweetheart.
55. "You don't like the girls?"
56. Commander
57. "Sandal" in this part of Colombia.
58. American Society for the Prevention for Cruelty of Animals.
59. A hearty stew.
60. Thick tripe soup.
61. "Don't take my son, please."
62. Ejercito de Liberacion Nacional, the second largest guerilla faction in Colombia, who specialized in kidnapping.
63. The priest.
64. A large Toyota SUV, with bench seats in back facing each other.
65. Go get fucked.
66. Unidad Antisecuestro y Extorcion de la Policia (Anti-Kidnapping and Extortion Police).
67. "It's okay."
68. Camper.
69. "Do you need anyone killed? I'll give you a discount."
70. "You don't know?"
71. "It's the Black and White Carnival."
72. Handmade, deep-fried smashed green bananas with soft cheese.
73. Venezuela's national currency.
74. "You're nothing but a fucking gringo. This ain't your land, faggot."
75. Slang for a "10."
75. For a fee this person would acquire legal documents for you, e.g., a liquor license, car registration, or passport, to name just a few.
76. Their national identification card, akin to a Social Security card in the

United States.

77. Lounge chair.
78. Bananas.
79. "Your boyfriend."
80. VOLLEYBALLGIRL.
81. Camel.
82. Luchino Visconti's classic 1969 Nazi film.
83. Prison guards.
84. Bureau of Prisons.
85. Urine analysis.
86. A prison cellmate. Not really a fair term because the cells in prisons were much more spacious than this one.
87. "Disgusting!"
88. Technically, ghats refer to the steps. But the people who live on these steps (there are dozens) are also referred to by this name.
89. The capital of the Venezuelan state of Nueva Esparta, of which the Island of Margarita is a part.
90. "What's next?"
91. Commissioner.
92. Luis Posada is a Cuban exile militant and former CIA agent. He is considered a terrorist by the FBI and the Government of Cuba, among others. He is widely considered responsible for the bombing of Cubana flight 455, which killed 73 people. He was arrested and jailed in Venezuela but escaped prison and landed in Miami. When the U.S. refused to extradite him to Venezuela or Cuba, President Chavez declared, "The U.S. has a double standard on its so-called war on terrorism." Today, Posada lives in Miami, where he openly attends Anti-Castro right wing meetings.
93. "Stop lying, whore!"
94. Special housing unit.
95. Pre-assigned access code.

For more documents and photos pertaining to this book, go to Gringothebook.com.

CPSIA information can be obtained
at www.ICGtesting.com
Printed in the USA
FFOW03n0347270817
39228FF